READING ACQUISITION AND DEVELOPMENTAL DYSLEXIA

ESSAYS IN DEVELOPMENTAL PSYCHOLOGY

North American Editors:
Henry Wellman
University of Michigan at Ann Arbor
Janet Werker
University of British Columbia

UK Editors:
Peter Bryant
University of Oxford
Usha Goswami
University of Cambridge

Essays in Developmental Psychology is designed to meet the need for rapid publication of brief volumes in developmental psychology. The series defines developmental psychology in its broadest terms and covers such topics as social development, cognitive development, developmental neuropsychology and neuroscience, language development, learning difficulties, developmental psychopathology and applied issues. Each volume in the series will make a conceptual contribution to the topic by reviewing and synthesizing the existing research literature, by advancing theory in the area, or by some combination of these missions. The principal aim is that authors will provide an overview of their own highly successful research program in an area. It is also expected that volumes will, to some extent, include an assessment of current knowledge and identification of possible future trends in research. Each book will be a self-contained unit supplying the advanced reader with a well-structured review of the work described and evaluated.

FORTHCOMING TITLES

Tager-Flusberg: *Autism and William's Syndrome*
Trehub: *Infants and Music*

Barrett: *Children's Knowledge, Beliefs and Feelings about Nations and National Groups*

RECENTLY PUBLISHED

Goldin-Meadow: *The Resilience of Language*
Inagaki & Hatano: *Young Children's Naïve Thinking about the Biological World*
Perez-Pereira & Conti-Ramsden: *Language Development and Social Interactions in Blind Children*
Bryne: *The Foundation of Literacy*
Meins: *Security of Attachment and Cognitive Development*
Siegal: *Knowing Children (2nd Ed.)*
Mitchell: *Acquiring a Conception of Mind*
Meadows: *Parenting Behavior and Children's Cognitive Development*

Langford: *The Development of Moral Reasoning*
Hobson: *Autism and the Development of Mind*
White: *The Understanding of Causation and the Production of Action*
Smith: *Necessary Knowledge and Constructivism*
Cox: *Children's Drawings of the Human Figure*
Howe: *Language Learning*
Sonuga-Barke & Webley: *Children's Saving*

For updated information about published and forthcoming titles in the *Essays in Developmental Psychology* series, please visit: **www.psypress.co.uk/essays**

Reading Acquisition and Developmental Dyslexia

Liliane Sprenger-Charolles, Pascale Colé,
and Willy Serniclaes

Ψ Psychology Press
Taylor & Francis Group

HOVE AND NEW YORK

MT

First published 2006 by Psychology Press,
27 Church Road, Hove, East Sussex, BN3 2FA

Simultaneously published in the USA and Canada
by Psychology Press
270 Madison Avenue, New York, NY 10016

Psychology Press is an imprint of the Taylor & Francis Group, an informa business

© 2006 Psychology Press

Typeset in Times by RefineCatch Limited, Bungay, Suffolk
Printed and bound in Great Britain by
MPG Books Ltd, Bodmin, Cornwall
Cover design by Lisa Dynan

This publication has been produced with paper manufactured to strict
environmental standards and with pulp derived from sustainable forests.

British Library Cataloguing in Publication Data
A catalogue record for this book is available from the British Library

Library of Congress Cataloging in Publication Data
Sprenger-Charolles, Liliane.
    Reading acquisition and developmental dyslexia / Liliane Sprenger-Charolles,
Willy Serniclaes and Pascale Colé.
        p. cm.
    Includes bibliographical references and index.
    ISBN 1-84169-592-0 (hardback)
    1. Dyslexia.   2. Developmental reading.   3. Reading – Remedial teaching.
I. Serniclaes, Willy.   II. Colé, Pascale.   III. Title.
    LB1050.5.S67 2006
    371.91′44 – dc22

                                                                    2006013994

ISBN 13: 978-1-84169-592-1
ISBN 10: 1-84169-592-0

3|8|07

Contents

Acknowledgements

We are grateful to Peter Bryant for encouraging us to write the present book, and to Usha Goswami for having very positively reacted to our project. We also want to thank Leo Blomert, René Carré, Séverine Casalis, Ghislaine Dehaene-Lambertz, Jean-François Démonet, Uli Frauenfelder, Pascal Mamassian, José Morais, Frank Ramus, Linda Siegel, Johanes Ziegler and an anonymous reviewer for very insightful discussions and/or comments. Also many thanks to our colleagues (especially Danielle Béchennec, Philippe Lacert and Elisabeth Samain) and PhD students (Caroline Bogliotti, Agnes Kipffer-Piquard, Souhila Messaoud-Galussi, and Victoria Medina). They have contributed in so many ways. Special thanks are extended to Vivian Waltz for her careful editing of most of this book, and for the many invaluable corrections she proposed, both in content and on technical and stylistic matters.

Introduction

The main objective of the present book is to provide a tentative framework to account for reading acquisition and developmental dyslexia in alphabetic systems. We chose to confine this book to alphabetic systems for two reasons. The first is clarity – it is easier to compare data from orthographies based on similar principles than to contrast languages that have fundamentally different writing systems, such as the alphabetic and logographic families. The second is prevalence – the alphabetic family is widespread, and even in countries with a non-alphabetic system, most children begin learning to read with the help of an alphabetic system as an intermediary.[1]

Some books on reading acquisition and developmental dyslexia have limitations which we will try to avoid. For example, certain books present studies carried out with children, and do not consider what is known about skilled reading (for example, Blachman, 1997; Snowling, 2000). A clear view of the processes on which skilled readers rely is necessary to understand the normal and disturbed time courses of reading development. For this reason, chapter 1 is devoted to research on skilled readers, and particular attention is paid to the relationships between written-word identification and reading comprehension. Another limitation of the research on reading is that most publications have been based on studies of English-speaking subjects in view of generalization to all writing systems. Clearly, the English language has a number of salient specificities that can influence reading and its acquisition. The significance of this issue has long been underestimated. Therefore, chapter 2 provides a survey of normal reading acquisition in different alphabetic writing systems. First, we present the principal characteristics of some of these writing systems. This is unusual in a book on reading, but we think it is essential for gaining a proper understanding of the impact of the linguistic environment on reading acquisition and developmental dyslexia. Then we examine the psycholinguistic literature, while relying on cross-linguistic studies to assess what is general and what depends on the individual characteristics of each language, and on longitudinal studies to assess developmental trends. This chapter takes a careful look at the grain size of reading processing units, from meaningless sublexical units such as letters, graphemes, onset-rhymes, and syllables, to meaningful lexical units such as morphemes and words.

The focus of chapter 3 is on the manifestations of developmental dyslexia. After presenting some methodological issues in the first section of this chapter, we describe the phenotypic performance pattern of developmental dyslexics in the second section, using group studies to underline what might be specific about the way these subjects process information during reading. The question of the existence and prevalence of subtypes such as phonological, surface, or mixed profiles is examined in the third and fourth sections, in the light of single and multiple case studies. An important part of these three sections is devoted to the compensatory strategies devised by dyslexics to cope with their deficits. As in the previous chapter, we rely as much as possible on both cross-linguistic data and longitudinal data to assess the stability of the dyslexic performance pattern across languages and over time as reading develops.

In chapter 4 we tackle the main explanations of dyslexia given so far. Explanations of dyslexia need cross-linguistic generality, but they should also specifically explain reading deficiencies that leave other functions unaffected. This leads us to compare the classic phonological explanation, which brings phoneme awareness deficits to bear, to two different perceptual theories – magnocellular theory where deficits in general sensory processes are at stake, and allophonic theory based on a specific mode of speech perception. The theories are compared on various criteria including reliability across studies and individuals, ability to predict long-term reading performance, and remedial potentialities. Based on the data presented in chapters 1 to 4, chapter 5 provides a plausible framework for explaining reading acquisition and developmental dyslexia, while considering the results of studies on skilled reading, and integrating behavioral and neuroimaging data.

CHAPTER ONE

What have we learned from studies with skilled adult readers?

In this introductory chapter, we discuss four aspects of written-word identification which play a crucial role in skilled reading: first, the effect of context in written-word identification; second, the automaticity of written-word identification (i.e., the written-word identification "reflex"); third, the time course of orthographic, phonological, and semantic code activation in written-word identification; fourth, the neural correlates of these processes.

This short overview of the literature breaks ground for an interpretation of reading as a highly specialized cognitive function. An emphasis on the automatic and autonomous nature of the written-word identification "reflex" in skilled reading defines the perspective that runs throughout the book and is essential to evaluating the theories and experimental findings that are presented here. Reading acquisition (chapter 2) and developmental dyslexia (chapter 3) are best understood when the focus is on written-word identification. In addition, a number of phenomena demonstrate the crucial importance of phonological factors in reading and suggest that dyslexia results from a phonological impairment (chapter 4). One critical issue is thus to understand how these factors enter into the word-reading "reflex" (chapter 5).

CONTEXT EFFECTS IN WRITTEN-WORD IDENTIFICATION

We know from reading expertise research that the seemingly effortless understanding of sentences or text is partly based on the automatic identification of written words. Such rapid and automatic word identification enables the skilled adult reader to recognize five words per second on average. This means that it only takes about a quarter of a second to recognize a written word from among the estimated 30,000 to 50,000 words in a reader's mental lexicon. The automaticity of written-word identification by skilled readers results in processing that is relatively independent of processing at the sentence level and becomes increasingly autonomous as reading expertise develops.

West and Stanovich (1978) demonstrated that, in skilled readers, sentence-context effects on written-word identification are not as strong because written-word identification occurs automatically. In their study, fourth and sixth graders as well as college students were asked to read target words (e.g., *cat*), as quickly as possible, in three conditions: (1) in a congruous sentence context with the prior display of a sentence context that was congruent with the target (e.g., the dog ran after the *cat*); (2) in an incongruous sentence context with the prior display of a sentence context that was incongruous with the target (e.g., the girl sat on the *cat*); (3) in a control condition with no sentence context but only the prior display of the word "the". The results presented in Figure 1.1 show that congruous contexts reduced target-word reading time in all three groups of readers (although the effect was much weaker for skilled readers), while incongruous contexts slowed the fourth and sixth graders down, but did not affect the adults.

Raduege and Schwantes (1987) contributed another piece of evidence in

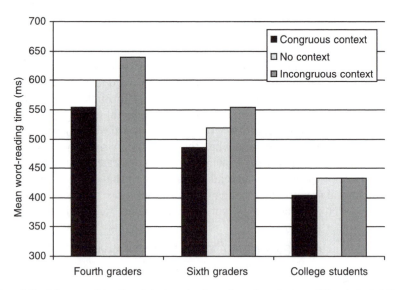

Figure 1.1. Mean word-reading time by school grade and context condition (adapted from West & Stanovich, 1978).

favor of the increasing autonomy of written-word identification processes and the decreasing role of contextual facilitation as reading ability develops. Third and sixth graders were asked to read words in a neutral context, a congruous sentence context, and an incongruous sentence context. Half of the words were presented during a training phase, and the other half were not. The third graders' results revealed a congruency facilitation effect of 120 ms on untrained words that dropped to as low as 47 ms on trained words. In contrast, for the sixth graders, there was no training effect (40 ms and 50 ms for trained and untrained words respectively). The latter finding suggests that written-word identification has become sufficiently automatic in sixth graders to prevent practice effects from occurring.

Some studies have also shown that heavy reliance on context is a defining trait, not only of beginning readers but also of individuals with more or less severe reading difficulties. For instance, in the study by Perfetti, Goldman, and Hogaboam (1979), skilled and less-skilled fifth graders were asked to read words presented either in isolation or in a story context. Figure 1.2 shows that the less-skilled readers made greater use of the written context than the good readers did.

In a study by Bruck (1990), college students who had been diagnosed as dyslexic during childhood were compared on context use to an adult control group matched on chronological age and to a child control group matched on reading age (sixth graders). The three groups of subjects were asked to read

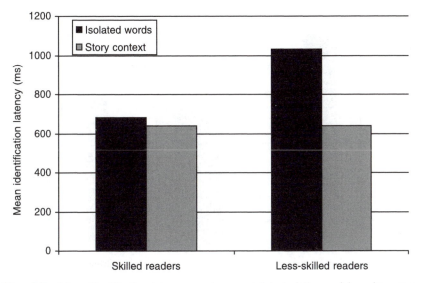

Figure 1.2. Mean identification latency: words presented in isolation and in written story context for skilled and less-skilled fifth graders (adapted from Perfetti et al., 1979).

words presented in a neutral context (e.g., "When I press the button, you will see the word _____") and in a sentence context (e.g., "The English language treats pigs with _____ [contempt]"). Figure 1.3a shows that the dyslexic adults relied heavily on context, probably to compensate for their poor written-word identification skills, which were below the norm for their chronological age or reading age, as measured by a word and pseudoword naming test (Figure 1.3b). Reliance on context may explain why Bruck (1990) observed high standardized comprehension test scores in adult dyslexic readers.

It thus seems that the role of context-based processing in written-word identification decreases as age and reading ability increases. More specifically, while sentence context can facilitate reading, the performance of more fluent readers seems to be dominated by rapid, automatic word identification. Such processes take place so fast that any effects arising from contextual factors – which take more time to process – are reduced. In less fluent readers, contextual and written-word identification processes occur at similar speeds, and both contribute to the performance levels observed. In fact, for skilled readers, facilitatory context effects disappear when the sentences used generate a meaningful but non-predictive context (Forster, 1981). This type of sentence predominates in everyday reading.

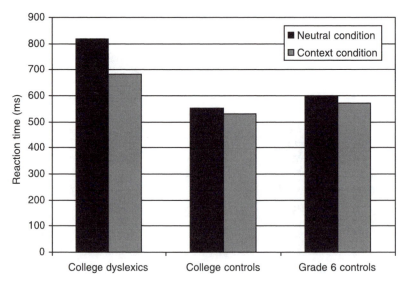

Figure 1.3(a). Mean reaction time to words presented in isolation and in context by reading ability, dyslexics and controls (adapted from Bruck, 1990).

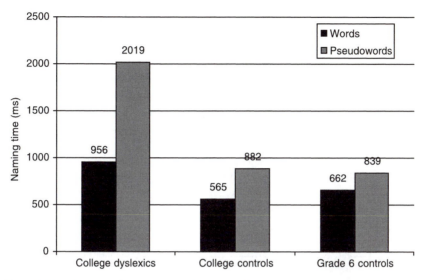

Figure 1.3(b).   Mean naming time to words and pseudowords by reading ability, dyslexics and controls (adapted from Bruck, 1990).

THE WRITTEN-WORD IDENTIFICATION "REFLEX"

One of the essential properties of automatic written-word identification, beyond mere rapidity, is its involuntary nature – it takes place without the mobilization of attentional resources (Laberge & Samuels, 1974; Perfetti & Zhang, 1995). The Stroop effect (1935) is considered by many researchers as an indicator of automatic processes in reading. In the Stroop test, subjects must rapidly name the color of the ink in which a word is printed; the word presented may itself be the word for a different color. The Stroop effect provides information about the level of automaticity of written-word identi-fication – the more automatic the processes involved, the less likely there is to be competition (and therefore interference) between the two color words activated (the written word presented, and the word for the ink color). West and Stanovich (1978) applied the Stroop test to sentences in order find out how "resistant" the automatic processes involved in written-word identifica-tion are to processing at the sentence level. They asked subjects to rapidly name the color of the ink used for one word in a sentence. The idea behind the combined use of context effects and Stroop effects is as follows: if the sentence context automatically primes a response other than the relevant color, then color-naming response time should be longer. However, if written-word identification processes automatically, the sentence context effect should be very reduced. Three context conditions were included: congruous, incongruous, and no context. Figure 1.4 illustrates the outcome: the context had a large effect on the color-naming times for fourth and sixth graders, but not for college students. The adults' performance thus suggests that context no longer interacts with automatic word-identification processes.

Ehri (1976) noted that even beginning readers processed printed words rapidly and automatically. She proposed a word interference task derived from the Stroop paradigm in which second graders, fifth graders, and junior high students were asked to name common objects and animals shown in labeled pictures. As illustrated in Figure 1.5a, the same drawing was presented with the correct label (congruous condition), an incorrect label (incongruous condition), or no label (control condition). The results, depicted in Figure 1.5b,

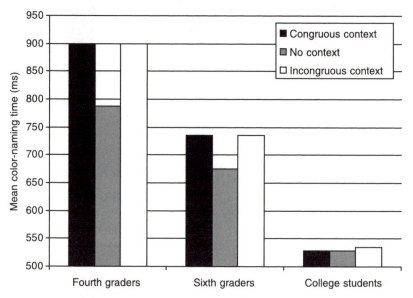

Figure 1.4. Mean color-naming time by school grade level and context condition (adapted from West & Stanovich, 1978).

Figure 1.5(a). Examples of the experimental conditions used by Ehri (1976).

indicated a congruency effect – response times to pictures with a congruous label were significantly faster than to pictures alone. Despite the subjects' efforts to ignore the words, the magnitude of this effect was constant for younger and older readers. The results also indicated an interference effect – pictures with misleading labels took significantly longer to name than pictures with no label (see Figure 1.5c).

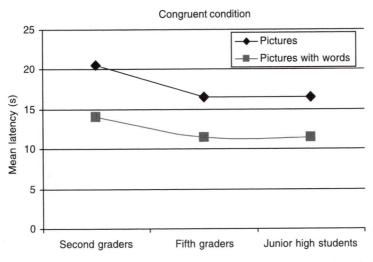

Figure 1.5(b). Mean picture-naming latency by stimulus condition (picture only and picture with a congruous word) and school grade (adapted from Ehri, 1976).

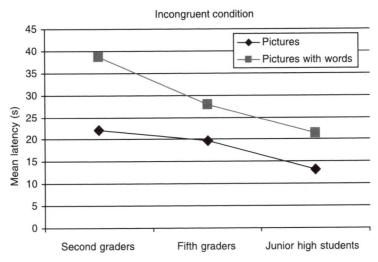

Figure 1.5(c). Mean picture-naming latency by stimulus condition (picture only and picture with an incongruous word) and school grade (adapted from Ehri, 1976).

In Guttentag and Haith's (1978) study, the interference effect reported by Ehri (1976) was found in first graders after only nine months of reading instruction. They suggested that the interference effects observed in their experiments and in Ehri's were the result of semantic interference due to the rapid processing of the meaning of the printed word. Indeed, the interference effect was a function of the semantic difference between the picture and the word: it was greater when the picture and word belonged to the same semantic category (picture of a dog / word *sheep*) than when the two belonged to different categories (dog / notebook). These results were found by the end of first grade, but not earlier. Thus, the interference effect is related to age and reading ability – it is stronger for beginning readers than for more skilled readers, because of the greater automaticity of written-word identification in older subjects.

TIME COURSE OF ORTHOGRAPHIC, PHONOLOGICAL, AND SEMANTIC ACTIVATION IN WRITTEN-WORD IDENTIFICATION

The above results indicate that written-word processing is fairly automatic in skilled readers. It remains to be understood exactly what these readers access during written-word identification. Models of skilled reading (Coltheart, Rastle, Perry, Langdon, & Ziegel, 2001; Plaut, McClelland, Seidenberg, & Patterson, 1996) and beginning reading (Harm & Seidenberg, 1999) both describe word identification as resulting from the activation of three essential codes in the mental lexicon: orthographic, phonological, and semantic. The orthographic code of a word contains the letters that compose it and their combinations in words (e.g., t + r + a + i + n). The phonological code stores individual phonemes and their combinations (e.g., /t/ + /r/ + /ei/ + /n/). The semantic code includes the conceptual knowledge necessary for word understanding.

Research in this domain has brought out three main facts. First, the activation of these codes by skilled readers follows a precise time course: the orthographic code is activated earlier than the phonological code, and the semantic code is activated later (Ferrand & Grainger, 1992, 1993; Perea & Gotor, 1997). Second, skilled readers activate phonological codes earlier and more automatically than do less-skilled readers (Booth, Perfetti, & MacWhinney, 1999). Third, disabled readers – and more specifically dyslexic readers – have trouble activating the phonological codes of written words (Booth, Perfetti, MacWhinney, & Hunt, 2000).

The time course of orthographic and phonological code activation during written-word identification has been examined primarily by way of rapid masked priming, which makes it possible to study early automatic processes in written-word identification. In general, this procedure involves the presentation of a target word, on which the subject must accomplish a certain task (usually naming or lexical decision). The target word is preceded by the very quick presentation (50 ms, for example) of a prime word (or pseudo-word), which may or may not share certain characteristics (orthographic or phonological) with the target. A mask composed of a series of hashmarks (#######) is displayed immediately before the prime, which is then followed by the target word. Since the prime cannot be consciously identified (because of the mask and the very brief exposure), the readers cannot make use of a predictive strategy in recognizing the target.

For written-word identification by skilled readers, Ferrand and Grainger (1992, 1993) showed that orthographic and phonological code activation is extremely fast (only a few tens of milliseconds of exposure to the prime suffice to trigger effects), and that the orthographic code is activated before the phonological code. They presented French adult subjects with target words preceded by three types of pseudoword primes: primes that were both orthographically and phonologically related (e.g., lont-LONG, pronounced identically in French: /lô/), pseudoword primes that were orthographically related but not homophonic with the target (e.g., lonc-LONG, pronounced differently in French: /lôk/-/lô/), and pseudoword primes that were unrelated (both orthographically and phonologically) to the target (e.g., tabe-LONG). The existence of a potential orthographic priming effect was determined by comparing the results for orthographically related primes to those of unrelated controls; a phonological priming effect was determined by comparing performance on orthographically and phonologically related primes to performance on orthographically related primes, by "subtracting" them from the orthographic primes. In their series of experiments (1992, 1993), the prime durations were 17, 33, 50, 67, 83, and 100 ms. We are interested here in the results obtained for exposures of 17 to 67 ms, since they can be compared with data from experiments involving beginning readers. In Figure 1.6, we can see that the time courses of orthographic and phonological activation were different, with orthographic codes being activated more rapidly. Orthographic facilitation effects were found for prime exposures between 17 and 50 ms, whereas phonological facilitation was noted only after 50 ms exposures.

The earlier activation of orthographic codes was also found by Booth et al. (1999) in beginning readers (mean age under 10) with prime exposure times of 30 and 60 ms. Figure 1.7a shows that the orthographic priming effect was greater than the phonological priming effect, regardless of prime exposure time. A study conducted by Grainger and Ferrand (1996) offers an indirect comparison between skilled and beginning readers. Figure 1.7b shows that for a 43 ms prime exposure and adult subjects, phonological priming effects were greater than orthographic priming effects, which no longer reached significance. In contrast, for beginning readers, orthographic priming effects

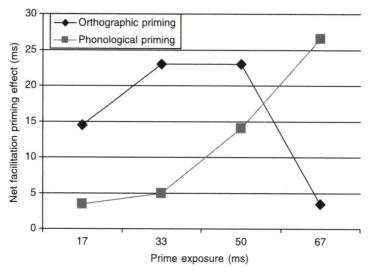

Figure 1.6. Net effects of phonological priming and orthographic priming in skilled adult readers, by prime exposure duration (adapted from Ferrand & Grainger, 1993).

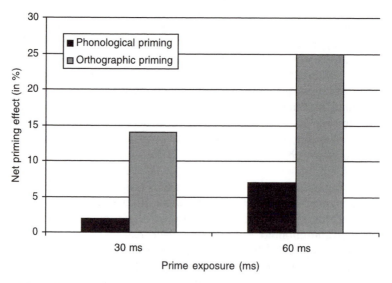

Figure 1.7(a). Net effects of phonological and orthographic priming in beginning readers (mean age < 10 years), by prime exposure duration. These effects were computed from accuracy scores (adapted from Booth et al., 1999).

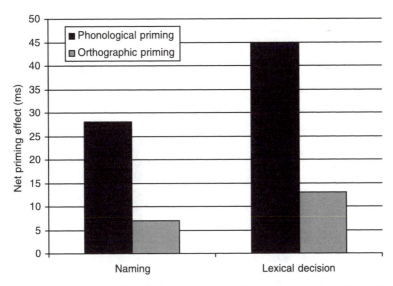

Figure 1.7(b). Net effects of phonological and orthographic priming in skilled adult readers for a prime exposure duration of 43 ms (adapted from Grainger & Ferrand, 1996).

remained greater than the effects obtained with phonological primes, which suggests that the activation of phonological codes is slower for beginning readers.

In the Booth et al. (2000) study, dyslexic children (mean chronological age 15) underwent the same experiment with a 60 ms prime exposure. Figure 1.8 summarizes the results and compares the dyslexic group to a control group matched on reading age (chronological age 9). The dyslexic children exhibited significantly lower overall accuracy levels than the control group. In addition, the control group was subject to greater phonological priming effects, which suggests that disabled readers have trouble activating the phonological code. Other findings have shown that difficulty in activating the phonological code of written words persists in adults diagnosed as dyslexics in childhood (Bruck, 1990; Elbro, Nielsen, & Petersen 1994; Snowling, Nation, Moxham, Gallagher, & Frith, 1997; Wilson & Lesaux, 2001).

Finally, other research has shown both for skilled adult readers (Perea & Gotor, 1997) and for beginning readers (Plaut & Booth, 2000) that semantic codes are activated later than orthographic and phonological codes, by at least 50 ms for skilled readers. It is not easy to compare these two populations, however, since the children's results were based on a long prime exposure time (800 ms).

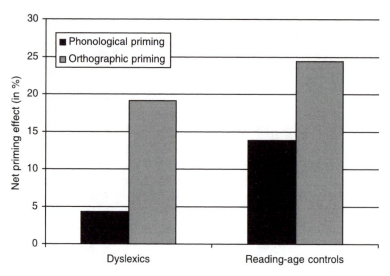

Figure 1.8.   Net effects of phonological and orthographic priming for a prime exposure of 60 ms, by reading ability. These effects were computed from accuracy scores (adapted from Booth et al., 2000).

DATA FROM FUNCTIONAL NEUROIMAGING STUDIES

A growing body of neuroimaging data on skilled and beginning readers corroborates the behavioral data summarized above. However, it is sometimes difficult from neuroimaging studies to get a clear picture of the brain areas involved in written-word identification. As underlined by Jobard, Crivello, and Tzourio-Mazoyer (2003) in their meta-analysis of neuroimaging research, this may be because an explicit definition of the theoretical framework is lacking (dual-route/single-route models of the written word) and there are many methodological variations across laboratories.

In the discussion that follows, we will therefore refer to a very general, widely accepted framework similar to that described by Démonet, Taylor, and Chaix (2004), Shaywitz and Shaywitz (2005) or Booth et al. (2003b) and Pugh et al. (2000). This model has been validated by a large number of consistent, frequently observed findings obtained through functional magnetic resonance imaging (fMRI) and positron emission tomography (PET).[1] Both of these techniques indirectly estimate changes in neural activity by measuring blood properties (i.e., blood flow or oxygenation) while subjects perform cognitive tasks; increased neural activity results in increased blood flow to the active region (see Demb, Poldrack, & Gabrieli, 1999). Local changes in blood properties thus provide an index of local changes in brain activity. The comparison of brain activity during experimental and baseline states can be used to establish direct correlations between active brain tissues and putative cognitive processes.

It is generally agreed today that in written-word identification by skilled readers, visual input is transmitted from the lateral geniculate nucleus in the thalamus to primary cortical areas (Brodmann's area or BA17) in the striate cortex, and to secondary areas (BA18) in the extrastriate cortex. From there, visual information has both a dorsal and a ventral pathway. These two pathways are left-hemisphere dominated. On the ventral route, centered in the posterior fusiform gyrus (BA37), it is assumed that activation is associated with automatic access to written-word forms (Cohen et al., 2000; Dehaene, Le Clec, Poline, Le Bihan, & Cohen, 2002). The dorsal route includes the angular (B39) and supramarginal (B40) gyri representing slower phonology-based assembly processes and also Wernicke's area (posterior BA22) which is thought to be responsible for the integration of written-word forms with semantic meanings. There is also one anterior component, located in the left inferior frontal gyrus (Broca's area, BA44, 45, 47) and connected to the two posterior pathways (ventral and dorsal), which is involved in phonological and articulatory output.

Event-related potential data (ERP) are consistent with the findings of computational and neuroimaging studies concerning the general time course of phonological, orthographic, and semantic information processing during single-word reading by skilled adults.[2] The ERP technique is used to study electrical activity in the brain and is based on electrical scalp recording of cortical area activation. Unlike neuroimaging techniques such as PET or fMRI, it offers high temporal resolution data pertaining to the type of processing under study, but with poor spatial resolution. The ERP technique thus provides a link between the temporal precision of chronometric approaches and the anatomical precision of neuroimaging approaches (Posner & McCandliss, 1999). Using the ERP technique, Bentin, Mouchetant-Rostaing, Giard, Echallier, and Pernier (1999) showed that accessing orthographic information[3] about written words in the fusiform gyrus takes about 200 ms, and McCarthy, Nobre, Bentin, and Spencer (1995) found that accessing phonological information in the superior temporal regions occurs at about 300 ms after word intake whereas accessing semantics in the temporo-parietal region occurs at about 400 ms (Kutas & Hilyard, 1984).

Coming back to fMRI studies, it seems increasingly evident (Booth et al., 2003b; Booth, Burman, Meyer, Gitelman, Parrish, & Mesulam, 2004; Pugh et al., 2000) that in normally developing readers the dorsal circuit predominates at first, and is associated with analytic processing aimed at integrating the orthographic features of printed written words with their phonological and lexical-semantic features. The ventral circuit constitutes a fast, late-developing word-identification system that underlies fluent written-word identification in skilled readers.

Using fMRI on 15 adults and 15 children (mean age 10.7), Booth et al. (2003b) found that during the processing of visually presented words, adults had more activation in the unimodal (only one type of information processing) visual areas of the fusiform gyrus (BA37) of the left hemisphere. The adults also exhibited selective activation in the fusiform gyrus during written-word tasks (compared to auditory word tasks), while the children did not. Thus, there appear to be developmental increases in the amount of fusiform gyrus activation devoted to visual processing. The lower activation found for children in this region is consistent with behavioral research showing that children are slow at processing orthographic and phonological information when they are reading words, and that skilled readers have developed very rapid written-word identification procedures.

In another fMRI study, Booth et al. (2004) investigated phonological-code activation using a rhyming task. Subjects were shown three written words and had to determine whether the final word rhymed with either of the first two words (jazz – last – has). This task, which requires grapho-phonological conversion, gave rise to greater activation in the angular gyrus of adults than of children (age 9–12), suggesting that skilled readers have more automatic access to phonological codes when reading words.

Lastly, the neural bases for the visual word identification reflex might be the "Visual Word Form Area" (VWFA), within the left occipito-temporal sulcus bordering the fusiform gyrus. This area has been shown to respond to visual words but not to a passive presentation of spoken words (Dehaene et al., 2002). Moreover, in Booth et al. (2003b) adults exhibited selective activation in the fusiform gyrus during a word-reading task, while children did not, thus suggesting that fusiform gyrus activation devoted to visual processing increases with development. Similar specialization can be acquired through experience in a specific visual domain (bird expertise) in the right fusiform gyrus, which has led McCandliss, Cohen, and Dehaene (2003) to suggest that the processes at work in the VWFA arise from a functional reorganization of visual circuits. Though not pre-tuned for word recognition, this region of the left visual cortex would exploit a pre-existing infero-temporal pathway for visual object recognition. The latter would undergo functional reorganization for coping with the demands of word reading.

Finally, this brain area could be devoted to written-word processing, whatever the writing system used, as suggested by a recent meta-analysis (Bolger, Perfetti, & Schneider, 2005), where the neuroimaging results for word reading within and across writing systems, including the English alphabetic writing system, the syllabic Japanese Kana system, and the logographic Chinese system, were examined. De facto, the region known as the Visual

Word Form Area shows strikingly consistent localization across tasks and across writing systems.

CONCLUSION

Findings supporting relatively autonomous written-word identification have led a number of researchers to advocate the separate investigation of written-word identification and reading comprehension, without completely dismissing the idea that these two processes may interact under certain conditions (the exact nature of the interaction(s) involved remains to be determined). In the area of reading acquisition, the assumption of autonomy implies that the primary challenge facing the beginning reader is to acquire automatic (rapid and irrepressible) written-word identification processes that require no attentional resources (Laberge & Samuels, 1974; Perfetti, 1985, 1994). It is the development of such automatic processes that will enable the reader to attain a level of skill comparable to his or her aural comprehension skills, by freeing the comprehension process from the decoding efforts needed in the initial stages of learning to read. Therefore, one of the major objectives in learning to read should be to acquire highly automatic reading "reflexes".

CHAPTER TWO

Reading acquisition in deep and shallow orthographies

The goal of reading is obviously to understand what is being read. However, this should not conceal the fact that the reading problems of children called "poor readers" or "dyslexics" are primarily due to difficulty identifying written words (see chapter 1). Moreover, subjects with reading disabilities rely on context to identify written words, precisely because they do not yet process written words automatically (see chapter 1). It is now widely agreed that reading comprehension requires both the ability to accurately and fluently identify written words and the ability to comprehend language in general (Gough & Tunmer, 1986). The processes involved in written-word identification are specific to reading, whereas those involved in reading comprehension are generally thought to be amodal, i.e., similar for spoken and written language. Indeed, Gernsbacher, Varner, and Faust (1990), who studied skilled readers with well-developed written-word skills, found an almost perfect correlation between their scores on spoken and written language understanding (0.92, see also Lecocq, Casalis, Leuwers, & Watteau, 1996). The main task facing beginning readers, then, is to find a means of understanding written texts as skillfully as they do the spoken language. They must first develop precise, rapid, and automatic written-word identification procedures. This allows them to allocate a large part of their processing capacity to text understanding.

To understand the problems facing beginning readers when they have to identify written words, it is necessary to determine precisely what is involved in reading acquisition in alphabetic systems compared with other writing systems. All writing systems transcribe units of the spoken language. What changes is the size of the basic units and their nature: these units can have meaning, such as words (lexical units), or can be meaningless, such as syllables or phonemes (sublexical units). Spoken language is, in fact, transcribed on three levels: the word or morpheme,[1] the syllable and the phoneme. In some writing systems (e.g., Chinese), words are basic units that cannot be split up. In other writing systems, words can be split up into sublexical units which are meaningless: i.e., syllables and graphemes. For example, the spoken word "chorus" contains two syllables (cho/rus) and five graphemes (ch-o-r-u-s). In a syllabic writing system (e.g., kanas of Japanese), syllables are basic units and cannot be split up. The basic units of an alphabetical writing system are graphemes, which transcribe the phonemes of the spoken language. Other writing systems transcribe phonological units by consonants and some morphological units by vowels, as in Arabic or Hebrew. Figure 2.1 presents a schematization of the main difficulties facing the beginning reader: the availability, consistency and size of units (or granularity) which connect the orthographical form of a word to its phonological form (Ziegler & Goswami, 2005).

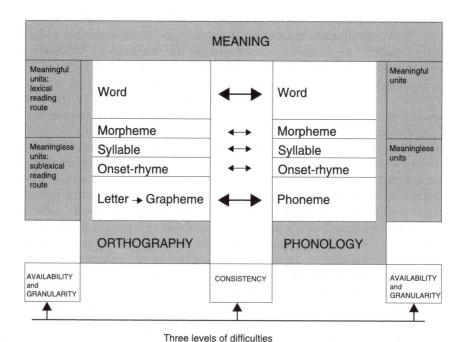

Figure 2.1.   Schematic description of the main problems facing beginning readers in alphabetical writing (adapted from Ziegler & Goswami, 2005).

The availability problem refers to the fact that, before learning to read, orthographic representations are not available, apart from a few words that children may have learned by heart. Also, not all phonological units are consciously accessible prior to reading. For instance, children do not have explicit access to phonemes that are the minimal distinctive features that make it possible to differentiate two words in a given language. Attending to phonemes requires a high degree of abstraction, since they are elements of spoken language that are rarely available as discrete units due to coarticulation. Indeed, phonemes are not pronounced one at a time, but in a single articulatory gesture within each syllable. For example, the word *resent* is not pronounced /r + i + z + e + n + t /, but /ri/ + /zent/. The consistency problem comes from the multiple pronunciations of some orthographic units and the multiple spellings of some phonological units, both of which slow down reading acquisition. In addition, the amount of inconsistency varies across languages and across different types of orthographic units. Granularity refers to the size of the processing unit. The problem here is that there are many more orthographic units to learn when access to the phonological system is based on larger grain sizes as opposed to smaller ones. In addition, the smaller grain-size units are meaningless (phoneme, onset-rhyme, syllable) while the larger ones are meaningful (words) or are at the interface between the semantic and formal aspects of language (morphemes). These units also differ in availability. For instance, the smallest meaningless phonological units (phonemes) are less available than the larger sized meaningful phonological ones (words). Achieving reading proficiency requires solving these three problems.

These considerations help us understand differences in the cost of learning to read using small versus large units. The use of a small number of graphemes and their corresponding phonemes gives children the opportunity to gain access to thousands of words they have heard but have never seen before. In such a case, children use small-size phonological units that are not readily accessible, but the memory load is not heavy. It is indeed supposed to be more economical to store this limited set of correspondences in memory than to learn an unlimited number of whole-word forms by heart, which is the case when access to the phonological system is based on larger grain sizes. In this case, children have to learn a very large number of words by rote memory. The memory load is thus tremendous, although the large-grain phonological units that children have to use are available, at least when the words are already stored in their phonological lexicon.

The main characteristic of all writing systems, except Chinese, is that two reading routes can be used to grasp written words: a lexical reading route (which relies on a large set of meaningful units), and a sublexical reading route (which relies on a small set of meaningless units). In alphabetic writing systems, reading high-frequency irregular words is generally used to assess the efficiency of the lexical reading route for two reasons: first, because these words are very frequent they are supposed to be stored in the internal lexicon of the reader; second, because these words are irregular their processing by another reading route (a sublexical reading route) leads to the production of regularization errors (*quay* read-aloud with a /kw/). The reading of unknown words (pseudowords) is mainly used to assess the efficiency of the sublexical reading route, because no lexical strategy is available unless these items are similar to words; e.g., either when they sound like a real word (like "taik", which sounds like the word "take") or when they share most of the spelling pattern of a real word (like "mable" which shares the same ending as the word "table").

The aim of this chapter is to provide a survey of the development of word reading in alphabetic writing systems. It is assumed here that the processes used by beginning readers depend both on general principles common to all languages, and on the specific characteristics of each language. In particular, no matter what language is being learned, reading acquisition strongly depends on the efficiency of the sublexical reading route (general principle), which in turn depends on the degree to which the writing system represents the spoken language it encodes (language specific). To illustrate these assumptions, we will first present the principal characteristics of some alphabetic writing systems (mainly English as compared to French, German, and Spanish). Then we will examine the psycholinguistic literature, while relying on cross-linguistic studies to assess what is general and what depends on the individual characteristics of each language, and on longitudinal studies to assess developmental trends.

A large part of this chapter is centered on a sublexical coding level whose writing units (letters, graphemes, rhymes, syllables) are not meaningful in themselves.[2] We will also present some studies dealing with another linguistic unit level, located at the interface between the formal and semantic aspects of a language, namely, its morphology, whether derivational (*dark*, *darken*, *darkness*, *darkroom*) or inflectional (used to indicate the plural of nouns and the person or tense of verbs, for instance).

ALPHABETIC WRITING SYSTEMS: LINGUISTIC DESCRIPTION AND STATISTICAL DATA

In alphabetic writing systems, the sounds of the spoken words are transcribed into written symbols (letters). For instance, the written form of the spoken French word /lak/ (with three sublexical phonological units, that is, three phonemes) is *lac* (with three sublexical writing units, that is, three graphemes). When children start learning to read, they have already largely mastered the spoken language. To acquire the skills specific to reading, they can thus rely on a limited set of correspondences between sublexical writing units and sublexical speaking units to figure out words already stored in their oral lexicon.

The ease of reading acquisition, however, is assumed to depend on the degree of transparency between graphemes and phonemes, which varies across languages, some of which have a more transparent writing system than others. In spite of this, research on reading has mainly been conducted with English-speaking participants, and reading models have been developed from this and generalized to all writing systems, or at least to alphabetic ones (see for example Coltheart, Curtis, Atkins, & Haller, 1993; Coltheart, Rastle, Perry, Langdon, & Ziegler, 2001; Harm & Seidenberg, 1999; Plaut et al., 1996; Seidenberg & McClelland, 1989; and for a developmental perspective, Frith, 1985, 1986; Goswami & Bryant, 1990; Harris & Coltheart, 1986; Marsh, Friedman, Welsch, & Desberg, 1981; Morton, 1989; Seymour, 1986). Clearly, English phonology and English orthography have a number of salient specificities that can influence reading and its acquisition. English is characterized by strong inconsistencies between spelling and sounds. According to Gelb (1952, p. 224):

> Many of our modern spellings are left-overs from a period in which a word could be spelled in several different ways, depending on the whim of the writer. There is no rhyme or reason for the English spelling of *height* as against *high*, *speak* as against *speech*, *proceed* as against *precede*, or *attorneys* as against *stories*. The preservation of these irrational spellings in modern English writing seems to be due to an old and inborn individualistic tendency, averse to accepting any bounds imposed by systematization.

Another difficulty in English word reading stems from the fact that word stress has to be taken into account to correctly pronounce vowels in words with more than one syllable. Vowels in unstressed syllables of polysyllabic words virtually disappear and are replaced by a neutral sound called schwa (Delattre, 1965). The problems posed by vowel reading in polysyllabic words may be the reason why most studies on reading in English, and most models of reading, pertain solely to one-syllable words.

The rest of this section describes the main differences between the orthography of English and other languages, especially French, German, and Spanish, while highlighting the significant features of these languages that might influence reading and its acquisition.

Main characteristics of English, French, German, and Spanish

Inheritance of the Greek and Latin alphabets

All alphabetic systems use a notation that includes consonants and vowels. These graphic units – called graphemes – correspond to phonemes, or families of sounds that indicate differences in meaning. For example, /t/ and /d/

are different phonemes in English, French, German, and Spanish; they differentiate *tin* and *din* in English, *toute* and *doute* in French, *tank* and *dank* in German, *tos* and *dos* in Spanish.

The writing systems of these languages used an alphabet which comes from the Semitic consonantal alphabet from which the Greek and then the Latin alphabets were derived. The Greek language had a number of particularities that made it difficult to transcribe using a consonantal alphabet. For example, clusters of two or three consonants are very common in Greek, so a Greek text in which the vowels are not systematically noted cannot be deciphered. The generally accepted interpretation of the origin of vowels is that the Greeks attributed a vocalic value to certain letters of the Semitic alphabet that they did not use, namely, *alpha* for /a/, *iota* for /i/, *upsilon* for /y/, *epsilon* and *eta* for /e/, *omikron* and *omega* for /o/, and a combination of *omikron* and *upsilon* for /u/ (Gelb, 1952). This set of vowels is sufficient to spell the 5 pure Spanish vowels, but does not cover the 14 or more pure vowels of spoken English, French, and German. To transcribe vowels, then, it was necessary to use a combination of letters (as in the French nasals *an, on*, etc.) or a letter with a diacritic mark (*u* and *ü* to differentiate /u/ from /y/ in German).

Phonological and orthographic structures of consonants

Most of the differences between the phonological and orthographic structures of English, French, German, and Spanish are related to vowels, not consonants (Delattre, 1965, 1966). For consonants, the ratio of the number of phonemes to the number of graphemes is almost the same in English, French, and German (20–24 to 50–60), with Spanish having the smallest difference (20–23 to 33). All four of these languages have similar inconsistencies (more than one pronunciation for one grapheme or more than one spelling for one phoneme), some of which are context dependent. For example, the letter *c* is pronounced /k/ when followed by the vowel *a, o*, or *u* or by a consonant, but is pronounced differently when followed by the vowel *i* and *e* in Spanish (*cerca*, /θ. . .k/), German (*circa*, /ts. . .k/), French (*cercle*, /s. . .k/), and English (*circle*, /s. . .k/). Likewise, the letter *g* may be /g/ or /ʒ/ in German, French, and English (e.g., *garage*, /g. . .ʒ/), and /g/ or /X/ in Spanish (*garaje, gente* /Xente/). However, in English, *c* and *g* followed by *e* or *i* can also be pronounced /k/ and /g/ or /dʒ/, respectively (for example, *celt* and *gift, get, gel*). Note also that in Spanish and French, *gu* is pronounced /g/, as in *guerra* or *gui*, and /gw/ or /gμ/ as in *guardia* or *aiguille*. The most important difficulty in German orthography is that the written voiced consonants (b, d, g, v, z, . . .) are usually pronounced as their voiceless counterparts (e.g., the *b* in *Ab* is pronounced /p/, the *d* in *Feld* is /t/, the *g* in *Tag* is /k/, the *v* in *Vater* is /f/, and the *z* in *Putz* is /s/).

A spelling difficulty shared by English and French is that many written consonants are silent. In English, for example, *kn*, *ps*, and *wr* at the beginning of a word become /n/, /s/, and /r/ (as in *know*, *psychology*, and *write*); the grapheme *gh* is silent before *t* (as in *fight*) and at the end of a word (as in *high*). Also, /t/ and /k/ disappear between /f/ or /s/ and /n/ or /l/ (as in *soften*, *castle*, and *muscle*). Moreover, *L* and *R* are not clearly articulated in a post-vocalic position, this phenomenon being stronger for *R* which merely lengthens the preceding monophthong (as in *barn*, *bird*, *board*). When the preceding vowel is a diphthong, a weak *R* appears (as in *bare* or *bear*). In French, silent consonants are mainly morphological markers located at the end of a word (as in *sot*, pronounced /so/, see p. 27). In Spanish, a written consonant can also be silent at the end of a word, particularly in the dialects spoken in southern Spain.

Another particularity of English and French written consonants, which mostly causes spelling problems, is that they can be doubled without clear phonological properties except in some cases. For instance, in both of these languages, *ss* corresponds to /s/, whereas the intervocalic *s* corresponds almost always to /z/ in French, not in English (e.g., *to use* and *use of*); in French, a double consonant modifies the pronunciation of a preceding *e* (*dette* /det/ versus *petit* /pəti/. For consonants, then, grapheme–phoneme correspondences (GPC) and phoneme–grapheme correspondences (PGC) are more complex in English than in French or German, and especially than in Spanish (see here above, see also Appendix in Sprenger-Charolles, 2003). As a whole, however, the differences between the four languages for consonants are not great compared to those of vowels.

Phonological and orthographic structures of vowels

Compared to Spanish, and to a lesser extent German and French, the reading of vowels in English causes major problems. In Spanish, the five monophthongs[3] are easily represented by the letters *a*, *e*, *i*, *o*, and *u*. In German, the 14 monophthongs are grouped into pairs (/a/a/, /e/ɛ/, /i/I/, /o/O/, y/Y/, /u/U/, /ø/ œ/). An umlaut can be used to transcribe these sets of phonemes (e.g., *ü* versus *u* for /y/ and /u/) but allographs are also found (e.g., *ü* and *uh* for /y/). Vocalic lengthening is usually achieved by doubling the vowel or by adding a silent *h* or a silent *e* after the vowel, as in *Bohne* or *Biene*, while a vowel followed by a double consonant is short, as in *offen*. This system is simpler for reading than for spelling because long vowels can be spelled in more than one way.

The spelling of French vowels is characterized by a high number of digraphs and by the presence of allographs (*o* also spelled *au*, *eau* . . .). But with the exceptions of *e* (which can be /e/ɛ/, /ə/ or /a/) and *en* (which can be /ĩ/ or /ã/), the French vocalic graphemes mainly correspond to only one phoneme (Catach, 1980; Véronis, 1986). Thus, grapheme–phoneme correspondences (GPC) are highly predictable. Phoneme–grapheme correspondences (PGC) are more difficult to manipulate because it is often necessary to choose between alternative spellings for a particular vocalic phoneme.

The English monophthongs are difficult to explain without taking into account the consonants that follow, the number of syllables, and word stress. In one-syllable words, short vowel GPCs exhibit few exceptions. However, to read correctly, one must know that short vowels cannot be found at the end of a word, that they are followed by a non-silent consonant, and that the post-vocalic *r* changes some of the preceding vowels. Long vowel spelling is complex. For example, there are many graphemes for /i:/ (*thEme, machIne, sEE, sEA, cAEsar, concEIve, nIEce, kEY, happY, pEOple,* and *subpOEna*). English also stands out clearly from the other three languages by the presence of schwa. This neutral vowel is found in German and French, but it is almost always written *e*. In English the majority of unstressed vowels turn out to be pronounced as a schwa, and according to Delattre (1965), over 50% of the vowels in connected speech are neutralized in this way. Therefore, a person reading English words would have correct pronunciation half the time if schwa was used instead of the vowel sounds corresponding to the specific vocalic graphemes. Yet, to spell the same words correctly, it is necessary to memorize the conventional graphemes.

Diphthongs (see note 3) do not exist in French. The Spanish spelling of the diphthongs has few exceptions, except that the letter *y* can be used at the end of a word instead of the letter *i* (*bailar/fray, boina/doy, beige/ley*). In German, alternative spellings are found for /ai/ (*LAIb, AmEIse*) and /oi/ (*erlÄUtern, hEUte*). The spelling of English diphthongs is highly unpredictable. They can be represented by a single-letter grapheme or by a digraph (for example: /ai/ is written *i* in *fine*, *y* in *try*, *igh* in *light*, and *uy* in *buy*). Moreover, all English vowels are more or less articulated in a constant movement. This phenomenon is not easy to represent graphically. According to Delattre's analysis (1965), the closest transcription of the English *do* is [dddəUUUuuuuw].

Nevertheless, English vowel spelling difficulties can be reduced if, instead of GPCs, correspondences between the onset of the word and its rhyme are taken into account (e.g., *ight*/ait/ in *night, fight, light, right, sight, tight*; *ake*/ eik/ in *make, cake, bake*). This may be why some researchers have assumed that subjects rely on this type of unit, especially when they start learning to read (Goswami & Bryant, 1990).

In sum, compared to German and French, English GPC and PGC for vowels are more complex, with Spanish being characterized by an almost one-to-one perfect mapping. In addition, word rhymes seem to have a specific status in English orthography.

Other differences between English, French, German, and Spanish

In English, German, and Spanish, words have some degree of phonetic independence, since every full word has its own stress pattern. However, the place of word stress is more variable in English than in German or Spanish (Delattre, 1965). This makes vowel reading harder because a schwa must be used in unstressed positions. In French, stress falls mainly on the word group, so readers cannot make stress errors when reading.

In addition, there is a preponderance of open syllables in French and Spanish, whereas in English and German most syllables have a closed structure (Delattre, 1965). Thus, in French and Spanish – but not in English or German – the rhyme unit is usually a vowel, and thus a phoneme. As a consequence, a model of reading that attaches importance to the role of rhyme units at the beginning of reading acquisition (see Goswami & Bryant, 1990) may be more suitable for English and German than for French and Spanish.

Finally, whereas English is clearly an outlier for grapheme–phoneme correspondences, French is the language that stands apart when it comes to the transcription of morphological markers. There are very few differences between the spoken and written languages at this level for Spanish, German, and English, whereas in French a large number of morphological markers which are not pronounced are used in the written language. This is true of derivational markers. For example, the *d* at the end of the French word *lourD* (heavy), from which is derived the word *lourdeur* (heaviness) is silent, whereas the *d* in the English word *kinD* (from which *kindness* is derived) is pronounced. In addition, at the end of a French word, the *s* that signals the plural (*tables*) is silent, as is the *s* that indicates the second person of verbs (*tu manges* [you eat]) whereas these written letters are pronounced in the English words *tables* or *he/she eats*. These differences between the spoken and written languages in French are due to its Romance origin. At first, French used inflection marks to indicate, for example, the person of verbs, as in Spanish (*cantO, cantAS, cantA, cantAMOS, cantAIS, cantAN*), whereas modern French relies on pronouns (*je, tu, il/elle, nous, vous, ils/elles*) as in English (*I, you, he/she, we, you, they*). However, in written modern French there are leftovers from the inflectional system of verbs, like the *s* and *nt* in *tu chantes* and *ils chantent* (neither of which are pronounced) or the *ons* and the *ez* in *nous chantons* and *vous chantez* (pronounced /ô/ and /E/, respectively).

From descriptive analyses to statistical data

The data presented above are purely descriptive. Statistical analyses have also been carried out, at both the rhyme and grapheme–phoneme levels. The consistency of the orthography-to-phonology (O–P) and the phonology-to-orthography (P–O) relationships were computed at the onset-rhyme level for French by Ziegler, Jacobs, and Stone (1996) and for one-syllable English words by Ziegler, Stone, and Jacobs (1997).[4] Regarding O–P rhyme consistency, a word was considered inconsistent when its orthographic rhyme could be read in more than one way (*int*, in the English words *pint* and *hint*; *emme* in the French words *femme* /fam/ [woman] and *flemme* /flem/ [laziness]). Regarding P–O rhyme consistency, a word was considered inconsistent when its phonological rhyme could be written in more than one way, e.g., /ip/ in the English words *deep* and *heap*, /o/ in the French words *sot* (silly), *seau* (bucket), *saut* (jump). In a synthesis of these analyses that also included data from German, Ziegler (1998; see Table 2.1a) found a significantly higher degree of O–P inconsistency in English than in either French or German, and higher proportions of P–O inconsistency in all three languages, but significantly much higher in French than in either English or German.

The statistical differences between English and the other two languages are not as great as might be expected according to our linguistic description based on grapheme–phoneme and phoneme–grapheme correspondences (GPC and PGC) and to the fact that the 40 English phonemes can be spelled in 1120 ways (Coulmas, 1996), whereas the 35 French phonemes have only 130 different spellings (Catach, 1980), the 40 German phonemes only 85 (Valtin, 1989), and the 29–32 Spanish phonemes only 45. The differences between the observed results at the rhyme level and the expected results at the phoneme level may be due to a strong decrease in inconsistency when rhymes in monosyllabic words are taken into account, particularly for English vowels (see also Treiman, Mullennix, Bijeljac-Babic, & Richmond-Welty, 1995).

Accordingly, English is characterized by a very low GPC consistency for vowels (Peereman & Content, 1998, 1999)[5] that increases drastically within rhymes (see Table 2.1b). In contrast, French vowel consistency is already high for words in isolation (GPC). However, PGC consistency for vowels is low in both English and French, and does not change significantly when rhymes are taken into account. For consonants, except in two cases (PGC consistency for final consonants both in English and French), GPC and PGC consistency is significantly higher than GPC and PGC consistency for vowels in both languages (see Table 2.1c). However, a fact that could bias the results is that only monosyllabic words were included in the Ziegler et al., and Peereman et al., databases, and at least for French, monosyllabic words represent only a small percentage (7%, that is, 2396 of the 36,000 words in the Micro Robert; see Content, Mousty, & Radeau, 1990; 9.5% or 4306 of the 45,080 words in MANULEX,[6] Lété, Sprenger-Charolles, & Colé, 2003).

Statistical and linguistic descriptions thus clearly indicate that English is a noticeable outsider because it has a deeper orthography than German, or even than French, at least for reading.

Table 2.1(a)
Consistency of orthography-to-phonology (O–P) and phonology-to-orthography (P–O) relationships at the onset-rhyme level for French, English, and German monosyllabic words (adapted from Ziegler, 1998)

	O–P consistency %	P–O consistency %
English	88	72
French	95	50
German	94	74

Table 2.1(b)
Vowel consistency at the grapheme–phoneme and phoneme–grapheme correspondence levels (GPC and PGC) and at the rhyme level (O–P and P–O). Adapted from Peereman and Content (1998)

	GPC consistency %	PGC consistency %
English	48	67
French	94	68

	O–P consistency	P–O consistency
English	91	67
French	98	58

Table 2.1(c)
Initial consonant (or consonant cluster) consistency and final consonant (or consonant cluster) consistency (adapted from Peereman and Content, 1998)

	GPC consistency %	PGC consistency %
Initial position		
English	95	90
French	95	99
Final position		
English	96	50
French	97	58

READING ACQUISITION: CROSS-LINGUISTIC STUDIES

In line with the above analysis, and if it is true that from the beginning of reading acquisition, children rely on connections between sublexical writing units and sublexical speaking units, the following hypotheses can be set

forth. First, if the degree of transparency of grapheme–phoneme correspondences (GPCs) has an effect on reading acquisition, quantitative differences should be found between Spanish, French, and English readers:
Spanish readers can be expected to outperform French readers, who in turn,
can be expected to outperform English readers. In addition, in most languages, spelling acquisition should be more difficult than reading acquisition
because GPCs are more transparent than PGCs, especially in French.
Second, if the processes implemented by beginning readers partially depend
on the specific characteristics of each language, qualitative differences can
also be predicted. More specifically, learning to read in a shallow orthography
(Spanish, German) should lead to the use of processing based on sublexical units (especially GPCs), whereas learning to read in a deep orthography (English) could lead to a greater reliance on processing based on lexical
units. Also, because of GPC inconsistencies in English vowels, we can expect
more errors on vowels than on consonants in that language, and greater
reliance on rhyme units, given that taking word rhymes into account reduces
this inconsistency. These two aspects may differentiate English readers from
non-English ones.

Quantitative differences between English and non-English beginning readers

According to most studies, the acquisition of sublexical reading skills in
English is slow and difficult. Mean accuracy for pseudoword reading at the
end of the first grade typically ranges from 20% to 60% (Jorm, Share,
MacLean, & Matthews, 1984; Juel, Griffith, & Gough, 1986; Siegel & Ryan,
1988). Because of the substantial specificity of English orthography, we
only examined comparative studies in which the items were matched across
languages, in order to take comparable spelling difficulties into account.

English-speaking versus German-speaking children

In the study by Wimmer and Goswami (1994), 7-, 8-, and 9-year-old
English- and German-speaking children were asked to read number words
that were similar in the two languages (e.g., *three-drei*). Pseudowords were
derived from these words by changing the initial consonant. When reading
the pseudowords, even the youngest German children made few errors, and
made even fewer than the oldest English children despite less reading experience. In another study, Frith, Wimmer, and Landerl (1998) asked 7-, 8-, and
9-year-old English and German children to read words that were similar in
spelling, pronunciation, meaning, and familiarity (e.g., *Summer/Sommer*).
Pseudowords were derived from the words by changing the initial consonant
(*Rummer/Rommer*). The English children performed less well than the

German ones, both on words (80% and 95% correct responses, respectively), and on pseudowords (59% and 88%), where their scores were even farther apart (29% difference), especially for the 7-year-olds (45% and 85%) where the difference between the two language groups was 40%. The same children were asked to read trisyllabic pseudowords with simple open syllables and no consonant clusters (e.g., *tarulo*, *surimo*). Accuracy and reaction times were computed. The scores of the 8-year-old English children were again lower than those of their German age mates, both on accuracy (70% and 99%, respectively) and on latency (4.3 s and 1.9 s respectively). These results suggest that the reading skills of German children are better than those of English ones, which can be expected given that English orthography is clearly deeper than German orthography.

English-speaking versus French- and Spanish-speaking children

In a cross-linguistic study, Canadian English- and French-speaking children were followed from 5.9 to 7 years of age (Bruck, Genesee, & Caravolas, 1997). Word and pseudoword reading was assessed at the end of the first grade. High-frequency, regular monosyllabic words whose spelling patterns are commonly taught to first graders were selected. Pseudowords were constructed by changing the first letter of the words. The French and English items were equated in terms of the number of letters and GPC difficulties. In spite of fewer pre-literacy opportunities and no reading instruction in kindergarten, at the end of the first grade the French-speaking children obtained higher scores than their English-speaking age mates on both words (76% versus 52%) and pseudowords (63% versus 36%).

In another study (Goswami, Gombert, & Barrera, 1998, Experiment 3), 7-, 8-, and 9-year-old English-, French-, and Spanish-speaking children were required to read monosyllabic and bisyllabic words, and pseudowords that were "analogs" of the words (in English, *tape* versus *fape*; in French, *voile* versus *roile*; in Spanish: *mientes* versus *lientes*). For each age level, the three language groups were matched as closely as possible on reading age and on knowledge of the real words from which the pseudowords were derived. For the words, the Spanish group's scores were higher than the French group's, which were higher than the English group's (94%, 86%, and 61%, respectively). Similar results were observed for the pseudowords (91%, 73%, and 31%). The negative impact of orthographic deepness is illustrated in Figure 2.2, which presents the results of the 7-year-old English-, French-, and Spanish-speaking children tested in the Goswami et al., study, and those of same age English and French speakers tested in the Bruck et al., study (1997).

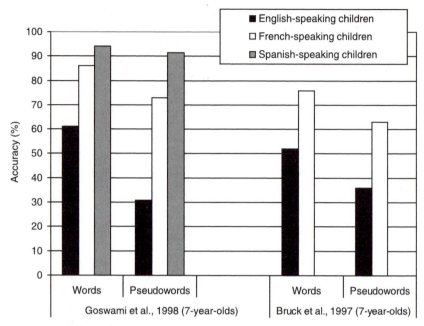

Figure 2.2.   Reading: accuracy (%) 7-year-old English-, French-, and Spanish-speaking children (Goswami et al., 1998) and same-age English- and French-speaking children (adapted from Bruck et al., 1997).

Other cross-language comparisons

In a large cross-linguistic study (Seymour, Aro, & Erskine, 2003), the reading skills of children who spoke 13 European languages (Greek, Italian, Spanish, Portuguese, French, German, Dutch, Norwegian, Swedish, Danish, Finnish, Icelandic, English) were assessed. Except for English and French, only first graders were examined. The English sample included children who were not held back by a social disadvantage (children with a low socioeconomic background were excluded) and whose reading scores were above the UK norms (the chronological ages and reading ages of the first graders were 5.6 and 6.2; the second graders, 6.6 and 7.2). The English-speaking first graders were the youngest children, whereas the English-speaking second graders were approximately the same age as the French, Spanish, Italian, Portuguese, Greek, Icelandic, and Dutch first graders, and were one year younger than the German, Norwegian, Swedish, Danish, and Finnish first graders.

Sets of very familiar high-frequency words were sampled from the reading materials used in the early stages of primary school in each language. These sets included 18 content words (mainly imageable nouns such as *home*, *school*, *bird*) and 18 function words (such as *them*, *about*, *out*, *many*). The items selected for the deeper orthographies were allowed to contain orthographic-ally complex features (diacritics, multi-letter graphemes, and irregularities). Two lists of pseudowords were also built, one consisting of one-syllable CV (consonant vowel), VC, or CVC items, and the other of two-syllable items with a VCV, CVCV, or VCVC structure. The items were formed by sampling dominant and consistent grapheme–phoneme correspondences in each lan-guage (one letter for one sound). Accuracy and processing speed were assessed. Processing speed was determined for the reading of each full list of items and was computed on all responses, whether correct or incorrect.

In the part that follows, we will mainly discuss the results obtained for reading accuracy, because it is difficult to compare processing times for lists where less than 35% of the words were read correctly (which was the case for the English-speaking first graders) to those where the correct response rate was 70% (other first graders, except pseudoword reading by the Danish children). The accuracy scores for the English, French, Spanish, and German (children from Austria) languages are presented in Figure 2.3. The statistical analyses reported in the paper (Seymour et al., 2003) indicated that, for word-reading accuracy, the English-speaking first graders' mean was signifi-cantly below those of the French, Danish, and Portuguese first graders, which were in turn significantly below the means of the children of all other lan-guages.[7] In addition, the results of the English-speaking second graders formed a subset with the Danish, Portuguese, and French (accuracy below 80%). For pseudoword reading, the scores of the English second-grade group (overall mean 63.5%) were below those of all Grade 1 samples other than the Danish.

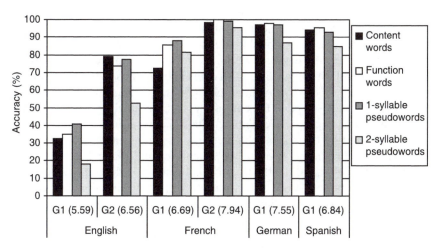

Figure 2.3. Reading: accuracy (%) for the English, French, Spanish, and German languages (adapted from Seymour et al., 2003).

At an equivalent age (around 6.6), the reading level of the English-speaking children was lower than that of most of the others, especially for the Spanish and French comparisons highlighted in this chapter. These results are all the more striking since the English group had benefited from one additional year of reading instruction, in addition to being a privileged sample because the children were not from socially disadvantaged homes and their reading scores were above UK norms.

However, it seems that the differences between anglophone and non-anglophone children are greater at the beginning of reading acquisition than later on. This was suggested in Aro and Wimmer's study (2003), where data from seven languages were analyzed. As above for the Seymour et al. (2003) study, only the results of the English-, French-, German-, and Spanish-speaking children will be presented here, and only those pertaining to accuracy.[8] Nine pseudowords derived from number words were generated for each language (*nour* from *four* in English, *zwier* from *vier* in German, *datre* from *quatre* in French, and *duatro* from *cuatro* in Spanish). In all school grades studied, the English-speaking children were the youngest,[9] but their mean reading age was above the national norms (nine months ahead in Grade 1 and at least one year ahead in the subsequent grades). As in the Seymour et al. (2003) study, the Spanish, French, and German readers outperformed the English ones (see Figure 2.4). Moreover, there was a large amount of variance in the results of the English-speaking children, 23% of whom read less than half of the pseudowords correctly, as compared to only 3 of the 649 children in the other language groups.

Another interesting aspect of the data presented in Figure 2.4 concerns the evolution of cross-language differences as the children got older. Whereas the English-speaking first graders differed by 37% from the French-, German-, and Spanish-speaking first graders combined, the English-speaking children's lag gradually decreased as school grade increased (from 20.5% in Grade 2 to 18% in Grade 3 and 4% in Grade 4). Similar results were found in the study by Frith et al. (1998) with English and German children, thus suggesting that the negative impact of English orthography gradually vanishes. However, the small differences observed at the end of these studies might be due to ceiling effects (see for example, Aro & Wimmer, 2003; Figure 2.4).

As suggested by the results obtained in cross-linguistic studies involving older children (mean age 9 years; see Pate, Snowling, & de Jong, 2004) or adults (Paulesu et al., 2001), the negative influence of orthographic inconsistency seems to be long-lasting. In these studies, processing time was examined, but contrary to the other studies, taking into account vocal reaction time between target onset and correct response onset (by means of a computer). The comparison between English- and Dutch-speaking children (Pate et al., 2004) brought out a lag in the English group on all measures (446 and 576 ms for word and pseudoword). Similar trends were reported in the study

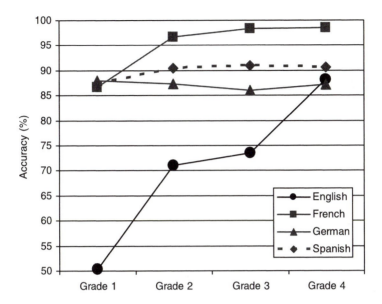

Figure 2.4.   Reading accuracy (%) for the English, French, Spanish, and German languages, Grades 1, 2, 3 and 4 (adapted from Aro & Wimmer, 2003).

The results for the English and German children are from Landerl and Wimmer's (2000) English- and German-speaking samples (Study 2) and Defior et al.'s (2002) Spanish-speaking sample, with approximately the same number of children per school grade as in France.

involving English-, French-, and Italian-speaking adults (Paulesu et al., 2001), where the differences between English and French or Italian controls were larger for pseudoword reading (90 and 260 ms respectively) than for word reading (30 and 120 ms respectively). These results further support the idea that reading acquisition strongly depends on the consistency of the orthography.

Qualitative differences between English and non-English beginning readers

The studies we have examined indicate that, in reading, non-English-speaking children outperform English-speaking ones. They also suggest that anglophone and non-anglophone children do not use the same reading procedures. For instance, in the Wimmer and Goswami (1994) study, a markedly lower correlation between pseudoword and word-reading scores was observed in the youngest English group (0.58) as compared to the youngest German group (0.93), thus suggesting that the English-speaking children, but not the German-speaking ones, relied on different reading processes for words and pseudowords. Similarly, correlations between words and pseudowords are very high for French children (0.84 in the middle of the first grade and 0.81 at the end; Sprenger-Charolles, Siegel, & Bonnet, 1998b). In addition, compared to children learning to read in a more transparent orthography, English-speaking children appear to be more sensitive to word frequency (Frith et al., 1998) and to make more lexicalization errors (the target item being replaced by another word, e.g., Ellis & Hooper, 2001; Frith et al., 1998; Spencer & Hanley, 2003). These results thus suggest that English-speaking children use top-down lexical representations to supplement error-prone bottom-up processes based on sublexical units.

From sublexical to lexical processing

The same tendency was found in a recent study in which the effect of pseudo-homophony was assessed in reading aloud and in silent reading (Goswami, Ziegler, Dalton, & Schneider, 2001). English-speaking and German-speaking children matched on reading level had to read pseudowords that sounded like real words (pseudo-homophones) and control pseudowords that included (+) or did not include (–) familiar rhyme chunks from real words (in English: *faik* [fake], *dake* [+], *koog* [–]; in German: *hunt* [hund], *tund* [+], *lunss* [–]). Since lexical retrieval is possible for pseudo-homophones, the effect of pseudo-homophony was assumed to have a positive impact on accuracy in reading aloud, and to lead to a high proportion of errors on homophone pseudowords in lexical decision tasks. In reading aloud, the expected facilitatory effect of pseudo-homophony was only observed for the English-speaking children (see Figure 2.5a). On the other hand, on the lexical decision task, the expected negative impact of pseudo-homophony was only observed for the German-speaking children (see Figure 2.5b). These results suggest that the activation of phonological information is quite automatic and difficult to inhibit for German-speaking children, but not for English-speaking ones, who rely to a larger extent on lexical retrieval.

The effect of item length is also considered to be an indicator of sublexical processing because this kind of reading process is assumed to be sequential and thus sensitive to item length. In the study by Goswami et al. (1998, Experiment 3), 7-, 8-, and 9-year-old English-, French-, and Spanish-speaking children were required to read monosyllabic and bisyllabic words and pseudowords. The results of the younger Spanish children (7 year olds) were already very high, and the presence of a length effect suggested that they relied on efficient sublexical processing, probably based on GPC. The length effect was found neither for the English readers nor for the French. However, the difference in length between short and long items was not the same across languages (for monosyllabic and bisyllabic items, 3.3 versus 6 letters in Spanish, 5 versus 5.8 in French, and 4.1 versus 5.7 in English). These differences may account for why the length effect was significant for the Spanish

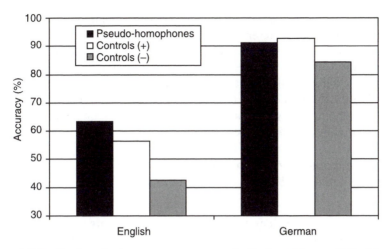

Figure 2.5(a).   Reading aloud: mean accuracy scores for 7-, 8- and 9-year-old English- and German-speaking children matched on reading level (adapted from Goswami et al., 2001).

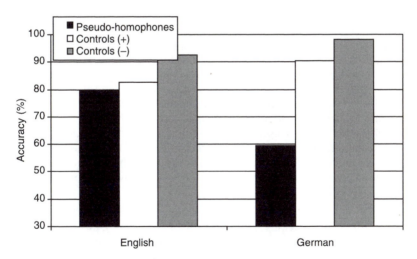

Figure 2.5(b).   Lexical decision: mean accuracy scores for 8- and 9-year-old English- and German-speaking children matched on reading level (adapted from Goswami et al., 2001).

children but not for the French. The nonsignificant effect of length observed for the English-speaking children suggests that they relied less on sequential processing than the Spanish-speaking children. This has also been found in comparisons between English-speaking children and children learning to read in a more transparent orthography, namely German (e.g., Goswami et al., 2001) and Welsh (e.g., Ellis & Hooper, 2001)

Taken together, the results for English-speaking children indicate reliance on top-down lexical representations, as suggested by the facilitatory effect of homophony in pseudoword reading aloud, the lack of a length effect, and lexicalization errors. The results of Spanish-speaking and/or German-speaking children indicate that they mainly rely on sublexical processing, as suggested by the negative impact of item length, the detrimental effect of pseudo-homophony in lexical decision, and the very high correlations between pseudoword and word processing.

From grapheme–phoneme correspondences to rhyme units

Another issue is the size of the units used in the sublexical reading procedure, which can be small such as a grapheme–phoneme or large such as an onset-rhyme or syllable. This issue was tackled recently by Ziegler and Goswami (2005) in the framework of their "psycholinguistic grain size theory". According to these authors (p. 11):

> The reduced reliability of small grain sizes in relatively inconsistent orthographies may well lead children to develop recoding strategies at more than one grain size. Such development of multiple recoding strategies will necessarily take longer than developing a single recoding strategy. For example, in English it has been argued that an important recoding strategy developmentally is the rhyme analogy strategy (Goswami, 1986, 1988). Following Glushko's (1979) definition of analogies in reading, Goswami showed that English children used orthographic chunks corresponding to rhymes to read novel words from early in the acquisition process (e.g., using *beak* as a basis for reading *peak*). This raises the question of whether rhyme analogies have any role to play in reading more consistent orthographies, where grapheme-phoneme recoding strategies alone are a perfectly efficient guide to pronunciation.

In addition, it is because of vowel GPC inconsistency in English that we can expect stronger reliance on rhyme units in this language, given that taking word rhymes into account reduces this inconsistency (see p. 26; see also Sprenger-Charolles, 2003). On the other hand, relying on rhyme units should not have a strong impact in languages that include words with clearly articulated vowels, and of course, languages that have mainly open syllables, such as French and Spanish as compared to English and German (Delattre, 1965).

This assumption leads us first to predict more reading errors on vowels than on consonants, especially in English – a result which has often been reported (Bryson & Werker, 1989; Fischer, Liberman & Shankweiler, 1977; Fowler, Liberman & Shankweiler, 1977; Fowler, Shankweiler & Liberman, 1979; Frith et al., 1998; Siegel & Faux, 1989). This has not been found for

French (Sprenger-Charolles & Siegel, 1997), German (Frith et al., 1998; Wimmer, 1993), or in Italian (Cossu, Shankweiler, Liberman, & Gugliotta, 1995). Moreover, differences related to orthographic deepness in the use of GPC versus rhyme units have been reported in cross-linguistic studies, with reliance on rhyme analogy being found for English-speaking and even French-speaking children, but not for children who speak Spanish, Greek, or German (Goswami et al., 1998; Goswami, Porpodas, & Wheelwright, 1997; Goswami, Ziegler, Dalton, & Schneider, 2003).

For example, in the study by Goswami et al. (1998, Experiment 3), 7-, 8-, and 9-year-old English-, French-, and Spanish-speaking children were required to read words and pseudowords that included (+) or did not include (–) familiar orthographic rhyme chunks from real words (in English, *tape*, *fape* [+], *faish* [–]; in French, *voile*, *roile* [+], *loave* [–]; in Spanish: *mientes*, *lientes* [+], *teslien* [–]). A significant analogy effect was found for both French-speaking and English-speaking children, but not for Spanish-speaking ones. However, the use of larger orthographic chunks had a more dramatic effect on pseudoword reading accuracy for the English group. Accordingly, for 7 year olds, the score increase due to the analogy effect was 20% on monosyllabic and 15% on bisyllabic pseudowords for the English speakers, as compared to 5% on monosyllabic and 3% on bisyllabic items for the French. As argued by Ziegler and Goswami (2005, p. 12), "The finding that French children as well as English children show rhyme analogy effects suggests that children learning to read inconsistent orthographies are indeed developing recoding strategies at larger grain sizes."

In our minds, this statement is only partially correct, because the nature of French orthography is such that French-speaking children cannot strongly rely on orthographic rhyme units. This contention is based on the results of a French study (Sprenger-Charolles et al., 1998b) in which analogous pseudowords were found to be read slightly, but significantly, better than non-analogous pseudowords (5% difference) in the middle of the first grade, as in the Goswami et al. (1998) study. However, the analogy effect was observed when frequency and lexicality had no impact on reading scores. It may therefore be rooted in a facilitatory effect of the oral lexicon, analogous pseudowords being constructed from high-frequency words that have preprogrammed articulatory codes (e.g., *mable* from *table*). This interpretation is supported by the lack of a comparable analogy effect in spelling, a modality in which articulatory codes do not directly interfere with the production of the correct response as it does in reading aloud. Further indicators that French-speaking children mainly process analogous and non-analogous pseudowords in the same way at the beginning of reading and spelling acquisition are the findings that in both reading and spelling graphemic length (comparison of pseudowords with one-letter graphemes to those with a digraph, such as *ou* /u/ or *ch* /ʃ/) had the same effect on analogous and non-analogous pseudowords, and that the correlations between these two types of pseudowords were very high (0.90 in reading and 0.86 in spelling).

By contrast, English-speaking children seem to rely on rhyme units, as suggested in the results obtained by Goswami (1986, 1988; for a review, see Goswami & Bryant, 1990) and more recently by Brown and Deavers (1999). In the latter study, children were asked to read pseudowords, all of which were consistent at the orthographic-rhyme level but which had either regular or irregular GPCs. If children use small units such as a GPC, then they should read the *a* of *dalk* as in *tap*, but if they use analogies based on larger units such as rhymes, they should read it as in *talk*. Brown and Deavers's (1999) results indicated that the children were in the process of developing a "flexible-unit-size strategy" based both on "small units" and "large units". The results they obtained for English-speaking children differed from those already reported for German (Frith et al., 1998; Goswami et al., 2001; Wimmer & Goswami, 1994), which suggest that German-speaking children rely on an efficient sublexical reading procedure based on GPCs. Goswami et al. (2003) assessed differences in the use of small (GPC) versus large (rhymes) units by English-speaking and German-speaking children matched as closely as possible on reading age (as evaluated on standardized reading tests). The rationale underlying this study was that the application of a reading procedure based on large units should be very successful for pseudowords that can be read using this type of unit (such as *dake* [cake, make] and *guff* [cuff, puff]) when only such pseudowords are included in the list, and vice versa for pseudowords that can be read using GPCs. If both types of pseudowords are mixed in a given list, switching from small to large units may be required. Thus, for English-speaking children, who are assumed to rely on multiple grain sizes, reading accuracy for both large and small unit pseudowords should be better if the pseudowords are presented "in blocks" by grain size, than if they are presented mixed together on the same list. On the other hand, the performance of German-speaking children should not be affected by this "blocking" manipulation. They should preferentially use small-grain sublexical strategies, so there should be no advantage of list blocking by grain size. As indicated in Figure 2.6, a strong pseudoword blocking effect was in fact observed for the English-speaking children but not for the German-speaking ones. As stated by Ziegler and Goswami (2005, p. 12):

> Blocking apparently helped the English readers to focus at a single grain size, which particularly increased recoding accuracy for large-unit items (like *dake*; here the child can use rime analogies to *make, cake, bake* etc.). German readers did not show these blocking effects despite the fact that special care was taken that, in principle, the German large-unit nonwords offered the same possibilities of applying higher-order correspondences as the English items (i.e., they

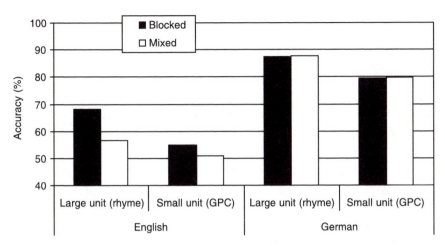

Figure 2.6. Mean accuracy scores (%) for 7-, 8- and 9-year-old children by language (English and German), pseudoword type (small units: GPC; large units: rhyme) and condition (blocked or mixed). Adapted from Goswami et al. (2003).

were matched to the English nonwords in terms of number of rime neighbors). The absence of a blocking effect for the German readers was taken as evidence that they already relied on general and efficient processing at the small unit level.

These results indicate that the low reliability of small-grain units (GPCs) in relatively inconsistent orthographies caused children to develop recoding strategies at more than one grain size. This has been found especially for English-speaking children, who rely strongly on rhyme units because taking them into account reduces vowel GPC inconsistency (Brown & Deavers, 1999; Goswami et al., 1997, 1998, 2003). On the other hand, GPCs are used in languages with clearly articulated vowels and mainly open syllables, such as Spanish (Goswami et al., 1998), Greek (Goswami et al., 1997), French (Goswami et al., 1998; Sprenger-Charolles et al., 1998b), and even German (Goswami et al., 2003) despite the fact that in German, as in English, there is a greater number of closed than open syllables and thus more opportunity to process rhyme units.

OTHER ISSUES CONCERNING SUBLEXICAL AND LEXICAL PROCESSING

The results reported so far indicate that compared to children learning to read in a transparent orthography, those learning to read in an opaque orthography exhibit lesser involvement of sublexical processing. In addition, they seem to rely on different types of phonological units, namely, large units such as rhymes rather than small ones such as graphemes and phonemes. However, besides rhyme units, there are other types of chunks below the word level that could contribute to reading acquisition, for instance, syllabic and morphological chunks.[10, 11] Since there are very few cross-language studies on these topics, we will examine the processing of syllabic and morphological chunks separately, along with another important question in the assessment of developmental dyslexia, that of the relationship between accuracy and processing time.

Syllabic-unit processing in reading acquisition

There are only a few studies that have examined the use of syllabic units in reading acquisition. This issue is far from trivial, since the size of the sub-lexical processing unit could change with reading level (see Colé, Magnan, & Grainger, 1999). In addition, reliance on the syllable could depend on the syllabic structure of the language. A finding to this effect was reported by Duncan and Seymour (2003), who asked 11-year-old English-speaking children to read aloud bisyllabic CVC-CVC, CV-CVC, and CV-CCVC words stressed on the first or second syllable. A significant effect of prosody and syllabic structure was observed. Children were more accurate at reading words that had the most frequent English stress pattern (that is, stress on the first syllable). They were also more accurate at reading words with the most frequent English syllabic structure (CVC-CVC items), especially when the stress was on the first syllable. Jimenez and Guzman (2003) reported similar results. They presented children with bisyllabic words that varied in positional syllabic frequency (hereafter PSF), which is the number of times a syllable appears in a particular position in a word (first, second, final, etc.). Spanish first and second graders were sensitive to PSF when reading aloud pseudowords (but not when making a lexical decision): pseudowords with a low PSF were read more slowly than ones with a high PSF.

In the French study by Colé et al. (1999), skilled readers (adults) and first graders were asked to decide whether a visual target presented on a computer screen was present at the beginning of a bisyllabic word displayed immediately after it.[12] The targets had a CV or CVC phonological structure which did or did not correspond to the first syllable of the following word (*ca* in *ca-rotte* versus *car* in *car-ton*). A syllable-compatibility effect, that is, shorter detection times when the target was equal to the first syllable of the word (*ca* in *ca-ramel* and *car* in *car-ton*) indicated that the participants relied on syllabic units. First graders did not show a syllable-compatibility effect when tested in February of the first grade; only target length influenced detection time (CV detected faster than CVC), suggesting GPC-based sublexical processing. When tested four months later (June), a syllable-compatibility effect was found, but only for the children with the highest reading level. On the other hand, for skilled readers, a syllable-compatibility effect was observed for low frequency words, but not for high frequency words. Taken together, these results suggest that, at least for reading acquisition in French, there is a first stage in which children mainly rely on GPCs. Then during the second stage (starting at the end of first grade), they gradually activate larger grapho-phonological chunks (syllabic units), and during the last stage they call increasingly upon the lexical procedure, at least for frequent words (Colé et al., 1999; see also Colé & Sprenger-Charolles, 1999).

To our knowledge, the only cross-linguistic study that compares the reading of polysyllabic words in beginning readers was conducted by Colé, Sprenger-Charolles, Siegel, and Jimenez-Gonzalez (2004). These authors ran a series of experiments on French-, English-, and Spanish-speaking first graders to test the hypothesis that the use of syllabic units depends on the structure of the language, item frequency, and the reading level of the children. French and Spanish have phonological properties that could encourage the use of syllabic units, since syllable boundaries are clear in these languages, unlike English, which is frequently ambisyllabic (Delattre, 1965). Syllabic processing is therefore expected to play a greater role in Spanish and French than in English. In addition, according to the results of the study by Colé et al. (1999) there should be an evolution from the use of grapho-phonemic units to that of syllabic units, and the chronology of this transition should depend on reading level (syllabic processing should be used earlier by beginning readers with a high reading level) and item frequency (syllabic processing should be used earlier for high-frequency items than for low-frequency ones).

To test these hypotheses, 85 anglophone, 60 francophone, and 47 hispanophone children, all 7-year-olds who were either above-average, average, or below-average readers, performed Colé et al.'s (1999) target-detection task. The same syllables were used in each language for both words and pseudowords (pseudowords representing one end of the word-frequency scale). The words chosen were pre-tested for familiarity to the children. The target letter group was always located in the first syllable of the words and pseudowords (e.g., for words, *pa* or *pan* in *panic* versus *panda* in English; *ca* or *car* in *carotte* versus *carton* in French and in *cara* versus *carne* in Spanish). In English and Spanish, the initial syllables were stressed, which was not the case in French, because syllabic word stress is not a relevant phonological variable. If moving from grapho-phonemic units to syllabic units depends upon the characteristics of the language, reading level, and item frequency, then the syllable-compatibility effect (1) should be greater in Spanish than in French (because the initial syllables were not stressed in French), and in both of these languages than in English (given the presence of ambisyllabicity in English); (2) this effect should be found both for above-average and average readers, but not for poor readers; (3) it should not be observed for pseudowords except in the best readers.

As expected, the syllable-compatibility effect was stronger in Spanish (mean 253 ms) than in French (126 ms), and above all, than in English (77.5 ms). In addition, significant differences within each language were observed as a function of the children's reading level and the type of item (word or pseudoword). As predicted, in Spanish, the syllable-compatibility effect was observed for both good and average readers on word reading, whereas it was found only for good readers on pseudoword reading (see Figure 2.7). In French (Figure 2.8), only the average readers exhibited a syllable-compatibility effect on words, and as for Spanish, this effect showed up for pseudowords solely in good readers. In English (Figure 2.9), average readers alone were sensitive to syllabic compatibility when they were reading words, but unlike the French and Spanish readers, no syllable-compatibility effect was found for pseudoword reading.

These results show that the use of syllabic units depends on the properties of the language. Spanish-speaking children seem to rely on such units to a greater extent than French ones, and particularly more than English ones. In addition, the transition from GPC to syllabic units for reading bisyllabic words also depends on both word frequency and reading level. For words, average readers seem to take syllabic units into account, whatever the language, thus suggesting that this type of chunk facilitates word reading at an intermediate stage of reading acquisition. The results are not clear-cut for

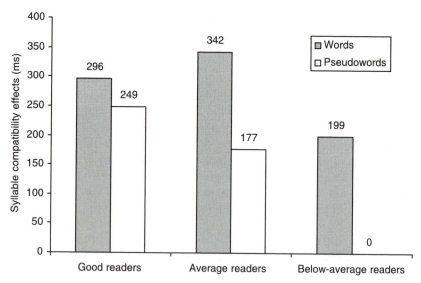

Figure 2.7. Syllable compatibility effects for Spanish first graders by reading level (adapted from Colé et al., 2004).

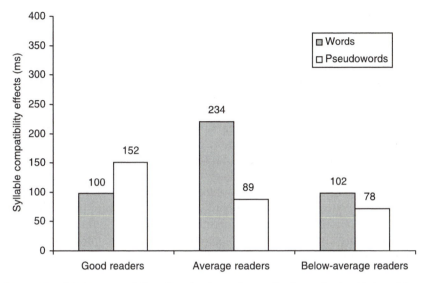

Figure 2.8.   Syllable compatibility effects for French first graders by reading level (adapted from Colé et al., 2004).

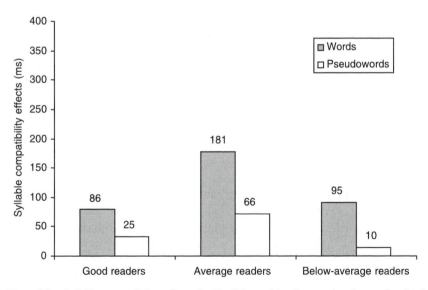

Figure 2.9.   Syllable compatibility effects for English-speaking first graders by reading level (adapted from Colé et al., 2004).

good readers, given that the syllable-compatibility effect was observed only for Spanish, perhaps because the Spanish writing system strongly encourages phonology-based reading processes. The fact that, for good readers of both French and English, no syllable-compatibility effect was found for words may be due to stronger reliance on lexical processing. In addition, a reading procedure based on syllable chunking is assumed to have been in place only recently, so this procedure cannot be applied to all words irrespective of their frequency. This would explain the lack of a syllable-compatibility effect for pseudowords in the three groups of average readers. In contrast, for good readers, this procedure would be sufficiently automatic to be used with new words, at least in the Spanish and French languages. In below-average readers, no syllabic-compatibility effect was found, no matter what language or type of item was being processed. Syllable-based processing may therefore be an intermediate kind of sublexical processing that is fairly well developed and can facilitate reading when written-word processing is not fully automatized.[13]

Between sublexical and lexical units: Morpheme processing

The morpheme is traditionally defined as the smallest unit of meaning in a language. There are two types of morphologically complex words, inflected and derived forms. Inflected forms are composed of a base, and one or two inflectional affixes that mark properties such as gender, number, tense, and person. Derived words are composed of a root and affixes such as the prefix *un-* in the word *unhappy*. Various linguistic criteria make it possible to distinguish inflectional affixes from derivational affixes, the main difference being that inflectional affixes are closely linked to the syntactic organization of the sentence in which they occur, whereas derivational forms do not have this close syntactic association.

Most researchers interested in reading consider that morphological processing comes into play only after several years of reading. For Seymour (1997), following Frith (1985, 1986), the morphological structure of words is only used in reading after the child has mastered grapho-phonemic decoding. Morphology is brought to bear essentially to compensate for the irregularity of certain words (which cannot be correctly read by simple conversion of graphemes to phonemes) and to make spelling easier. For these researchers, the use of morphological units in written-word identification is a sign of skilled reading. In fact, many studies have shown that skilled adult readers perform an automatic morphological analysis of complex words as they read (Alvarez, Carreiras, & Taft, 2001; Barber, Dominguez, & De Vega, 2002; Bertram & Hyönä, 2003; Bertram, Schreuder, & Baayen, 2000; Colé, Segui, & Taft, 1997; Hyönä, Vainio, & Laine, 2002; Longtin,

Segui, & Hallé, 2003). Most research into the role of morphology in learning to read has therefore focused on more advanced reading levels (after three or five years of instruction). Apart from a few studies on French (Marec-Breton, Gombert, & Colé, 2005), Italian (Burani, Marcolini, & Stella, 2002), and German (Verhoeven, Schreuder, & Baayen, 2003), the work has largely been carried out on English-speaking readers, seemingly without cross-linguistic comparisons.

Although there are not many studies on the role of morphological processing in the early stages of learning to read, two main orientations in the research can nevertheless be identified. The first focuses on the role of *morphological awareness* in word identification. Morphological awareness was defined as the capacity to reflect on and explicitly manipulate the morphological structure of the words orally (Carlisle, 1995). Note that this definition is based on the conventional definition of *phonological* awareness. The links between reading and morphological awareness will be examined later, along with the connection between phonological awareness and reading (see pp. 56–65). The second research orientation focuses directly on the processes involved in complex word reading. This issue is addressed in the next part of this section, which examines the processing of inflected and derived forms.

Inflected-form processing

There is very little data on how inflected forms are processed by beginning readers. Most of the work so far has examined the acquisition of spelling (e.g., Green, McCutchen, Schwiebert, Quinlan, Eva-Wood, & Juelis, 2003; Nunes, Bryant, & Bindman, 1997). In one of the first studies in this domain, Laxon, Rickard, and Coltheart (1992) showed that English 7- to 9-year-old readers processed inflected words and derived forms morphologically (although the authors' description does not always make the distinction between these two morphological types). They found that suffixed words (like *dancer* or *locked*) read aloud gave rise to significantly fewer errors than pseudo-suffixed words (like *dinner* or *wicked*, in which the -*er* and the -*ed* are not suffixes). These results were obtained for better and poorer readers, as we can see in Figure 2.10: both groups produced fewer errors on the first type of word. Laxon et al. also found that, regardless of a child's reading level, derivational forms ending in -*er* were read aloud with fewer errors than inflected forms ending in -*ed*, whereas this difference was not observed in adult readers. Children's difficulty here can be explained in terms of rules governing the pronunciation of the -*ed* ending in English, which are relatively complex, since three different phonological realizations are possible. The results thus suggest that for readers at this stage in the learning process, the reading of morphologically complex words is dependent on phonological factors.

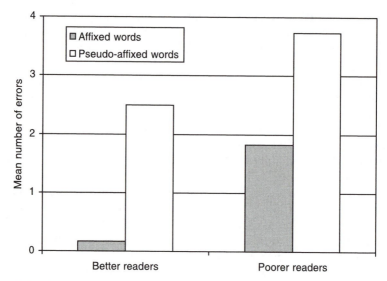

Figure 2.10. Mean number of errors on affixed and pseudo-affixed words by reading level (adapted from Laxon et al., 1992).

More recently, Feldman, Rueckl, DiLiberto, Pastizzo, and Vellutino (2002) examined the processing of inflected words by English fifth graders. These authors proposed a target completion task in which the target (t_n, for example) was preceded by a matching prime (*turn*), an orthographically-related prime (*turnip*), or a morphologically-related prime (*turned*). In the last case, the prime was morphologically related but could be orthographically opaque (*ridden* for the target *ride*, with *riddle* as an orthographic control). Priming effects were evaluated by comparing each prime condition with a control situation in which the target was presented with no prime at all. The results, presented in Figure 2.11, indicate a morphological facilitation effect. However, this effect was stronger with transparent primes, which suggests that at this relatively advanced school level, morphological processing continues to be influenced by phonological factors.

Derived-form processing

A facilitatory effect of morphology has also been found in tasks involving derivational morphology, as in the study with Italian children by Burani et al. (2002). These authors compared reaction times on lexical decision and reading aloud tasks, with pseudowords made up of a base and illegally combined derivational suffixes (e.g., *donn-ista*), and non-affixed pseudowords (e.g., *dennosto*). They obtained identical results for both tasks in all groups studied (third to fifth graders): the "morphological"

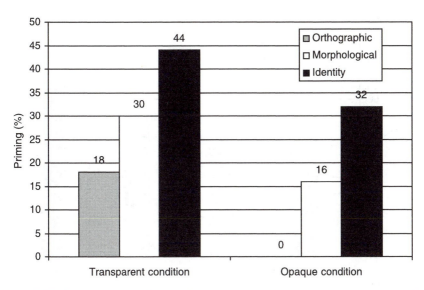

Figure 2.11. Net effects of morphological, orthographic and identity priming in fifth graders by morphological relationship transparency (adapted from Feldman et al., 2002).

pseudowords were pronounced more rapidly than the "non-morphological" ones.

Mann and Singson (2003) showed that suffixed word reading is dependent on phonological constraints up to the fifth grade, echoing findings obtained for inflected forms (Feldman et al., 2002; Laxon et al., 1992). English third-through sixth-grade readers were asked to read aloud suffixed words that were either phonologically transparent (*quickly*) or phonologically opaque (*easily*). The results, presented in Figure 2.12, indicated that the transparent words were read more accurately than the opaque suffixed forms, but the phonological transparency effect was only found for the third and fourth graders. The authors accounted for the large improvement in the reading of opaque suffixed forms by fifth graders in terms of Anglin's (1993) observation, that children's reading material contains more morphologically complex words at the fifth-grade level.

Despite these findings, Mann and Singson (2003) also showed that readers carry out a morphological analysis of derived words as early as the third grade. Children were asked to read aloud suffixed words whose base was frequent or infrequent but whose "surface" form (the complete derived word) was of comparable frequency to the other words on the list. The bases of the "high-base" words occurred 70 or more times per million (such as *movement/* base *move*) and the bases of the "low-base" words occurred less than once per million (*equipment/* base *equip*). Figure 2.13 shows that already in third grade,

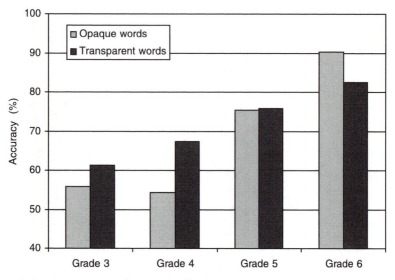

Figure 2.12. Accuracy on reading aloud suffixed derived words by phonological transparency and school grade (adapted from Mann & Singson, 2003).

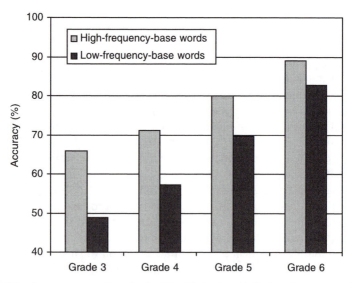

Figure 2.13. Accuracy on reading aloud suffixed derived words, by base frequency and school grade (adapted from Mann & Singson, 2003).

the children were sensitive to the frequency of the base of derived words, and that they decoded the low-base words less successfully than comparable words with high-frequency bases. Thus, as early as third grade, suffixed words appear to be parsed as *base* + suffix during reading.

Carlisle and Stone (2003) reported similar data. These authors showed that English second- and third-grade readers (as well as fourth- to sixth-grade ones) were able to use the morphological structure of suffixed words. They read suffixed words like *windy* faster (Figure 2.14a) and with greater accuracy (Figure 2.14b) than pseudo-suffixed forms like *candy*.

The studies reviewed above indicate that children use morphological chunks when reading (both inflected and derived forms), and that this phenomenon occurs irrespective of the orthographic transparency of the language (for instance, in Italian, German, French, and English). The processing of morphological markers seems to be acquired gradually between the end of the second (or third) grade and the end of primary school. However, until a relatively advanced school grade, the processing of such units continues to be influenced by phonological factors. We can hypothesize that this kind of processing is lexical in nature, and that children acquire it gradually, in accordance with phonological constraints, up through the end of elementary school.

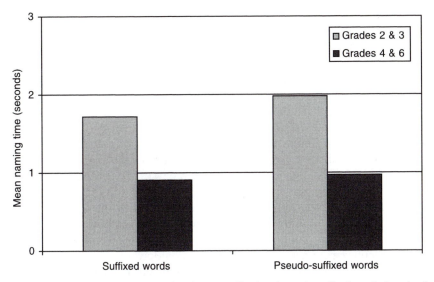

Figure 2.14(a).   Reading: mean naming time on suffixed and pseudo-suffixed words, by school grade (adapted from Carlisle & Stone, 2003).

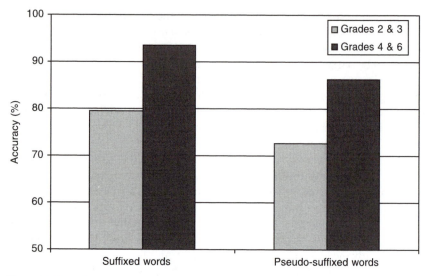

Figure 2.14(b).   Reading: accuracy scores on suffixed and pseudo-suffixed words, by school grade (adapted from Carlisle & Stone, 2003).

Trade-off between sublexical and lexical processing

Given that the efficiency of a skill depends on both accuracy and speed, it is important to take both of these measures into account in assessing reading ability, especially since the results obtained for accuracy do not always paint the same picture as those obtained for processing speed. This critical issue for the assessment of reading disabilities (see chapter 3) is clearly illustrated by the results of a longitudinal study in which non-reading French kinder-gartners were followed for four years (Sprenger-Charolles, Siegel, Béchennec, & Serniclaes, 2003). Reading performance on pseudowords, as well as on frequent regular and irregular words,[14] was examined after four months of reading instruction, and then again at the end of each school year (Grades 1, 2, 3, 4). The results are presented in Figure 2.15a (mean error percentages from the middle of Grade 1 to the end of Grade 4)[15] and 2.15b (mean laten-cies on correct responses, from the end of Grade 2 to the end of Grade 4). Reliance on the sublexical reading route was assessed by the significance of the regularity effect (difference between regular and irregular words); reliance on the lexical reading route was assessed by the significance of the lexicality effect (difference between regular words and pseudowords).

For accuracy, the most important developmental change was observed between the first two test sessions. In the middle of Grade 1, scores on regular words and pseudowords were not significantly different (43% and 50% correct responses respectively), but they were higher than on irregular words, where the scores were quite low (5% correct responses). The presence of a strong

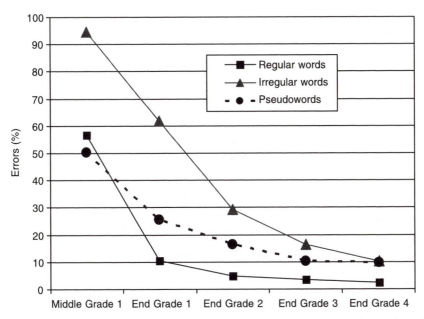

Figure 2.15(a).   Reading: mean number of errors (%) on regular words, irregular words and pseudowords, by school grade (adapted from Sprenger-Charolles et al., 2003).

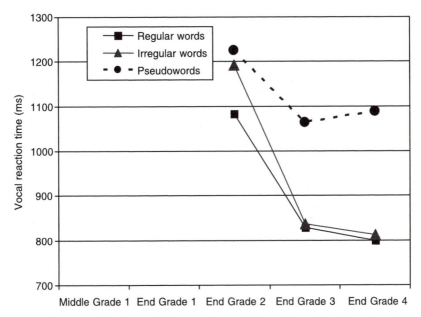

Figure 2.15(b).   Reading: latency (ms) on regular words, irregular words and pseudowords, by school grade (adapted from Sprenger-Charolles et al., 2003).

regularity effect, together with the lack of a detrimental effect of lexicality, indicates that at that time, reading mainly depended on the sublexical procedure. Between the middle and the end of this grade, the picture changed considerably. Progress was observed for all three types of items, but was greater for regular words than for pseudowords and irregular words (gains of 46%, 25%, and 33% respectively). At the end of Grade 1, the regularity effect was still significant (89% and 38% correct responses for regular and irregular words, respectively), and a detrimental effect of lexicality emerged (89% and 74% correct responses for regular words and pseudowords, respectively). Thus, indicators of reliance on both sublexical and lexical processing were found at this stage. The fact that the scores for regular words almost reached the upper limit at the end of this grade might be explained by the double benefit of regularity and frequency of exposure. Neither frequency of exposure alone nor regularity alone was sufficient, as suggested by the lesser progress on irregular words and pseudowords. These data also help explain why reading acquisition is better and faster when the language's graphophonemic relationships are relatively transparent as in Spanish or German.[16]

From the end of Grade 2 to the end of Grade 4, both accuracy and latency were taken into account. The expected detrimental effect of lexicality was always significant, whether the measure was accuracy or speed. Regularity, however, had different effects on these two measures. For accuracy, the regularity effect remained significant until the last test session (see Figure 2.15a). This effect was also significant on latency at the end of Grade 2, but was no longer so after the end of Grade 3 (see Figure 2.15b).

Reliance on the lexical reading route was thus suggested here by the very early lexicality effect (by the end of Grade 1 for accuracy, and by the end of Grade 2 for processing time, i.e., as soon as it could be accurately taken into account). Regarding the regularity effect – which is one of the indicators of reliance on the sublexical reading route – the effect on accuracy remained consistently significant until the end of the study, and the effect on latency, until the end of second grade. The fact that, starting at the end of third grade, regularity had different effects for accuracy and latency, but lexicality did not, might be explained by the ability of latency to capture the effects of articulatory codes, which are more encapsulated for words than for pseudowords (see Marmurek & Rinaldo, 1992; Rastle, Harrington, Coltheart, & Palethorpe, 2000). This clarifies why regular words were processed more rapidly than pseudowords, and why, when the regularity effect was still significant for accuracy (end of Grades 3 and 4), words read correctly, regular or not, were read at the same speed.

These results indicate that both word frequency and word regularity facilitate reading, and that the combination of the two helps the most, although at first the regularity effect is stronger than the frequency effect, perhaps because frequency effects are item-specific while regularity effects are based on generalization from other items. At the early stages, then, word frequency does not contribute much to consistent item processing, but regularity matters a lot.[17] The results also suggest that reliance on sublexical processing does not decrease, even when there are signs that the orthographic lexicon is being built. In addition, the respective weights of sublexical and lexical processes seem to change as reading skills improve, although the two processes appear to evolve differently for different types of items (regular words, irregular words, and pseudowords) and different measures (accuracy and speed). Thus, rather than being independent components of written-word identification (Coltheart et al., 2001), these two reading procedures may be reciprocally related, as suggested by connectionist models (Harm & Seidenberg, 1999; Plaut et al., 1996). However, the weight of the sublexical reading procedure is higher than that of the lexical reading procedure in the beginning of learning to read.

These results, as well as those reported in the previous part of this chapter (cross-language studies), indicate that phonology is at the core of reading acquisition. In the last section of this chapter, we will present other data suggesting that reliance on the sublexical reading route constitutes a bootstrapping mechanism for reading acquisition, and that learning to read also depends on the quality of the child's phonological representations.

BOOTSTRAPPING MECHANISMS IN READING ACQUISITION

The weight of early phonological reading skills

Evidence that phonological reading skills constitute a bootstrapping mechanism for reading acquisition is provided by longitudinal studies, which have shown that children who had accurate phonological reading scores when they began learning to read (attested by their pseudoword reading scores) later obtained the best results in reading, even on irregular words (Byrne, Freebody, & Gates, 1992; Jorm et al., 1984; Juel et al., 1986; Juel, 1988; Sprenger-Charolles, Siegel, & Béchennec, 1998a). Other longitudinal data have highlighted the fact that early pseudoword reading captures the major part of the unique variance of later word-reading skills (Manis, Custodio, & Szeszulski, 1993; Sprenger-Charolles et al., 2003).

Additional evidence can be found in studies entailing different kinds of training, where it has been shown that phonological training is more efficient than visual training. For instance, young nonreaders learned to read words more easily when they were associated with phonological clues than when the same items were associated with visual clues (Ehri & Wilce, 1985; Laing & Hulme, 1999; Rack, Hulme, Snowling, & Wightman, 1994). Similar results were obtained with older children (second graders) in Share's (1999) study on

Hebrew, a language considered to have nearly perfect one-to-one letter–sound correspondences when all vowels are written out. The experimental paradigm consisted of multiple presentations of target words to second graders. The targets were pseudowords representing fictitious names of cities, animals, flowers, and so on, embedded in short texts. Three days later, each child was asked if he or she remembered the story and was presented with four alternative spellings of the target item (the original target spelling, a homophonic foil, and two visually similar foils, one with a letter substitution and one with a transposition of two letters). Target spellings were more often correctly identified, more quickly read, and more accurately spelled than even the homophonic foils (Experiment 1). However, conditions designed to minimize phonological processing (for example, irrelevant concurrent vocalization in Experiment 2) significantly reduced the degree of orthographic learning. The contribution of pure visual exposure (non-alphabetic symbols replacing the original Hebrew letters in the target words, Experiment 4) was found to be very small. It thus seems that even in a very transparent orthography "phonological recoding may well represent the cutting edge of reading development not merely for the beginner, but throughout the entire ability range" (Share, 1999, p. 97).

The weight of early expertise in phonemic awareness

Phonological awareness is defined as a skill that enables one to identify the phonological components of a language and to manipulate them. The components in question are meaningless segments: syllables, phonemes, and infrasyllabic units such as the onset and the rhyme of a word. Phonological awareness is thought to be what enables beginning readers to realize that spoken words are composed of sound sequences, which in turn could enable them to understand that – at least for alphabetic writing systems – the most basic sounds (phonemes) correspond to written symbols such as letters (a, t) and letter groups (ou, ch). The ability to segment spoken words into their most elementary units thus seems indispensable to make appropriate use of grapho-phonemic correspondences. In the following part, we will first examine the different levels of phonological awareness (syllabic, infrasyllabic, and phonemic) and then how these levels are related to reading acquisition.

Phonemic and syllabic awareness across languages

Some studies on syllabic and phonemic awareness have shown that phonemic awareness is more difficult for children than syllabic awareness, which develops at around the early age of four. This might be because of the fact that phonemic awareness requires a high degree of abstraction, since it focuses the child's attention on elements of spoken language that are rarely available as discrete units due to coarticulation. De facto, phonemes are not pronounced one at a time, but in a single articulatory gesture within each syllable. This phenomenon makes it difficult to identify the phonemes in spoken words, and explains why children do not perform well on tasks that measure phonemic awareness before reading acquisition, as shown by Liberman, Shankweiler, Fischer, and Carter (1974) for English-speaking children. As we can see in Table 2.2, similar results have been found for various other languages, where syllabic awareness scores are higher than phonemic awareness scores prior to literacy teaching, but not after reading acquisition (except in some cases, especially in Japanese).

A look at Table 2.2 calls for several comments. Both before and after reading acquisition, most children, especially Italian and Turkish ones, exhibit

Table 2.2(a)
Syllable and phoneme awareness: mean percentage of correct responses

Units	Kindergarten Syllable	Phoneme	First grade Syllable	Phoneme
Language				
English[b]		48		74
English[d]	63.5	63	75	75.6
French[c]		45		98
German[b]		17.5		69
Italian[a]	77	34.4	88	93.1
Turkish[d]	93.5	67.1	97.5	94
Japanese[e]		91		43

Table 2.2(b)
Percentage of subjects who reached the criterion of six consecutive correct responses

Units	Kindergarten Syllable	Phoneme	First grade Syllable	Phoneme
Language				
English[a]	48	17	90	70
Italian[a]	80	27	100	90
Japanese[e]		100		10

a = from Cossu et al., 1988; the English data are from Liberman et al., 1974 (counting task);
b = from Mann and Wimmer, 2002 (deletion task);
c = from Sprenger-Charolles et al., 2000 (deletion task);
d = from Durgunoglu and Oney, 1999 (counting task);
e = from Mann, 1986 (counting task; the results are not for syllables, but for mora, which are the rhyme units of the language that more or less correspond to syllable).

high levels of syllabic awareness. The results observed in these languages contrast sharply with those reported for English-speaking children, whose syllabic awareness is low, probably because of the complexity of the vowels and syllabic structure of their language. The impact of the language itself is also apparent in the case of phonemic awareness. For instance, Turkish kindergartners have remarkable phoneme-awareness skills for pre-readers. Durgunoglu and Oney (2002) pointed out that the use of vowels to indicate morphological changes (e.g., pluralization) "forces" Turkish children to notice phonemic changes in the spoken language prior to reading, and that one consequence of this is that excellent letter–sound recoding skills typically develop by the fifth month of first grade, despite teaching methods that start "from the whole". In contrast, the Italian-, German-, French-, and English-speaking children were found to reach a high phonemic-awareness level mainly after reading acquisition, thus suggesting that this awareness results from the fact that they learned to read in an alphabetic system. Support for this explanation can be found in studies involving children who learned to read in non-alphabetic writing systems like Japanese (Mann, 1986). We will come back to the question of the links between early phonemic awareness and reading acquisition in a next part of this chapter.

Onset-rhyme versus phonemic awareness

The "rhyme" is the end of a syllable including the vowel and the consonant(s) that follow. Simple rhymes include only one vowel (e.g., there are two simple rhymes in the written word *very*: /e/ and /i/). Complex rhymes include one or more consonants (/est/ in *rest*). From this definition, it follows that a rhyme unit corresponds to a phoneme in the case of a simple rhyme, in such a way that in languages where there is a preponderance of open syllables (e.g., French and Spanish), the majority of rhyme units are single phonemes. This is not the case in languages where most syllables have a closed structure (e.g., English and German).

Most studies in this field have been conducted with English-speaking children, where there seems to be a developmental trend from syllabic to infra-syllabic units, with conscious access to phonemes being the latest stage in the process. The existence of such a developmental sequence was demonstrated in some recent studies by Anthony and his colleagues (Anthony, Lonigan, Burgess, Driscoll, Phillips, & Cantor, 2002; Anthony, Lonigan, Driscoll, Phillips, & Burgess, 2003; Anthony & Lonigan, 2004). For example, Anthony et al. (2003), who tested a large number of participants (more than 1000 children) between the ages of 2 and 6, investigated the order of acquisition of various phonological awareness skills, while holding constant the type of operation performed (blending or deletion, for instance). The results indicated that children mastered syllabic-level skills before onset-rhyme skills, which in turn were mastered before phonemic-level skills. Similar trends were reported in another study (Carroll, Snowling, Hulme, & Stevenson, 2003) in which preschoolers were followed between age 4 and age 5. Moreover, children's performance on rhyme tasks is consistently higher than on phonemic tasks (e.g., for 5-year-olds: Goswami & East, 2000; for 5- and 6-year-olds: Hulme, Hatcher, Nation, Brown, Adams, & Stuart, 2002; for 4- and 5-year-olds: Muter, Hulme, Snowling, & Taylor, 1998; for 6-year-olds: Nation & Hulme, 1997).

Reliance on onset-rhyme in spoken language may be more specific to English, however. For example, Dutch-speaking pre-readers and first graders seem not to treat onset and rhyme as cohesive units, at least in tasks that tap explicit awareness (Geudens & Sandra, 2003). In addition, not only the type of task (more or less explicit) but also the phonological properties of the items may have an effect on the availability of such units (see Geudens & Sandra, 2003; Treiman & Cassar, 1997).[18] This issue is still under debate (for a discussion, see Ziegler & Goswami, 2005).

The fact that rhyme tasks are mastered earlier and better than phonemic tasks by pre-readers and beginning readers does not allow us to determine which is the best predictor of future reading skills. Some specialists have reported data supporting the hypothesis that phonemic awareness is the most important factor (Duncan, Seymour, & Hill, 1997; Hulme, Muter, & Snowling, 1998; Hulme et al., 2002). Others have presented data suggesting that the most important factor is awareness of larger units such as onset-rhymes (Bradley & Bryant, 1983; Bryant, MacLean, Bradley, & Crossland, 1990; Goswami & East, 2000).

Apart from the landmark paper by Bradley and Bryant (1983), the only other study that has often been quoted as providing evidence of the incidence of early rhyme awareness on later reading skills is Bryant et al.'s (1990) article. Children were followed from age 4.7 to age 6.7, and were seen twice in between (5.7 and 5.11). Rhyme and alliteration skills were assessed during the first two test sessions, phonemic skills (deletion and counting) during the third test session, and reading at the end of the study. The rhyme and alliteration tests predicted later phonemic skills once the effects of age, verbal skills, intelligence, and social background were factored out. Also, after controlling for these extraneous variables, phonological awareness (at the rhyme, alliteration, and phoneme levels) accounted for part of the variance in reading. According to the authors, these data suggest that: (1) sensitivity to rhyme leads to phoneme awareness, which in turn affects reading; (2) rhymes make a direct contribution to reading that is independent of the connections between reading and phonemic awareness. Making a direct comparison between the predictive power of rhyme and phoneme awareness is difficult, since these two abilities were not examined at the same time. In addition, according to some authors (Snowling, Hulme, Smith, & Thomas, 1994; Wagner & Torgesen, 1987), the task used by Bryant et al. to assess rhyme awareness (the oddity task) may not be as clean a measure of this awareness as rhyme perception and production (see Muter et al., 1998). For us, the main problem is probably due to the fact that the tasks used by Bryant et al. (1990, see Bradley & Bryant, 1983) tapped as much phonemic as rhyme awareness. Indeed, to find out the "odd word" among *sun*, *gun*, *rub* (rhyme oddity) or *see*, *sock*, *hat* (alliteration oddity) implies some awareness of the phonemic structure of these words.

In the Muter et al. (1998) study, rhyme perception and production and phonemic awareness were assessed at the onset of the study (Time 1) when the children were nonreaders (4.3 years old) and were then re-examined one and two years later (Times 2 and 3: ages 5.3 and 6.3, respectively). Reading and spelling were examined at Times 2 and 3. The relationships to reading and spelling outcomes at the end of the study are presented in Table 2.3.

Phonemic skills at Times 1 and 2 were far more highly correlated with the reading and spelling scores obtained at Times 2 and 3 than were rhyming skills. However, the result pattern changed for the outcomes at the end of the study. At that time (Time 3), the correlations between rhyming performance and reading and writing performance reached the significance level, but the correlations between segmentation skills and reading or spelling remained significant. Phonemic awareness thus seems to be important for understanding the principle of the alphabet in the very early stages of reading acquisition. The replication of these results in another study (Hulme et al., 2002) reinforces this interpretation. In that study, rhyme and phoneme skills as predictors of future reading performance were assessed on the same tasks and with the same stimuli, in such a way that the stimuli and task requirements were not confounded with levels of phonological analysis. As in the

Table 2.3

Relationships between rhyme and phonemic awareness at Time 1 (age: 4.3, the children were nonreaders), Time 2 (age: 5.3) and Time 3 (age: 6.3), and reading and spelling scores (adapted from Muter et al., 1998)

	Reading (Time 3)	*Spelling (Time 3)*
Language		
Time 1		
Rhyming	0.07	0.04
Segmentation	0.29	0.40*
Time 2		
Rhyming	−0.01	0.22
Segmentation	0.62**	0.60**
Time 3		
Rhyming	0.50*	0.45*
Segmentation	0.39*	0.62**

* and ** significant at levels 0.01 and 0.001.

Muter et al. study, phoneme awareness was found to be a better predictor of early reading skills than rhyme awareness, and this held true even when the effects of initial reading skills and verbal abilities were controlled.

Regarding the last test-session results in the Muter et al. (1998) study, the findings may be due to the fact that the children were readers by then. As suggested in cross-linguistic studies, English-speaking children use rhyme units to read because the consistency of English spelling increases when rhymes are taken into account. This could cause reading scores at that stage to be more strongly correlated with rhyme awareness. Cross-linguistic studies that examine both rhyme and phoneme awareness and written-word process-ing at both the GPC and rhyme-unit levels would allow us to determine whether this finding holds mainly for anglophones. Keep in mind, however, that even English-speaking children are confronted with an alphabetic writing system when learning to read, the main principle of such systems being that graphemes represent the phonemes of the spoken language. Thus, the finding that phonemic awareness is a better predictor of reading acquisition than rhyme awareness is not surprising.

Links between phonemic awareness and reading acquisition

The links between reading and phonemic awareness were investigated in greater depth by Alegria, Morais, and their staff (Alegria & Morais, 1979; Alegria, Pignot, & Morais, 1982; Morais, Cary, Alegria, & Bertelson, 1979; Morais, Bertelson, Cary, & Alegria, 1986). In one study, Alegria and Morais (1979) compared the phonemic and syllabic awareness skills of same-age children, tested either in the third month of reading instruction (November) or in the sixth month (February). The two groups therefore differed in their reading experience. The February group did better on phonemic aware-ness tasks than the November group. This points out a clear reading-instruction effect on phonemic awareness. In a second study, Alegria et al. (1982) assessed the effects of teaching method on phonemic awareness. French-speaking children being taught to read using a phonological or a global method were given phonological tasks involving the manipulation of syllables or phonemes. After a few months of reading instruction, the children taught phonologically were better at manipulating phonemes (58.3% success rate, compared with 15.4% for the global group). As noted in the previous study, this result was not found for tasks involving syllabic manipu-lation. In addition, Morais et al. (1979) examined adult Portuguese speakers who were either illiterate or who had acquired literacy late. Higher scores on a phonemic manipulation task were obtained by late literate subjects (72% correct answers, compared with 19% for the illiterate group). This result was replicated in other studies, which also indicated that illiterate adults had similar syllabic manipulation skills to the late-literacy group (Morais et al., 1986). We can conclude from these studies that simple maturation does not determine the development of the phonemic awareness necessary for understanding the principle of the alphabet. Rather, it is through reading acquisition that phonemic awareness is acquired.[19]

Yet the development of phonemic awareness is one of the most important factors in successful reading acquisition. Several studies have shown that phonemic awareness is one of the best predictors of future reading level (Kirby, Parrila, & Pfeiffer, 2003; Parrila, Kirby, & McQuarrie, 2004; Schatschneider, Fletcher, Francis, Carlson, & Foorman, 2004; Share, Jorm, MacLean, & Matthews, 1984). Another argument in favor of the importance of phonemic awareness in learning to read is found in the research on dyslexic children. Various studies have shown that in phonemic awareness tasks, the scores obtained by disabled readers are significantly below those obtained by average readers matched on chronological age and/or on reading level (for English: Bradley & Bryant, 1983; Bruck, 1992; Fawcett, & Nicolson, 1994; for German: Wimmer, 1993; for French: Colé & Sprenger-Charolles, 1999; Lecocq, 1991). Moreover, longitudinal studies indicate that deficient phonemic awareness can be observed in future dyslexics even before they learn to read (Lundberg & Hoien, 1989; Wimmer, 1993, 1996; Sprenger-Charolles, Colé, Lacert, & Serniclaes, 2000).

Results of training studies

The strongest argument supporting the role of phonemic awareness in reading acquisition comes from training studies. In a meta-analysis of 52 training studies (Ehri, Nunes, Willows, Schuster, Yaghoub-Zadeh, & Shanahan, 2001a, see also Ehri, Nunes, Stahl, & Willows, 2001b), the "size" of the effect of phonemic-awareness training on reading acquisition was calculated. The effect size indicates how much the mean of the trained group exceeds the mean of the control group in standard deviation units. To judge the strength of an effect size, Cohen's (1988) values are commonly used. An effect size of $d = 0.20$ is considered small, an effect size of $d = 0.50$, moderate, and an effect size of $d = 0.80$ or above, large.

The average effect size of phonemic-awareness training on reading turned out to be moderate ($d = 0.53$). However, the effect was greater for the English-speaking students than for the non-anglophones,[20] at least on the immediate post-test ($d = 0.63$ versus 0.36) although not on the follow-up test ($d = 0.42$ versus 0.47). The reasons for the larger effect size in English may be that the English writing system is not as transparent as in the majority of the other languages tested, so phonemic-awareness training may make a bigger – and immediate – contribution to clarifying the links between graphemes and phonemes in English.

The effect size was also large for at-risk children ($d = 0.86$), and was even larger on the follow-up post-test ($d = 1.33$). The likely explanation of this increase is that the children in the at-risk groups were generally kinder-gartners or first graders selected on the basis of their low level of phonemic awareness and poor pre-reading skills. It may therefore have taken time following training for their reading skills to develop and for them to draw the greatest amount of benefit from the phonemic-awareness instruction. These results support the hypothesis that development of phonemic aware-ness is a significant factor in determining successful reading acquisition. By comparison, the effect size was smaller for disabled readers ($d = 0.45$) and much smaller on the follow-up post-test ($d = 0.28$). The difference between these two groups may be due to the fact that, unlike the at-risk children, the disabled readers were trained after their disability was discovered (and thus, after reading acquisition). This last finding suggests that a phonemic aware-ness deficit is indeed at the core of reading disability, and that such a deficit is difficult to remedy in children with this disability, as indicated by the much smaller magnitude of the phonemic-awareness training effect in that popula-tion ($d = 0.62$) than in the at-risk children ($d = 0.95$). Above all, disabled readers may have trouble transferring what they learned during training to the reading process (Vellutino, Fletcher, Snowling, & Scanlon, 2004).

Finally, greater effects were obtained if, in addition to phonemic training, the children had to manipulate letters ($d = 0.67$), this effect remaining signifi-cant on the second post-test ($d = 0.59$). This result, also noted in another meta-analysis (Bus & Van Ijzendoorn, 1999), suggests that the development of phonemic awareness is an important factor in learning to read, but it is not a sufficient condition.

Conclusion

The results presented above were discussed by Castles and Coltheart (2004; see also Marshall & Cossu, 1991) in a recent incisive paper entitled "Is There a Causal Link Between Phonological Awareness and Learning to Read?", where the authors present two main arguments suggesting that the answer is no. First, they noted that in most longitudinal studies, the children's pre-reading skills were not assessed, in which case it cannot be ruled out that at Time 1, the children were already using their reading skills to improve their phonological awareness scores. If so, then the only statement that can be made is that reading at Time 1 predicts reading at Time 2. Castles and Coltheart identified 18 studies in which the children's pre-reading level was in fact assessed (e.g., Bradley & Bryant, 1983; Caravolas, Hulme, & Snowling, 2001; Cardoso-Martins, 1995; Elbro, Borstrom, & Peterson, 1998; Hulme et al., 2002; Muter et al., 1998; Perfetti, Beck, Bell, & Hughes, 1987; Stuart, 1995; Wagner, Torgesen, & Rashotte, 1994; Wagner et al., 1997). As we stressed above, they reported that evidence for a unique contribution of syllabic awareness and rhyme awareness is very limited, in contrast to what has been observed for phonemic awareness. Among the studies they selected for close scrutiny, not a single one that included phonemic awareness measures failed to find evidence of a unique contribution of that skill on subsequent reading or spelling.

In their second criticism, Castles and Coltheart (2004) underlined that phonemic awareness and reading cannot be shown to be linked unless it is demonstrated that training in phonemic awareness specifically affects reading skills. They noted several reports of successful transfer of phonemic-awareness training to reading (e.g., Fox & Routh, 1984; Lundberg, Frost, & Peterson, 1988; Schneider, Kuespert, Roth, & Vise, 1997; Treiman & Baron, 1983) and added that some studies suggest that this effect is specific to reading (Lundberg et al., 1988; Schneider et al., 1997). However, they conclude that these positive results cannot establish causality unequivocally until it is shown, first, that the training effect is still observed when children with above zero reading and spelling skills are removed from the sample, and second, that this effect is due to pure phonemic-awareness training and not to training in several types of phonological units. The most important criticism lies in the fact that Castles and Coltheart (2004), like Marshall and Cossu (1991), deny that explicit knowledge of sublexical phonological units is necessary for acquiring the reading module. They state:

> It would seem to be clear that some skill or set of skills tapped by phonemic awareness tasks is closely related to reading acquisition and that those who do not read well are lacking in the same skill or set of skills. The question at issue concerns precisely what the skills are that are being tapped and, especially, whether they necessarily include such a process as explicit phoneme awareness.
>
> How might one adjudicate between a theory of reading in which phonemic awareness is a pre-existing skill that is then used to assist the formation of links with graphemes, and one in which explicit awareness of phonemes is acquired only at the point at which their link with graphemes is learned, and not before. It is likely that the window of time in which these two possibilities will be distinguishable will be small. One clear prediction however is that knowledge of letter-sound connections . . . will be at least as good, or even a better predictor of subsequent reading and spelling achievement than phonemic awareness on its own.
>
> (Castles & Coltheart, 2004, p. 105)

This conclusion sounds much like the ones drawn in the meta-analyses proposed by Ehri et al. (2001a, see also 2001b) and Bus and Van Ijzendoorn (1999) who, relying on the fact that greater training effects were obtained if in addition to phonemic training the children had to manipulate letters, suggest that phonemic awareness is an important factor in learning to read, but not a sufficient condition. Moreover, in our minds, it is not the explicitness or implicitness of the phonemic tasks that counts, but the types of operations needed to understand and use an alphabetic writing system. This issue has not been carefully examined. To map a grapheme to a phoneme, for instance, one must be able to isolate the phoneme in the speech stream and also to have learned well-specified phonemic categories. The former skill has been largely investigated in studies using different types of tasks (deletion, counting, etc.), but not the latter, which can be assessed by phonemic discrimination or phonemic categorization tasks. We will examine this issue in chapter 4. In the last part of this chapter, we will look at another question, in order to provide an indirect answer to the issue raised by Castles and Coltheart (2004): how is reading achievement affected by morphological awareness as compared to phonological awareness?

From phonemic to morphological awareness

Reliance on morphological knowledge in reading, and especially in reading comprehension, may be important at two levels. First, the morphemes that make up derived words carry semantic information that is crucial for retrieving the meaning of the words. Second, inflection markers contain critical information for syntactic parsing. Relatively few studies have investigated the links between morphological knowledge and the development of reading, and in most cases the distinction is not made between inflectional and derivational morphological knowledge.

In one of the first studies in this domain, Carlisle and Nomanbhoy (1993) showed that morphological knowledge is put to use in word reading as early as the first grade. Two morphological tasks were used. In the word-relationship judgment task, the child had to decide whether or not two words presented orally were connected (e.g., *freshen-freshly, funny-funnel*). In the production task, the child had to complete a sentence presented orally by providing the inflected or derived form of an initially-presented base word (e.g., *drive, this man is a . . . driver*). Performance on these two tasks accounted for the children's ability to read words to a small (4%), but significant, extent. However, the contribution of phonological awareness was greater (37%).

Muter, Hulme, Snowling, and Stevenson (2004) observed different trends in a two-year longitudinal study beginning shortly after the children had started their first year of formal schooling. In their morphological task, the experimenter uttered two sentences, a stem sentence followed by a second sentence in which the final word was omitted. The child was required to supply the missing word and to use inflection rules (e.g., *Here is a tree, here are three. . .*). The written-word identification skills of the first and second graders were predicted by earlier measures of letter knowledge and phoneme sensitivity, but not by morphological awareness, assessed by the morphological generation task. The same knowledge measured in first grade did predict reading comprehension in second grade, however.

The results of a French longitudinal study (kindergarten through second grade; see Casalis & Louis-Alexandre, 2000) corroborate the Carlisle and Nomanbhoy (1993) findings on written-word identification and the Muter et al. (2004) findings on reading comprehension. Inflectional morphological knowledge in kindergarten accounted for 5.7% of the first-grade variance on a standardized reading test (Bat-Elem: Savigny, 1974) and 22% of the second-grade variance in written comprehension (ECOSSE: Lecocq, 1996). In another French study, Colé, Royer, Leuwers, and Casalis (2004) followed children between the first and second grades using Carlisle and Nomanbhoy's (1993) task, designed to measure implicit word-relationship judgments involving no conscious manipulation of morphological knowledge by the child. Performance was found to be related to reading level as early as the first year of primary school. This was not the case for performance on explicit tasks such as the base extraction task (which require the child to find a smaller word in a derived word), which was not found to determine reading level until second grade.

The involvement of morphological knowledge nevertheless seems to be greater for older children than for younger ones. This was suggested, for instance, by Deacon and Kirby's (2004) four-year longitudinal study (Grades 2 to 5). Children had to complete a sentence with an inflected form. After controlling prior measures of reading ability, verbal and nonverbal intelligence, and phonological awareness, morphological skills in Grade 2 were found to contribute significantly to pseudoword reading and reading comprehension in Grades 3 through 5. In a study on second, third, and fourth graders, Fowler and Liberman (1995) also observed significant correlations between morphological abilities and word and pseudoword reading. After controlling for effects related to age and vocabulary size, a hierarchical regression analysis revealed that morphological abilities accounted for 42% and 34% of the variance on word and pseudoword reading, respectively.

According to other studies, the contribution of morphological knowledge to word reading increases between the third and sixth grades, whereas that of phonological knowledge decreases over the same period, but remains significant (Mahony, Singson, & Mann, 2000; Shankweiler et al., 1995). A decrease in the involvement of phonological knowledge was also observed in the study by Singson, Mahony, and Mann (2000), where this knowledge explained 36% of the reading variance in third grade, 4% in fourth grade, 3.2% in fifth grade, and only 1% in sixth grade. On the other hand, Carlisle (2000) found that morphological knowledge contributed significantly to the variance in third-grade reading comprehension (43%) and rose to 55% in fifth grade.

Taken together, these results suggest that morphological knowledge is used gradually and increasingly in written-word identification. More

generally, while phonological awareness is crucial for understanding the principle of the alphabet – which explains why phonological awareness is more
significant for younger children than for older ones – morphological awareness seems to enter into play in reading acquisition later on. The data also
suggest that the role of morphological knowledge is different from that of
phonological knowledge.[21] Because of its linguistic properties, morphological
knowledge may be involved in the development of reading comprehension,
but also (and further research is needed to confirm this hypothesis) in the
development of the lexical reading route.

SUMMARY AND CONCLUSION

Our main assumptions here were that the procedures used in learning to read
depend both on some general principles common to all languages, and on the
specific characteristics of each language. In particular, no matter what language is being learned, reading acquisition depends on the efficiency of the
sublexical reading route (general principle), which in turn depends on the
degree to which the writing system represents the spoken language it encodes
(language specific).

The descriptive and statistical data presented in the first section indicate
that, as far as grapheme–phoneme correspondences are concerned (GPCs),
English orthography is an outlier – GPCs are more transparent in Spanish,
in German, and even in French than they are in English. Therefore, significant differences could be expected between non-anglophone beginning
readers and anglophones. In contrast to children learning to read in more
transparent writing systems, English-speaking learners are in fact characterized by: (1) later mastery of the procedures necessary to process the written
word; (2) lesser involvement of the sublexical reading route; (3) reliance on
different types of phonological units, especially large units such as onset-
rhymes rather than just small units like GPCs; (4) recourse to lexical
retrieval, probably to supplement error-prone bottom-up processes based on
GPCs.

More precisely, cross-linguistic studies indicate that English-speaking
children perform reading tasks less well than do children who speak Spanish
(e.g., Goswami et al., 1998; Seymour et al., 2003), French (e.g., Bruck et al.,
1997; Goswami et al., 1998), or German (e.g, Frith et al., 1998; Wimmer &
Goswami, 1994). In addition, the gap between anglophone and non-
anglophone children and adults is larger for pseudowords than for words,
that is, when it is not possible to rely on lexical knowledge (for children:
Bruck et al., 1997; Frith et al., 1998; Goswami et al., 1998; Seymour et al.,
2003; Wimmer & Goswami, 1994; for adults: Paulesu et al., 2001). These
results show that GPC opacity has a long-lasting negative effect on reading
that is not only quantitative, but also qualitative.

Other qualitative differences have been observed between anglophone and non-anglophone beginning readers. For instance, the dissociation between the sublexical and lexical procedures is greater for English-speaking children than for children who speak other languages, as suggested by the lower correlations between pseudoword and word reading in English than in German (e.g., Wimmer & Goswami, 1994) and in French (Sprenger-Charolles et al., 1998b). In addition, the frequency effect is more noticeable in English than it is in German (Frith et al., 1998; Goswami et al., 2001). Similarly, while homophony with real words increases homophone-pseudoword accuracy scores in reading aloud tasks for English-speaking children (e.g., Frith et al., 1998; Goswami et al., 2001), it leads to a high error rate on the same items in lexical decision tasks for German-speaking children (Goswami et al., 2001), thus suggesting that the activation of phonological information is quite automatic and difficult to inhibit for German-speaking children but not for English-speaking ones, who rely to a larger extent on lexical retrieval.

Other discrepancies between anglophone and non-anglophone readers have been noted. In particular, the nature of the units used by children also depends on their importance and their consistency in the language. In English, it is probably because taking word rhymes into account reduces the inconsistencies of grapheme–phoneme correspondences that beginning English readers make greater use of rhyme units (Brown & Deavers, 1999; Goswami et al., 1997, 1998, 2003), unlike beginners in languages with a shallower orthography who rely on grapheme–phoneme correspondences. This is true of Spanish, Greek, and French (Goswami et al., 1997, 1998; Sprenger-Charolles et al., 1998b), and even German (Goswami et al., 2003), despite the fact that in German, as in English, there are a greater number of closed than open syllables and thus more opportunity to process rhyme units.

In contrast, syllable-based processing seems to play a more important role in languages where syllable boundaries are clear as they are in French and Spanish for example, unlike English which is often ambisyllabic (Colé et al., 2004), and to be frequent for the better beginning readers (Colé et al., 1999, 2004). Syllable-based processing may therefore be seen as an intermediate type of sublexical procedure that facilitates reading when written-word processing is not yet fully automatized.

As regards the use of morphological reading units, the studies reviewed indicate that children rely on morphological chunks to read, and that this phenomenon occurs irrespective of the orthographic transparency of the language (in English: Feldman et al., 2002; Laxon et al., 1992; in Italian: Burani et al., 2002; in French: Colé et al., 2004). Until a relatively advanced school grade, however, the processing of such units continues to be influenced by phonological factors. Furthermore, the relationship between morphological awareness and learning to read is weaker at the beginning of reading acquisition (Carlisle, 1995; Carlisle & Nomanbhoy, 1993; Casalis & Louis-

Alexandre, 2000) than later on (Fowler & Liberman, 1995; Mahony et al., 2000; Shankweiler et al., 1995; Singson et al., 2000), and the predictive power of morphological awareness increases with reading level (Carlisle, 2000; Mahony et al., 2000; Singson et al., 2000) while that of phonological awareness decreases (Singson et al., 2000). In addition, the role of morphological awareness appears to be different from that of phonemic awareness. These data can be explained by the fact that phonemic awareness is crucial for understanding the principle of the alphabet, and is thus more significant for beginning readers than for older ones. On the other hand, because of its linguistic properties, morphological knowledge may be involved not only in the development of reading comprehension, but also in the acquisition of the lexical reading route. Note also that no cross-language differences have been found in the research on this topic. However, these two issues (the use of morphological reading units and the relationship between morphological knowledge and learning to read) have been addressed in only a small number of studies, most of which involved English-speaking children and none of which were cross-linguistic, at least to our knowledge. Further research is clearly needed in this domain.

Whatever the opacity of the orthography, it has nonetheless been shown that early reliance on phonology-based reading procedures constitutes a bootstrapping mechanism for future reading acquisition. Evidence of this is provided by longitudinal studies (e.g., for English-speaking children: Byrne et al., 1992; Jorm et al., 1984; Juel et al., 1986; Manis et al., 1993; for French-speaking children: Sprenger-Charolles et al., 1998a, 1998b, 2003), and by the fact that phonological training is more effective than visual training, not only for beginning readers (Ehri & Wilce, 1985; Laing & Hulme, 1999; Rack et al., 1994) but also for older children (Share, 1999). In addition, among the pre-reading abilities linked to reading acquisition, phonemic awareness has been shown to be the best predictor of future reading level, and evidence for the unique contribution of syllabic awareness and rhyme awareness is very limited, even in English (e.g., Caravolas et al., 2001; Duncan et al., 1997; Hulme et al., 1998, 2002; Kirby et al., 2003; Muter et al., 1998; Schatschneider et al., 2004; Wagner et al., 1994, 1997; but see Bradley & Bryant, 1983; Bryant et al., 1990; Goswami & East, 2000). We also know that the level of phonemic awareness in disabled readers is significantly lower than that of average readers matched on chronological age and even on reading level (e.g., for English: Bradley & Bryant, 1983; Bruck, 1992; for German: Wimmer, 1993; for French: Sprenger-Charolles et al., 2000). Furthermore, longitudinal studies indicate that deficient phonemic awareness skills can be observed in future dyslexics even before they learn to read (e.g., Wimmer, 1993, 1996; Sprenger-Charolles et al., 2000). The strongest argument supporting the causal role of phonemic awareness in reading acquisition comes from training studies (see the meta-analyses by Bus & Van Ijzendoorn, 1999, and by

CHAPTER THREE

Reliability and prevalence of dyslexic reading deficits

The data presented in the previous chapter showed that reading acquisition depends on the efficiency of phonological skills. If a phonological deficit is at the core of developmental dyslexia (Ramus, 2003; Snowling, 2000), then developmental dyslexics will have trouble mapping spellings to sounds. Furthermore, if reading acquisition depends on the consistency of spelling-to-sound correspondences, it might be more difficult for English-speaking dyslexics than for Spanish-, German-, or French-speaking ones to master these correspondences. These are the topics approached in the present chapter. After a description of some methodological issues, we will examine the results of different types of studies (group studies, single case studies, and multiple case studies), conducted in various languages to evaluate the reliability and prevalence of the dyslexic performance pattern.

SOME METHODOLOGICAL ISSUES

Developmental dyslexia refers to a developmental disorder of suspected congenital or hereditary origin, in contrast to acquired dyslexia, which is a disorder resulting from brain injury after the onset of reading. However, the word "developmental" does not mean that this disorder will disappear with maturity. In fact, a noticeable characteristic of dyslexia is its persistence across the lifespan, although appropriate remedial treatment as well as compensatory strategies may help dyslexics partially overcome their reading deficit. Note that a child who has trouble learning to read is not always a dyslexic. Indeed, reading difficulties can have different origins, including mental retardation; visual or hearing impairment; poor mastery of the native language; inadequate educational opportunities; a penalizing social, cultural, or economic background; and emotional disturbances. It is only after the elimination of these potential causes of learning disabilities that it becomes possible to speak of dyslexia. In this chapter, the definition of developmental dyslexia will be re-examined, along with other methodological issues that should allow us to understand some inconsistencies in the current literature on this topic. In particular, we will point out the different types of studies (group studies, single case studies, multiple case studies), types of comparisons (with average readers of the same age or same reading level), and types of measures (e.g., accuracy and processing speed) used to highlight dyslexic deficits.

How is developmental dyslexia defined?

The since often-quoted definition of dyslexia was first proposed at a meeting of the World Federation of Neurologists held in 1968 and was summarized by Critchley (1970) in the following terms: Specific developmental dyslexia is a disorder manifested by difficulty in learning to read despite conventional instruction, adequate intelligence, and socio-cultural opportunity. It is dependent upon cognitive disabilities which are frequently of constitutional origin (see also World Health Organization, 1993). This "exclusionary" definition is not operational in helping diagnose dyslexia, since it provides no criteria for specifying the deficit of dyslexics. Other definitions have therefore been proposed. Some take into account the lag between the reading level and the cognitive level of dyslexics. The sole definition not based on exclusionary criteria involves evaluating the efficiency of dyslexic reading skills.

Definition based on the IQ discrepancy criterion

If we assume that there is a significant correlation between IQ and academic outcomes in the normal population, the reading level of children with a high intelligence level should be above the mean of same-age peers, and the reading level of children with a low intelligence level should be below the mean. When the correlation between IQ and reading is known, it becomes possible to predict the reading level of any given child from his or her chronological age. A child whose reading scores are lower than the expected level is thus considered to have a reading disability.

Several studies have questioned the validity of the IQ discrepancy criterion (Klicpera & Klicpera, 2001; Siegel, 1992; Stanovich & Siegel, 1994). The main argument is that this definition presupposes the existence of qualitative differences in reading behavior between dyslexics and non-IQ-discrepant poor readers, who have both low reading scores and low IQ scores. There are no great differences between IQ-discrepant and non-discrepant poor readers in measures of recoding skills (e.g., Vellutino, Scanlon, & Lyon, 2000). This point was corroborated in a review of nearly 50 studies (Stuebing, Fletcher, LeDoux, Lyon, Shaywitz, & Shaywitz, 2002), which casts doubt on the validity of the discrepancy criterion. In addition, it is well known that IQ, especially verbal IQ assessed by vocabulary size, improves with reading acquisition and thus leads to a gradual increase in the differences between good and poor readers. To explain this phenomenon, Stanovich (1986) evoked the "Matthew" effect (the rich get richer and the poor get poorer). The more students practise reading, the more they encounter new words, so readers who are reading well increase their vocabulary. In contrast, children with low reading skills have slower vocabulary development. This finding allows us to hypothesize that older dyslexics with an average verbal IQ probably had an above-average verbal IQ before reading acquisition. These subjects are therefore the ones most likely to have developed adequate compensatory strategies.

Definition based on the efficiency of dyslexic reading skills

A more recent definition of dyslexia that takes behavioral indicators of the dyslexic reading deficit into account has been proposed. This definition relies on the fact that the most convincing manifestation of dyslexia is failure to develop the ability to automatically recognize isolated written words out of context (Gough & Tunmer, 1986; Perfetti, 1985; Stanovich, 1986, 2000; Stanovich & Siegel, 1994). In line with this idea, the Orton Dyslexia Society of the USA (now called the International Dyslexia Association) contended that dyslexia is one of several distinct learning disabilities. It is a specific language-based disorder of constitutional origin, characterized by difficulties in single word decoding, usually reflecting phonological processing difficulties. These difficulties in single word decoding are often unexpected in relation to age or other cognitive abilities; they are not the result of generalized developmental disability or sensory impairment. Thus, dyslexics constitute only part of the poor reader population, which comprises all individuals whose reading level is inadequate with respect to social requirements. Some of the few epidemiology surveys suggest that almost 5% of all children are dyslexics.[1]

Other issues

A crucial issue in developmental dyslexia is the existence of subtypes of dyslexia. Boder (1971, 1973) was one of the first researchers to tackle this problem. Children had to read words aloud. Words read rapidly were assumed to be part of the child's sight vocabulary. When a word was not read immediately, the child was given 15 more seconds to decode it. Then a spelling test was given on the words the child was unable to read. The analyses dealt with the errors on the spelling test. According to the results, there were three groups of dyslexics: dysphonetic dyslexics, who were not able to spell words unless they were in their sight vocabulary (60% of the cases); diseidetic dyslexics, whose deficit was linked to the memorization of the shape of the written word (10%); and double deficit dyslexics, who suffered from the most severe impairment since they could not draw upon either phonological or visual skills. However, this well-known study was biased by the fact that the dyslexic classification was based on spelling skills rather than reading skills.

Since this multiple case study, most publications on developmental dyslexia have been either group studies or single case studies in which the reading-skill deficits of dyslexics were mainly assessed in the framework of the dual-route model (Coltheart et al., 1993, 2001). According to this model, written words can be processed either by a lexical procedure or a sublexical procedure. The reading of high-frequency irregular words (which can be read by sight) is generally used to assess the efficiency of the lexical reading route, and the reading of unknown words (pseudowords) is mainly used to assess the efficiency of the sublexical reading route. Dyslexics are characterized as "phonological dyslexics" when their sublexical reading route is impaired but not their lexical reading route, and vice versa for "surface dyslexics". Other dyslexics suffer from disturbances in both reading routes. These studies raise some methodological issues.

Group studies, single case studies, and multiple case studies

Group studies and single case studies occupied a preponderant position in the research on dyslexia until recently. The goal of group studies is to characterize the phenotypic performance pattern of developmental dyslexics by underlining what is specific about the information processing of these subjects, as a group. The mean scores of a group of dyslexics and a group of average readers are compared, and statistical analysis are used to evaluate the presence of significant differences between the two groups on the skills assessed. The observed differences are said to be "robust" when the same results are almost systematically replicated across studies. Studies based on this type of analysis do not postulate that every participant in each of the two groups exhibits the same behavior. A significant difference between average readers and dyslexics may in fact be due to only some children. For example, it is possible for the two groups' scores to differ significantly in pseudoword reading even if only 50% of the dyslexics show evidence of a pseudoword-reading deficit. If so, it is illegitimate to assume that the deficit observed in the dyslexic group is prevalent. This issue is addressed again later in the present chapter and in chapter 4.

Group studies clearly differ from single case studies, which look solely at individuals. The main goal of these studies is to show that it is possible to find "double dissociations" in developmental dyslexia, as in acquired dyslexia, which is a strong argument in favor of the dual-route model of reading. The dyslexics enrolled in such studies are assumed to exhibit either a phonological profile with impaired sublexical reading skills but well-preserved lexical reading skills, or a surface profile with impaired lexical reading skills but well-preserved sublexical reading skills. However, these studies suffer from two shortcomings. First, only typical cases with strong dissociations between lexical and sublexical reading skills are enrolled, mixed profiles never being taken into account. Second, the question of the prevalence of these different profiles (dissociated or not) is not examined.

To assess the prevalence of the various profiles, it is necessary to conduct multiple case studies that include dyslexics who have not been selected to fit a certain profile, i.e., all dyslexics should be eligible and their individual profiles then investigated. Such studies could allow us to overcome the drawbacks of group and single case studies. Like single case studies, multiple case studies examine individual cases, but they include several cases not selected a priori for the typicality of their profile; like group studies, multiple case studies look at a broad population assumed to be representative of the larger population of individuals with dyslexia. As such, they can assess the prevalence of the different profiles, whether dissociated, such as phonological and surface dyslexia, or mixed, which have almost always been ignored in single case studies.

Chronological age and reading level comparisons

Another issue is that, both in group and in single case studies, dyslexic performance has mostly been compared to that of same-chronological-age controls. This poses two significant problems. First of all, from the landmark papers by Bryant and Impey (1986) and Stanovich (1986), reading level is known to have an impact on vocabulary size and phonemic awareness. Therefore, the finding of differences in these skills between dyslexics and same-chronological-age controls may just be a consequence of the lower reading level of the dyslexics. Second, there are processing trade-offs between reliance on sublexical and lexical reading procedures, depending on the overall written-word identification level attained. This is clearly illustrated by the results presented in chapter 2 (Figure 2.14b). For example, the regularity effect on processing time is significant at the end of the second grade, but not one or two years later, thus suggesting a change in the reading procedures used by children between the ages of 8 and 10. Consequently, it seems difficult to compare the reading skills of 10-year-old average readers to those of 10-year-old dyslexics with a reading level typically obtained by 8-year-old average readers.

Insofar as the main question in this domain is whether or not the reading system itself develops differently in developmental dyslexics, dyslexics must be compared to same reading-level controls (Bryant & Impey, 1986; Snowling, Bryant, & Hulme, 1996a). In order to understand the relevance of such a comparison, think of a two-tray scale with weights on both sides. The left tray represents sublexical reading skills and the right tray represents lexical skills. The total weight of the two skills is similar for dyslexics and younger children of the same reading level. However, the imbalance between the two trays may not be the same for these two groups, and the imbalance may not be the same for all dyslexics. For instance, phonological dyslexics are assumed to exhibit an imbalance with a greater deficit on the sublexical-skill side, whereas surface dyslexics are assumed to exhibit an imbalance with a greater deficit on the lexical-skill side. If we find the same imbalance, say, for surface dyslexics and reading-level controls, then we may conclude that surface dyslexics exhibit a developmental lag because they behave like younger children of the same reading level. On the other hand, if the imbalance is not the same for phonological dyslexics and reading-level controls, then the phonological dyslexics exhibit a behavior not observed in average same-level readers, so we may conclude that their reading skills deviate from the normal developmental pattern.

Measuring skill efficiency: Accuracy and speed

In most studies on developmental dyslexia, only reading accuracy has been assessed, not reading speed. Thus, a dyslexic with a high accuracy level on pseudoword reading, for example, could be considered as having unimpaired sublexical reading skills, even when that accuracy level comes with a very slow processing time. This could be the case for dyslexic adults or for dyslexics who speak languages other than English, who might perform like their unimpaired peers on non-timed measures of written-word identification while suffering from a phonological deficit that makes their reading less automatic, more effortful, and thus slower. However, according to some researchers, processing speed can only be used when the number of correct responses is not too low, for example, above 50% in reading aloud tasks (e.g., Olson, Forsberg, Wise, & Rack, 1994). This point could explain why, in most dyslexic child studies, especially ones in English, only accuracy scores are taken into account. Indeed, the mean percentage of correct responses observed in English studies is often very low, unlike the studies involving Spanish-, German-, or French-speaking dyslexics, as indicated by the results presented in this chapter.

The preceding statement presupposes that accuracy scores and processing speed fall along a continuum (see also chapter 2, pp. 52–55). A clearly different approach to reading speed is proposed in the so-called "double deficit" hypothesis (Bowers & Wolf, 1993; Wolf & Bowers, 1999; Wolf, Bowers, & Biddle, 2000; Wolf, Goldberg O'Rourke, Gidney, Lovett, Cirino, & Morris, 2002). More precisely, these authors assume that there are two independent sources of reading dysfunction, one related to phonological processing (usually assessed by accuracy scores in phonological awareness tasks), the other related to lexical access (usually assessed by processing speed in the rapid automatic naming (RAN) of highly frequent items). In classic RAN tasks, a set of five pictures of high-frequency words or colors, or a series of five digits or letters, are presented ten times in a different order on a sheet of paper. Children have to name them as accurately and rapidly as possible. Two main types of evidence have been presented in support of the double-deficit hypothesis. First, naming tasks have been found to explain unique variance in reading beyond that explained by phonological awareness. Second, phonological awareness and rapid naming appear to be differentially related to reading skills, the former to accuracy scores and the latter to processing speed.

However, these pieces of evidence have been challenged (Wagner et al., 1997; Schatschneider, Carlson, Francis, Foorman, & Fletcher, 2002; Vellutino et al., 2004). Wagner et al. (1997), for example, found that a second-grade measure of phonological awareness explained unique variance on fourth-grade, non-timed and timed word reading when performance on second-grade reading measures was controlled. This was not true for the rapid naming of letters or digits. Similar findings were obtained with third-grade predictors and fifth-grade reading measures. Also, the relationships between RAN task scores and reading were stronger for letters and digits than for objects or colors (see also, Parrila et al., 2004). As suggested by Wagner et al. (1997), it is possible that including alphanumeric stimuli makes these RAN tasks "mere proxies for individual differences in early literacy and print exposure" (p. 476), which explains why the predictive power of these skills vanishes when reading skills are taken into account. In addition, non-timed measures (of phonological awareness and short-term memory, for example) were compared to timed measures on RAN tasks. To ensure that there were two entirely different deficits in dyslexia, one related to phonological skills and the other related to naming speed, it would be necessary to use timed measures in both cases. Finally, the theoretical underpinning of the timing mechanism assumed to be involved in both rapid naming and reading is unclear. This issue will be re-examined later (see pp. 134–139).

Other limitations of studies in the field of
developmental dyslexia

One important finding in the current literature is that reading acquisition and reading disabilities depend on the consistency of grapheme–phoneme correspondences (see chapter 2; see also, Ziegler & Goswami, 2005). Most studies on developmental dyslexia have been conducted with English-speaking participants. This poses a huge problem since among the languages with an alphabetic writing system English has the deepest orthography. It is thus necessary to examine languages with a shallower orthography if we hope to understand what, in developmental dyslexia, depends on general principles common to all languages and what depends on the specific features of each language.

These issues are taken into account in the present chapter, which first presents the most outstanding results of group studies, then examines the findings of single case studies, and finally looks at the results of multiple case studies. In addition, since the manifestations of dyslexia are assumed to be influenced by the transparency of the orthography, we will present the results of cross-linguistic studies as often as possible, along with studies involving non-English-speaking participants. Special attention will be paid to the link between accuracy and processing speed, but only when the data are sufficiently reliable. More specifically, as in the previous chapter, we will look primarily at speed on correct responses, assessed item by item on a computer, that is, vocal reaction time in reading aloud tasks or response time in silent reading tasks.

GROUP STUDIES

The goal of group studies is to characterize the phenotypic performance pattern of developmental dyslexics by underlining what is specific about the information processing of these subjects, as a group. Dyslexics are assumed to rely more strongly on their lexical knowledge when reading because their weak phonological skills are assumed to impede the normal development of the sublexical reading route. Consequently, on the one hand, they are expected to have trouble reading pseudowords because no lexical strategy is available unless these items are similar to words. On the other hand, the regularity effect, i.e., the difference between regular words and irregular words, should be weaker for dyslexics than for controls. This statement is based on the assumption that the normal use of the sublexical reading route results in the widely observed advantage of regular words over irregular words, at least in the initial stages of reading acquisition in English (e.g., Backman et al., 1984; Waters et al., 1984) and French (see Figure 2.14a from Sprenger-Charolles et al., 1998b; see also Leybaert & Content, 1995), two languages where the regularity effect can be assessed.

We will begin by reviewing the literature on these two issues. Special attention will be accorded to studies with reading-level matching. As often as possible, we will refer to cross-linguistic studies or studies conducted in languages other than English. The last sections will be devoted to the relationships between accuracy and processing time in developmental dyslexia, and to the compensatory strategies devised by dyslexics to cope with their deficits.

Lexicality and regularity effects

The pseudoword-reading deficit in dyslexia: Meta-analyses of English studies

Reading pseudowords requires good phonological skills and is especially problematic for dyslexics. When such a disability is found, even in comparison to reading-level controls, it means that the developmental trajectory of the dyslexic is deviant. This issue was thoroughly assessed in two reviews on studies with reading-level matching: the qualitative analysis by Rack, Snowling, and Olson (1992) and the quantitative meta-analysis by Van Ijzendoorn and Bus (1994).

Rack et al. (1992) classified studies into two sets: those where dyslexics were found to lag behind younger children of the same reading level, and those where no difference was observed. The first set included 10 studies involving a total of 428 dyslexics and a similar number of average readers (e.g., Baddeley, Ellis, Miles, & Lewis, 1982; Siegel & Ryan, 1988; Snowling, 1981). The dyslexics were between 1.3 and 5 years older than the reading-level controls (median: 2.5 years). Group differences in pseudoword-reading accuracy ranged from 9% (Baddeley et al., 1982) to 43% (Snowling, 1981), with a median of 19%. The other set included 6 studies involving 276 dyslexics and a similar number of reading-level controls (e.g., Beech & Harding, 1984; Szeszulski & Manis, 1987; Treiman & Hirsh-Pasek, 1985). Age differences between the groups ranged between 1 and 4 years (median: 3) and differences in pseudoword reading ranged from 0 (for the high reading age; Szeszulski & Manis, 1987) to 15% (for the low reading age; Szeszulski & Manis, 1987), with a median of 4%. Rack et al. (1992) argued that the differences between these two sets of studies might be due to the test used to match the groups and the type of pseudowords. It seems that the null results were mainly obtained in studies in which dyslexics were matched with reading controls on the basis of connected-text reading or simple regular-word reading. In addition, differences seem to be found more often when the pseudowords are phonologically complex than when they are simple, that is, short or analogous to real words.

The validity of these explanations was assessed by Van Ijzendoorn and Bus (1994) in their meta-analytic study, which re-examined the results of the studies examined by Rack et al. (1992). The entire population was composed of 1183 subjects, half of whom were dyslexics. Van Ijzendoorn and Bus first calculated how much the mean of the dyslexics lagged behind the mean of the reading-level controls in number of standard deviations. As explained in chapter 2, to estimate the strength of an effect size, Cohen's (1988) values are commonly used, an effect size of 0.20 being considered small, an effect size of 0.50, moderate, and an effect size of 0.80 or above, large. For the whole set of studies reviewed by Van Ijzendoorn and Bus the combined effect size ranged from 0 to 1.03, with a mean of 0.48. The combined effect size for studies that found a deficit was 0.66. However, the combined effect size for studies that supposedly did not find a pseudoword deficit in dyslexics compared to reading-level controls, although small (0.27), was significant (p <0.005). Thus, the combination of those studies that, individually, did not find a significant phonological deficit in pseudoword reading, did exhibit this deficit.

Regarding the impact on the results of the factors that Rack et al. (1992) underlined as being assumed to make a difference between the studies, Van Ijzendoorn and Bus first examined the type of pseudowords used, their complexity (one versus more than one syllable), and their similarity to real words (change of one versus more than one letter). In fact, these factors did not make a difference in the effect size. In contrast, the nature of the reading test used to match the groups was found to have a strong influence on the effect size. The effect size was smaller in studies relying on the reading of words in context or easy-to-read words (0.23) than in studies relying on the reading of more complex words (0.62). The use of a verbal IQ test was also found to be a factor that determined the magnitude of the effect (when verbal IQ was assessed: 0.84; when not assessed: 0.37). This discrepancy could be due to the possibility that dyslexics develop different reading strategies, depending upon their verbal IQ. This meta-analysis thus clearly supports Rack et al.'s (1992) main conclusion, that there is extremely strong evidence for the phonological deficit hypothesis.

The regularity effect in dyslexia: Meta-Analyses of English studies

If the development of the lexical reading route depends on the efficiency of the sublexical reading route (chapter 2), and if a phonological deficit is at the core of developmental dyslexia, then not only the sublexical reading skills of dyslexics but also their lexical reading skills, can be assumed to be impaired. The main option for them would thus be to learn words by sight (or by heart). Therefore, dyslexics should show no strong advantage of regular words over irregular words in reading. Indeed, the regularity effect provides an index of the subject's use of spelling-to-sound correspondences to pronounce familiar words. If dyslexics are less able to use this kind of knowledge, they should at least exhibit a smaller regularity effect than average readers (Manis, Szeszulski, Holt, & Graves, 1990; Olson, Kliegel, Davidson, & Foltz, 1985). Despite the apparent validity of this prediction, a regularity effect of equal magnitude has been observed for both dyslexics and reading-level controls in most studies (e.g., Bruck, 1988; Olson et al., 1985; Snowling, Goulandris, & Defty, 1996b; Stanovich, Nathan, & Zolman, 1988).

Comparisons of the size of the regularity effects found for dyslexics and reading-level controls were examined in a meta-analytic review by Metsala, Stanovich, and Brown (1998) that included 17 studies and more than 1000 participants, with 536 disabled readers and 580 reading-level controls. Combined effect sizes were calculated in standard deviation units. Based on the assumption that a larger sample size is associated with a smaller variance and therefore more precise estimates of the size of the concerned effect, weighting procedures were used to accord more weight to studies with a smaller conditional variance.

The main effect size for the entire population was 0.63 (unweighted: 0.74), and, contrary to predictions, this effect was not significantly smaller for dyslexics (weighted: 0.58; unweighted: 0.64) than for reading-level controls (weighted 0.68; unweighted: 0.85). Even for the eight studies that individually reported a difference between dyslexics and reading-level controls (e.g., Frith & Snowling, 1983; Murphy & Pollatsek, 1994; Siegel & Ryan, 1988; Szeszulski & Manis, 1987), the combined weighted effect size for the dyslexics (0.44) was not significantly different from the one observed for the reading-level controls (0.67). In addition, word frequency was found to have an impact on the magnitude of the effect, with effect size increasing as word frequency decreased. However, even in studies that used words of a relatively high frequency, the mean effect size was above zero, in line with the results reported by Jared (1997) showing that regularity can in fact affect the reading of high-frequency words.

Lexicality and regularity effects in dyslexia: An English example

This section gives an example of a longitudinal study in which the effects in English of lexicality and regularity were assessed at the same time (Snowling et al., 1996b). The main characteristics of the population, and the results obtained for the reading tasks, are presented in Table 3.1 and Figure 3.1. At the beginning of the study, dyslexics and younger same-reading-level (RL) controls were matched pairwise on reading age. At that stage, the dyslexics were much older than the controls and had benefited from remedial help. Their pseudoword-reading scores (40%) did not differ significantly from those of the RL controls (35%), thus suggesting a pattern of delayed but not deviant development.

Table 3.1
Lexicality and regularity effects in English: longitudinal data (adapted from Snowling et al., 1996)

	Dyslexics	Reading-level controls
Time 1		
Chronological age	9.6	6.8
Reading age (BAS)*	7.3	7.3
Pseudoword reading (%)	40.2	35.2
Regular-word reading (%)	50.1	50.1
Irregular-word reading (%)	31.3	39.8
Time 2 (two years after onset of study)		
Reading age (BAS)*	8.8	10.2
Pseudoword reading (%)	55.5	76.9
Regular-word reading (%)	76.4	92.4
Irregular-word reading (%)	56.1	76.8

* BAS: British Ability Scale, word reading.

The most striking finding was that, while the dyslexics performed similarly to the younger RL controls at Time 1, they improved very little between sessions and were clearly worse at Time 2 (two years after the first reading-level match), especially for pseudoword reading (see Figure 3.1). The dyslexics improved by only 15% (rising from 40% to 55%) versus 42% for the RL controls (from 35% to 77%), making for an improvement difference of 27%. This difference was less marked for regular words (16%) and irregular words (12%) than for pseudowords: for regular words, the increase was 26% for the dyslexics (going from 50% to 76%) and 42% for the RL controls (from 50% to 92%), and the irregular-word increase was 25% for the dyslexics (from 31% to 56%) versus 37% for the RL controls (from 40% to 77%). Thus, even when a pseudoword-reading deficit was not observed in dyslexics compared to younger children of the same reading level, the difference in the improvement rates of these two groups across sessions suggests that dyslexics have considerable difficulty mapping graphemes to phonemes without the help of lexical knowledge. Therefore, such a deficit appears to be a clear signature of developmental dyslexia.

In contrast, the regularity effect was significant for both groups and both test sessions, and was not qualitatively different for dyslexics than for reading-level controls. Thus, as reported in the Metsala et al. (1998) meta-analysis, dyslexics and reading-level controls exhibited comparable regularity effects.

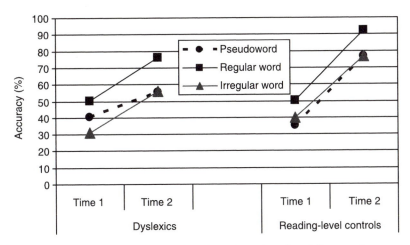

Figure 3.1   Regular word, irregular word, and pseudoword reading: follow-up of a group of dyslexics and a group of same-reading-level controls (Time 2: two years after the first assessment). Adapted from Snowling et al. (1996b).

Lexicality and regularity effects in dyslexia: A French example

Lexicality and regularity effects were also examined simultaneously in a study on French dyslexics (Casalis, 1995) whose reading age was two years below their chronological age according to a standardized reading test (Lefavrais, 1967). The children had average nonverbal IQs (assessed by the Raven Matrices, PM 47), and children with other potential causes of learning disabilities were eliminated (e.g., linguistic or sensori-motor deficits). Two groups of dyslexics whose reading scores reached the level obtained at either the end of first grade or at the end of second grade were matched to two groups of reading-level controls. The participants were asked to read 20 regular words and 20 pseudowords matched in terms of length and orthographic complexity (ten 5–6 letter monosyllabic items, and ten 6–8 letter bisyllabic items in each category), plus 40 regular words and 20 irregular words. Accuracy and latency on correct responses were measured. The results are presented in Table 3.2.

The regularity effect was significant and equally strong in all groups, as observed in the Snowling et al. (1996b) study and in the Metsala et al. (1998) meta-analysis. On the other hand, French children read pseudowords less accurately and less rapidly than words, and the lexicality effect was stronger for dyslexics, both on accuracy and on processing speed,[2] again, as already observed in English studies (Snowling et al., 1996b; Rack et al., 1992; Van Ijzendoorn & Bus, 1994) as well as in more recent French studies (Casalis, 2003; Grainger, Bouttevin, Truc, Bastien, & Ziegler, 2003; Sprenger-Charolles

Table 3.2

Lexicality and regularity effects in French: cross-sectional measures of accuracy rate (mean) and latency on correct responses (in ms) (adapted from Casalis, 1995)

	Dyslexics reading level Grade 1	Reading-level controls Grade 1	Dyslexics reading level Grade 2	Reading-level controls Grade 2
Chronological age	9.5 (8.2–11.11)	6.6	11.11 (9.7–15.4)	7.6
Reading age	6.8	6.6	7.7	7.6
Lexicality				
Short word	87% (2052 ms)	96% (1464 ms)	96% (997 ms)	99% (987 ms)
Long word	80% (2625 ms)	92% (2085 ms)	96% (1106 ms)	98% (1189 ms)
Short pseudoword	56% (3561 ms)	83% (2212 ms)	80% (1656 ms)	94% (1596 ms)
Long pseudoword	47% (3908 ms)	84% (2529 ms)	67% (2012 ms)	87% (1873 ms)
Regularity				
Regular word	60% (2860 ms)	83% (2266 ms)	91% (1233 ms)	91.5% (1184 ms)
Irregular word	38% (3003 ms)	53% (2399 ms)	64% (1437 ms)	71% (1246 ms)

et al., 2000). Thus, as regards their phonological reading skills, the group of dyslexics in that study exhibited a deviant developmental pattern.

Conclusion

The presence of a strong deficit in pseudoword reading, together with equivalent spelling-to-sound regularity effects in dyslexics compared to younger children of the same reading level is inconsistent with what can be predicted on the basis of dual-route model of reading (Coltheart et al., 2001). Given the very large overlap between the studies reviewed by Rack et al. (1992), Van Ijzendoorn and Bus (1994), and Metsala et al. (1998), and the fact that other studies assessed lexicality and regularity in the same children (e.g., English: Snowling et al., 1996b; French: Casalis, 1995), this surprising pattern of findings cannot be attributed to the characteristics of the participants involved. In addition, Metsala et al. (1998) noted that a similar tendency was obtained in the initial simulations using the Seidenberg and McClelland (1989) connectionist network. The network was found to reproduce the classic regularity effect, whereas its performance on pseudoword reading was poorer than observed in skilled readers (Besner, Twilley, McCann, & Seergobin, 1990). Its failure in pseudoword reading was attributed to the nature of the representations used to implement this connectionist model, which were triplets of letters and sounds. As suggested by subsequent research, improvement in pseudoword reading could be obtained with more appropriate input and output representations that would allow the network to capture generalizations at the grapheme–phoneme level (Plaut et al., 1996). The poor performance on pseudoword reading and the presence of a regularity effect can therefore be attributed to the poor phonological representations of the Seidenberg and McClelland (1989) network. The same argument can be forwarded to account for the pattern of findings observed in developmental dyslexics. Chapter 4 provides an in-depth examination of this issue.

Concerning the regularity effect, as noted in the previous chapter, both word frequency and regularity help children learn to read, with a combination of the two helping the most. At the beginning, though, the regularity effect is stronger than the frequency effect, perhaps because frequency effects are item specific, whereas regularity effects are based on generalization from other items. Accordingly, items that can be processed by relying on both the lexical and sublexical reading routes, namely regular words that are frequent, may be easier to read, even for dyslexic children, because there are two main keys to accessing them. Moreover, keep in mind that when dyslexics have to read words, the availability of semantic information might provide them with a vital compensatory strategy (see pp. 5–7, 130–131, 184).

Cross-linguistic studies

Cross-linguistic studies involving anglophone and non-anglophone dyslexics are very rare. To our knowledge, the first one was published by Lindgren, De Renzi, and Richman (1985) and included more than 1000 English-speaking and about 500 Italian-speaking 11-year-old children. Reading ability was assessed on the reading comprehension test used in the International Evaluation of Educational Achievement (IEA; Thorndike, 1973), which consists of 8 reading passages and 50 multiple-choice questions. Based on the test scores, dyslexia appeared to be significantly more prevalent in the United States than in Italy. For example, when children with a WISC full-scale IQ greater than or equal to 85 and a reading comprehension score at least one standard deviation below the WISC IQ were defined as dyslexics, there were 7.3% dyslexics in the US and 3.6% dyslexics in Italy. The children's decoding skills were also assessed, but because of differences between the English and Italian tests, especially in item numbering and scoring, the authors themselves acknowledged that the results of the two national groups were not easy to compare. Nevertheless, within each country, 59% of the English-speaking dyslexics scored at least one standard deviation below the national mean in pseudoword reading, whereas only 25% of the Italian-speaking dyslexics did. Note that the pseudoword-reading deficit of the Italian-speaking dyslexics (and even that of the English-speaking ones) may have been underestimated due to the use of accuracy scores only. Another finding was that, in both countries, most of the differences between dyslexics and average readers were found in verbal processing. Thus, although the deficit of

English-speaking dyslexics seems to be more severe than that of Italian-speaking dyslexics, the cross-language similarities among dyslexics appear far greater than the differences.

The same conclusion came out of a study by Landerl, Wimmer, and Frith (1997) that examined the reading and phonological processing abilities of English-speaking and German-speaking dyslexic children (age 11–12) whose reading level was delayed by about 3–4 years. Each group was compared with a control group matched on reading level (8 years). All cross-language comparisons were based on a set of stimuli matched on meaning, pronunciation, and spelling (e.g., *boat-Boot, motor-Motor, quality-Qualität*). There were 96 words and 96 pseudowords, the latter created by changing the consonantal onset of words (e.g., *brind* from *blind*). Item length varied in number of syllables (1, 2, or 3 syllables, with 32 items per length).

The German-speaking dyslexics read the most difficult items (three-syllable pseudowords) more accurately than the English-speaking dyslexics read the easiest ones (one-syllable words). The increase in errors with increasing length was larger for English-speaking than for German-speaking dyslexics, especially on pseudowords: the error percentage on 3-syllable pseudowords climbed up to about 70% for English-speaking dyslexics while remaining as low as 20% for the German-speaking dyslexics. In Table 3.3a, the scores of the three syllable lengths were combined. As compared to younger children of the same reading level, the English-speaking dyslexics made many more errors for pseudowords. A similar result was obtained for the German-speaking dyslexics, where a small but significant difference between dyslexics and reading-level controls was found for pseudowords.

These results clearly reflect the impact of the orthographic-consistency difference between English and German. However, no matter how consistent or inconsistent the orthography, the dyslexic reading deficit mainly showed up on pseudoword reading, even compared to same reading-level controls. In addition, the differences between the English- and German-speaking dyslexics were mainly due to the misreading of English vowels. As already noted (see chapter 2), in English – but not in German – the grapheme–phoneme correspondences of vowels are highly inconsistent. In this light, the finding of 324 instances of incorrect pronunciations of the first vowel among the word errors made by English-speaking dyslexics but only 20 such vowel misreadings by German-speaking dyslexics in the present study is not surprising.

Another cross-linguistic study involving 10- to 11-year-old English- and German-speaking dyslexics was conducted more recently (Ziegler, Perry, Ma-Wyatt, Ladner, & Schulte-Körne, 2003). The main differences between these two studies were that only monosyllabic words and pseudowords were used in the Ziegler et al. study, and vocal reaction times on correct responses were computed using a voice key system. Also, according to the data presented in Tables 3.3a and 3.3b, the dyslexics in the latter study seem to be less

Table 3.3
Cross-linguistic comparison (a. adapted from Landerl et al., 1997); (b. adapted from Ziegler et al., 2003)

(a) Landerl et al. (1997)

	Number (% boys)	Age	Reading level percentile	Words % errors	Pseudowords % errors
German					
Dyslexics	18 (78)	11.7	12	7	14
RL controls	18 (56)	8.8	17 (56)[1]	5	10
Effect size				2	4
English					
Dyslexics	18 (83)	12.3	8	37	52
RL controls	21 (57)	8.3	8 (50)[1]	32	35
Effect size				5	17

(b) Ziegler et al. (2003)

	Number (no. of boys)	Age	Reading age	Words % errors	Pseudowords % errors	Words latency ms	Pseudowords latency ms
German							
Dyslexics	19 (13)	10.4	7.6	6.9	21.6	1490	2168
RL controls	20 (11)	7.9	7.6	11.7	21.7	1277	1585
Effect size				−4.8	−0.1	213	583
English							
Dyslexics	30 (22)	10.9	7.6	25.2	51.4	1746	2673
RL controls	16 (6)	8.4	8.2	23.7	50.1	1513	2133
Effect size				1.5	1.3	233	540

[1] The first mean is based on the scores of average readers of the same chronological age as the dyslexics (and indicates that the reading level of the RL controls is similar to the reading level of the dyslexics). The second score is the mean percentile in comparison to the norm group of same-age children (and shows that the RL controls are normally developing readers).

impaired than those in the former study: the difference between the dyslexics and the reading-level controls was only two and a half years in the Ziegler et al. study, versus three to four years in the Landerl et al. study. Ziegler et al. (2003) once again reported that dyslexic children in both countries exhibited a specific pseudoword-reading deficit even compared to younger children of the same reading level (see Table 3.3b). However, this deficit emerged only on latency, not on accuracy, and was similar in size across languages. These results suggest that, at least when the pseudowords were not too difficult, and when the level of reading impairment was not too severe, even the English-speaking dyslexics were able to correctly map each graph-eme to the appropriate phoneme, in such a way that their phonological deficit only showed up as slow pseudoword reading.

A similar pattern has been reported for English-, French-, and Italian-speaking dyslexic adults compared to average adult readers (Paulesu et al., 2001). Reading speed (vocal reaction time) was assessed for words and pseudowords. When the relative effect sizes (z-scores) were compared across orthographies, the pseudoword-reading deficit of the Italian-speaking adult dyslexics was no different from that of the French- or English-speaking adult dyslexics, despite the greater orthographic consistency of Italian. However, as Figure 3.2 shows, the more opaque the orthography, the greater the severity of the dyslexic reading impairment. A striking finding was that the Italian-speaking dyslexics' scores fell between those of the French- and English-speaking average readers. In addition, their reading impairment was not as great as that of the French-speaking dyslexics, which in turn was not as great as that of the English-speaking dyslexics. Regardless of orthographic opacity, however, the dyslexic reading impairment (compared to chronological-age controls) was twice as great on pseudowords as on words. These results suggest that English-speaking dyslexics do not differ from non-English-speaking ones in their underlying phonological impairment, but seem to differ in the expression of that impairment.

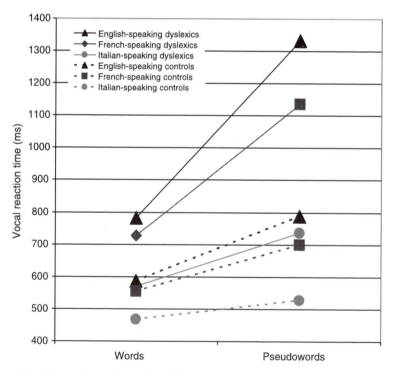

Figure 3.2 Word and pseudoword reading: cross-linguistic comparison between English, French, and Italian dyslexics and chronological-age controls (adapted from Paulesu et al., 2001).

The pseudoword deficit in languages other than English

A deficit in pseudoword reading has often been reported for languages other than English, but mostly on the basis of processing time (in Spanish: Jimenez-Gonzalez & Valle, 2000; in German: Wimmer, 1993, 1995; in Dutch: Van der Leij, Van Daal, & De Jong, 2002; in French, Casalis, 1995, 2003; Grainger et al., 2003; Sprenger-Charolles et al., 2000). In the study by Jimenez-Gonzalez and Valle (2000), for example, a sample of 80 participants was selected and divided into two groups: 40 dyslexics (chronological age 9) and 40 younger average readers at the same reading level (chronological age 7). As expected, there were differences between the dyslexics and the reading-level controls, especially on pseudowords, and mainly in terms of processing speed.

Similar results had already been reported for German. The findings of a study involving dyslexics and average readers in Grades 2, 3, and 4 are presented in Table 3.4 (Wimmer, 1993). Even the younger dyslexics made very few errors in pseudoword reading (17%). In the comparison between Grade 4 dyslexics and Grade 2 controls of the same reading level, the pseudoword-reading deficit was only observed on processing time. In addition – and again, as expected – the processing-speed difference was found for pseudoword reading only, not for text or content-word reading.

In a second study (Wimmer, 1995), the author also found that 10-year-old German-speaking dyslexics obtained rather high reading accuracy

Table 3.4

Median reading time per word and error percent in each school grade (adapted from Wimmer, 1993)

	Grade 2		Grade 3		Grade 4	
	DYS	Controls	DYS	Controls	DYS	Controls
Number	23	127	22	119	29	113
Age	8.5	8.4	9.4	9.4	10.5	10.3
Reading time (centile)	7	57	4	51	4	48
Sex ratio (% male)	83	55	86	47	62	55
Time per word						
Text reading	1.46	0.68	1.01	0.53	0.75	0.43
Content word	1.77	0.83	1.20	0.73	0.90	0.60
Pseudoword	3.75	2.17	2.81	1.71	2.63	1.54
Errors (%)						
Text reading	7	1	1	1	0	1
Content word	7	0	0	0	0	0
Pseudoword	17	8	8	4	4	8

DYS = dyslexics

scores on pseudowords in comparison to what is typically found among English-speaking dyslexics. However, the German-speaking dyslexics did exhibit a specific pseudoword-reading deficit. In particular, their speed on pseudowords was impaired in comparison to younger children matched on frequent-word reading speed. The pseudoword deficit was observed both on pseudowords that bore little resemblance to existing German words and on pseudowords that were analogous to short, frequent content words. According to Wimmer (1995), these results suggest that German-speaking dyslexics do not differ from English-speaking ones in their underlying phonological impairment, but seem to differ in the expression of that impairment.

Other ways to account for non-anglophones dyslexics' reading deficits

The studies reviewed above indicate that a specific phonological impairment characterizes the reading performance of dyslexics. Some researchers nonetheless contend today that the typical dysfluency problem found in dyslexics who are learning regular orthographies is due to the fact that these children suffer from surface dyslexia. This new interpretation has been proposed to account for results observed in German (Hawelka & Wimmer, 2005; Hutzler & Wimmer 2004; Wimmer & Mayringer, 2002) and Italian (Judica, De Luca, Spinelli, & Zoccolotti, 2002; Zoccolotti, De Luca, Di Pace, Judica, Orlandi, & Spinelli, 1999).

Processing speed and non-anglophone dyslexics' reading deficits

In two large studies with German-speaking children (Wimmer & Mayringer, 2002), a substantial number of participants with marked dissociations between reading and spelling were identified. According to the authors, these dissociations were expected because German has a high degree of regularity in the grapheme-to-phoneme direction (forward regularity) but not in the phoneme-to-grapheme direction (backward regularity). High forward regularity allows for reliance on sublexical reading skills, whereas low backward regularity requires reliance on orthographic memory representations in spelling.

In the Wimmer and Mayringer (2002) study, phonological awareness, phonological memory, and naming speed were assessed at school entry, and subtyping based on reading fluency and spelling accuracy was applied three years later. Reading fluency was assessed from the reading of a short story (57 words) and of two word lists (simple words and compound words such as *Wohnzimmer* [living room]). A composite syllable-per-minute score based on these subtests was used to establish reading fluency. Errors were not taken into account because reading accuracy was close to the ceiling level. For the spelling task, the words were chosen in such a way that reliance on simple phoneme-to-grapheme correspondences would not result in correct spelling (e.g., *kommt* could be misspelled *komt, komd, gomd, kohmmt, kom*, or *kont*). The children also had to read pseudowords, for which accuracy and speed were recorded; the latter measure was for the entire list of items, whether or not the responses were correct.

There were 415 children in Study 1 and 230 in Study 2. Children were assigned to the single reading-fluency-deficit group when their word-reading rate was below the sixteenth percentile and their spelling accuracy was above the twenty-fifth, to the single spelling-deficit group when they had the opposite pattern, and to a third group called the double-deficit group when they had both deficits. In the first study, there were 83 disabled children, 28% of whom fell into the first group, 22% into the second, and 51% into the third. The percentages in the second study, which included 54 disabled children, were 35%, 28%, and 37%, respectively. Dysfluent reading in the absence of spelling problems was associated with an earlier naming-speed deficit and thus could be due to specific impairment in building memory representations for words. In contrast, a specific spelling deficit was associated with an earlier deficit in phonological awareness and phonological short-term memory, and thus may be related to a phonological impairment.

However, the scores of the group with an assumed single reading-fluency deficit were also found to significantly differ from those of the control group on spelling accuracy, so the spelling skills of these children were not firmly in place. Likewise, the group assumed to suffer from a single spelling deficit performed significantly below the controls on pseudoword reading, at least according to the results of the second study on accuracy, so their reading skills were not well established. In addition, processing speed on the phonological tasks was not assessed in either study, whereas for the RAN only, processing speed was examined. Thus, the observed differences might be due to the type of measure rather than to the type of task.

Visual processing and non-anglophone dyslexics' reading deficits

Other data supporting the hypothesis that the typical dysfluency problem found in dyslexics facing regular orthography is not due to a phonological impairment have come from eye movements studies (in Italian: De Luca, Di Pace, Judica, Spinelli, & Zoccolotti, 1999; De Luca, Borrelli, Judica, Spinelli, & Zoccolotti, 2002; Judica et al., 2002; in German: Hawelka & Wimmer, 2005; Hutzler & Wimmer, 2004). As Rayner (1998) explained in his review of the literature, we cannot be sure that the atypical pattern of eye movements most often observed in dyslexics (longer fixation duration, more backward and forward regressions) is a cause rather than a simple consequence of reading disabilities. This remark applies to all of the studies cited in the present section, especially since they relied on comparisons with average readers of the same chronological age, unlike the studies mentioned earlier (except Paulesu et al., 2001, and Lindgren et al., 1985).

In addition, some results obtained in these studies are in fact entirely compatible with the phonological hypothesis. Indeed, the extent of spelling-to-sound consistency was found to have effect on the mean fixation duration, which was shorter in Italian than in German. For example, the average duration of all fixations during passage reading by 12-year-old Italian dyslexics was 290 ms, that is, 56 ms longer than for normal readers (De Luca et al., 1999). The German dyslexics were about two years older, but their mean fixation duration during passage reading was 360 ms, exceeding normal readers by 175 ms (Hutzler & Wimmer, 2004). More dramatic were the Italian–German differences for pseudoword reading. Even though these studies were not cross-linguistic and the methodology used to examine eye movements was not the same (thereby limiting the validity of the comparisons), as Hutzler and Wimmer (2004, p. 241) themselves stated this pattern of findings does not allow a straightforward interpretation as surface dyslexia. The higher number of fixations and the prolonged fixation duration exhibited by the dyslexic participants were found not only for words (as expected from the surface dyslexic account) but also, and even more massively so, for pseudowords. Moreover, future dyslexics, as compared to future average readers, had deficits on tasks requiring phonological processing (especially, pseudoword repetition, rhyme awareness, and rapid naming) even before learning to read (e.g., Hawelka & Wimmer, 2005).

In summary, the data supporting these new ways of accounting for reading deficits in non-anglophone dyslexics are scarce, controversial, and difficult to reconcile with the large body of findings showing that a severe phonological reading deficit is the main characteristic of developmental dyslexia, even in languages with a shallow orthography.

An example of a compensatory reading strategy in dyslexics

Most research on developmental dyslexia has focused on describing and understanding the deficits that characterize dyslexics. This research has looked at deficits both in the skills associated with learning to read (such as phonemic awareness) and in the reading process itself (see pp. 78–92). Two related topics have received relatively little attention, namely the skills associated with learning to read that develop normally or quasi normally in dyslexics, and the compensatory reading strategies that allow these individuals to read despite their cognitive deficit (Bruck, 1990). One area of research in which these two topics have nonetheless been addressed is morphology. It has been shown in the related studies that dyslexics have rather preserved morphological knowledge that they use in morphology-based compensatory reading strategies.

There are at least three reasons why dyslexics might rely on such a morphology-based strategy. First, morphemes (stems and affixes) are meaningful units that appear very frequently in many morphemically complex words. For example, in French, the base *lait* (milk) is contained in many words such as *laitage* (dairy product), *laitier* (milkman), *allaiter* (to breast-feed), etc. It is reasonable to assume that when reading, dyslexics are sensitive to the mapping of frequent letter sequences (like those that make up morphological units) to their meanings. Since dyslexics have difficulty making use of the phonological structure of words, they could rely on morphological units and their relationships with meanings.

The second reason is rooted in empirical arguments supporting an independent role of morphological awareness in learning to read. Some longitudinal studies have shown that morphological performance makes a contribution to explaining the variance in reading tasks that is small but significant and is added to the contribution of phonological abilities (see chapter 2, pp. 65–67). Thus, morphological awareness appears to be more than a mere extension of phonological abilities.

Finally, as mentioned above, studies conducted in various languages, including English (Fowler & Liberman, 1995; Shankweiler et al., 1995), Danish (Elbro, 1989), and French (Casalis, Colé, & Sopo, 2004), have shown that dyslexics' performance on tasks assessing their morphological knowledge is systematically better than when predicted on the basis of their phonological awareness. Morphological knowledge may therefore be used more efficiently by dyslexics to recognize written words than phonological knowledge.

Morphological awareness in dyslexics

Casalis et al. (2004) showed that while dyslexic French children perform poorly on tasks that require phonological processing, they do better on tasks that assess their morphological knowledge. In this study, the performance of 33 dyslexics was compared to that of two normal-reading control groups matched on chronological age or reading age. All groups were administered reading, phonological, and morphological tests. In the reading tasks, the children had to read aloud regular and irregular words and pseudowords. In line with previous reports, both control groups outperformed the dyslexics on pseudoword reading.

To measure their phonological awareness, the children had to pronounce what remained once the first phoneme of short or long pseudowords had been removed (as in *dri->ri* or *groupal->roupal*). Morphological awareness was tested using a morphological blending task, a suffix-deletion task, and a sentence-completion task requiring a morphological derivation. In the morphological blending task, the children had to pronounce a morphologically complex word given its base and affix, pronounced by the experimenters (e.g., *nettoie* and *age* to make *nettoyage* [cleaning]). In the suffix-deletion task, the children had to say the base of a suffixed word pronounced by the experimenter. In half of the cases, morphemic segmentation required deleting the final syllable (*jour-nal/jour* [daily/day]); in the other half, morphemic segmentation involved an intrasyllabic segmentation at the end of the word (e.g., *sa-gesse/sage* [wisdom/wise]). The first condition was called the preserved-syllable condition and the second, the broken-syllable condition. This procedure was chosen to focus on syllabic constraints in base identification. In the sentence-completion-with-derivation task, the children had to complete a sentence with either a derived word given the base (in half the cases), or with a base word given the derived word (in the other half). In half of the items, the base did not undergo a phonological change in the derived form (as in *poli/politesse,* [polite/politeness]). In the other half, the base did undergo a phonological change (as in *vieux/vieillesse* [old/oldness]). The context of the sentence was neutral (i.e., provided no semantic clues, as in *politeness/ this boy is . . .*).

As Figure 3.3a shows, the phonological abilities of the dyslexic children were deficient. By contrast, they had developed good morphological skills despite their phonological impairment. More specifically, their performance on the morphological blending and sentence-completion tasks corresponded to their reading-age level. However, it should be noted that performance on the morphological tasks was affected by the difficulty of the phonological processing required by the task. On the suffix-deletion task (Figure 3.3b), the dyslexic children's performance did not differ from that of the matched-reading-age children, but was worse when the suffix required a phonological segmentation that did not fit with the word's syllable structure.

Bryant, Nunes, and Bindman (1998) reported additional results with grammatical awareness tasks that assessed more general morphological knowledge. Using longitudinal methods, they found that children who later displayed severe reading problems did not differ in grammatical awareness performance from chronologically and reading age matched groups in the first years of reading acquisition although they were worse in tasks that evaluate knowledge of phonologically based letter–sound correspondences.

Several studies also indicated that dyslexic children are sensitive to the meaning conveyed by morphological units. For instance, in the study by Casalis, Matthiot, Bécavin, and Colé (2003) a modified sentence-completion-with-derivation task was used with a three-choice response format that alleviated the need for participants to come up with the derived or pseudo-derived

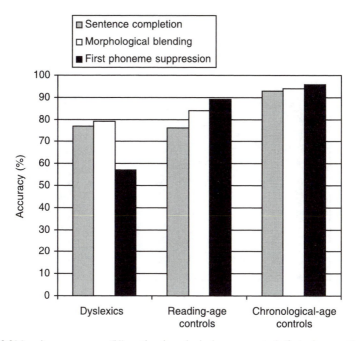

Figure 3.3(a).   Accuracy scores (%) on the phonological awareness task (first-phoneme deletion) and on the morphological awareness tasks (morphological blending and sentence completion), for dyslexic children and control groups of readers matched on chronological age and reading age (adapted from Casalis et al., 2004).

form (an example for words: *le poisson nage grâce à ses* . . . [the fish swims with its . . .] *nageoires* [fins (swim+suffix, correct word)], *nageurs* [swimmers], *nageottes* [to swim badly]; an example for pseudowords: *l'homme qui pache est un* . . . [the man who fashes is a . . .] *pacheur* [fasherman], *pachon* [fashering], *pachoir* [fasheral]). This experimental design was chosen for two reasons. The first was that the dyslexics did not have to pronounce pseudowords, which would introduce a difficulty that is phonological and not morphological in nature. The second was that this design made it possible to focus the child's attention on analyzing the suffix, since all of the choices shared the same base. As Figure 3.4 shows, the results obtained suggest that dyslexic children are particularly sensitive to the meaning of affixes. Their performance was comparable to that of younger children matched on reading age in the word condition. All three groups had worse performance in the pseudoword condition. However, the dyslexics' performance did not differ from that of their chronological-age controls, and was better than that of the younger children with the same reading level.

In summary, the studies presented here suggest that dyslexic children have developed a capacity to analyze morphological units orally that is superior to

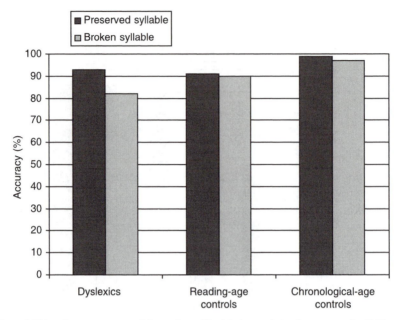

Figure 3.3(b). Accuracy scores (%) on the suffix-deletion task in the preserved-syllable and broken-syllable conditions, for dyslexic children and control groups of readers matched on chronological age and reading age (adapted from Casalis et al., 2004).

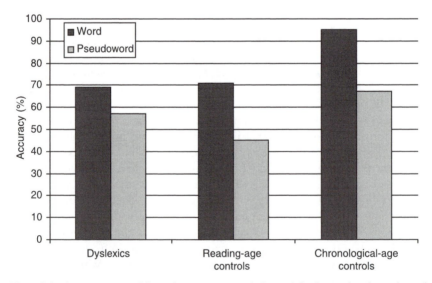

Figure 3.4 Accuracy scores (%) on the sentence-completion task in the word and pseudoword conditions, for dyslexic children and control groups of readers matched on chronological age and reading age (adapted from Casalis et al., 2003).

that predicted on the basis of their phonological abilities. Moreover, it appears that tasks requiring a deeper analysis of meaning are performed much better than tasks based on manipulations of form. These results (see also Champion, 1997; Nagy, Berninger, Abbott, Vaughan, & Vermeulen, 2003) reveal a relatively high degree of sensitivity to morphological information in dyslexics. We can conclude that morphemes may be used in a compensatory reading strategy, with the morphological information captured in written words being more available to dyslexics than phonological information. This was also suggested in the study on adolescent dyslexics conducted by Elbro and Arnbak (1996).

Morphological processing in reading

Elbro and Arnbak (1996) compared the reading performance of Danish adolescent dyslexics and normal reading-age matched controls. They found that semantically transparent compound words (such as *sunburn*) were read faster and more accurately than were semantically opaque compound words (such as *window*), but only by the dyslexics. Moreover, their measure of morphological dependency (based on the observed use of morphology in word reading) was positively correlated with reading comprehension, again, only for the dyslexics. These results suggest that dyslexics use a compensatory reading strategy which is based on the recognition of morphological units. They also suggest that this strategy is based on the meaning conveyed by the morphemes.

In a second experiment using a reading comprehension task, Elbro and Arnbak (1996) provided some additional data in support of this hypothesis. They compared the sentence-reading performance of another group of adolescent dyslexics to that of normal readers matched on reading age. Sentences were displayed under five conditions (word-by-word, morpheme-by-morpheme, syllable-by-syllable, letter-by-letter, and a control condition in which the whole text was visible). The presentation of the chunks of text was controlled by the reader via a button. At the end of the sentence, five pictures were presented on the screen, and the reader was asked to select the one that fitted the best. Reading performance, assessed in terms of accuracy (number of correctly read sentences, as indicated by the choice of the correct picture) and latency (average time in milliseconds taken to read a word in a correctly read sentence), was measured in each condition (the letter-by-letter condition proved to be too difficult and was not included in the statistical analyses). A complementary measure (reading power) that combined accuracy and latency (number of correctly read words per minute) was also calculated. In Figure 3.5, only reading power is shown.

The performance of the two groups did not differ in the control and word-by-word conditions. However, while the dyslexics read significantly faster and

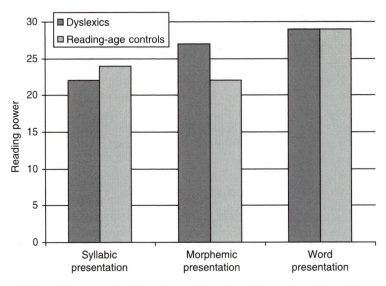

Figure 3.5 Reading power (number of correctly read words per minute) in each sentence-presentation mode, for dyslexic children and control groups of readers matched on reading age (adapted from Elbro & Arnbak, 1996).

with more overall reading power in the morpheme condition than in the syllable condition, no such differences were found in the normal controls. In addition, the dyslexics read practically as well in the morpheme condition as in the whole-word condition (the reading-power difference was non-significant). Thus, the dyslexics found more support for reading in the morpheme condition than did the younger average readers, who read better in the word condition than in the morpheme condition. A word-decoding pre-test (word reading aloud) showed that the reading-age group outperformed the dyslexic group, and that the latter group had serious trouble using phonological information during the decoding phase. These results thus suggest that dyslexics are able to compensate for their word-decoding difficulties when reading coherent sentences and thereby achieve a higher level of reading comprehension than would be expected from their word-decoding skills. Written-morpheme identification may be one way in which dyslexics manage to compensate for their basic phonological difficulties as they read sentences.

Recent results obtained with college students who had been diagnosed as dyslexics during childhood confirmed these conclusions. This population constitutes an ideal case for testing the hypothesis of a compensatory reading strategy based on morphology. Students have received intensive exposure to the written language, and despite their reading deficit they manage to go to college. One can thus assume that they overcame their handicap by developing compensatory strategies, one of which may be morphologically based. There are very few behavioral studies on compensatory reading strategies in dyslexic adults, but the work by Bruck (1990) cited in chapter 1 shows that these readers rely heavily on sentence context to decode words, and that reliance on context is six times greater than in reading-age-matched children (sixth graders). In another study, Colé, Leuwers, and Sprenger-Charolles (2005) used EVALEC (Sprenger-Charolles, Colé, Béchennec, & Kipffer-Piquard, 2005) to assess reading and reading-related skills in college students with a childhood diagnosis of dyslexia, and in two control groups matched on chronological age or reading age. The results showed that the cognitive deficits found in dyslexic children persisted into adulthood (for similar results, see for example Snowling et al., 1997). Figure 3.6a reveals a phonological deficit in adults with a childhood diagnosis of dyslexia, in the areas of syllabic and phonemic awareness and phonological short-term memory, but also (see Figure 3.6b) in both the sublexical reading procedure (as assessed by pseudoword reading) and the lexical reading procedure (as assessed by regular and irregular word reading).

In the second experiment of the same study, the authors tested the hypothesis of a compensatory reading strategy based on morphology in adult dyslexics. All three groups participated in a morphological priming

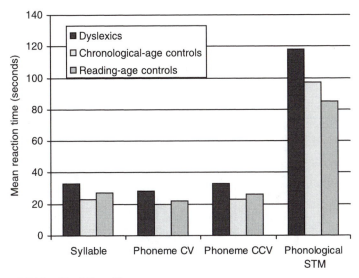

S.T.M. = Short-Term Memory

Figure 3.6(a). Mean reaction time (in seconds) on tests of syllabic and phonemic awareness (with CV and CCV one-syllable pseudowords) and phonological short-term memory, for dyslexic college students and control groups of readers matched on chronological age and reading age (adapted from Colé et al., 2005).

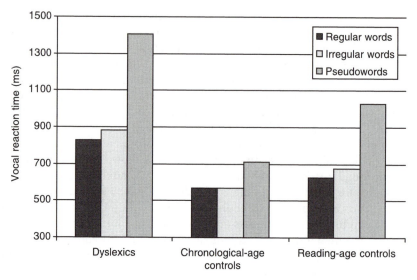

Figure 3.6(b). Mean vocal reaction time (in ms) on regular and irregular words and on pseudo-words, for dyslexic college students and control groups of readers matched on chronological age and reading age (adapted from Colé et al., 2005).

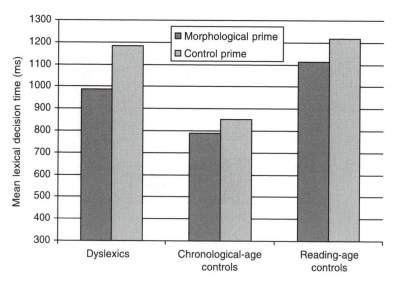

Figure 3.6(c). Mean lexical decision time (in ms) on suffixed target words, by priming condition (morphological and control), for dyslexic college students and control groups of readers matched on chronological age and reading age (adapted from Colé et al., 2005).

experiment in which they made lexical decisions on target words that were morphologically related (*coiffeur-coiffure* [hairdresser-hairdo]) or unrelated (*bloquer-coiffure* [block-hairdo]) to word primes. Both the dyslexic group and the adult controls exhibited morphological priming facilitation, but a significantly larger effect was obtained with the dyslexics. For the reading-age control group, the effect was only marginally significant (see Figure 3.6c).

The adult dyslexics were more sensitive to the morphological relationship between the primes and targets than were the normal reading-level-matched and chronological-age-matched controls. This finding suggests that adult dyslexics have developed a morphologically based compensatory reading strategy to enhance written-word identification. Along with the results obtained by Elbro and Arnbak (1996), it also suggests that this compensatory reading strategy is based on the frequency-sensitive extraction of the smallest units of meaning (stems and affixes) that make up complex targets. Further research is needed to test this hypothesis. If these findings are confirmed, they could have important implications for remedial treatment of dyslexia. Indeed, training in morphological awareness, independently of phoneme awareness, has already been found to have a positive effect on reading comprehension in dyslexic students (Arnbak & Elbro, 2000).

Summary and conclusion

Group studies indicate that a specific phonological impairment characterizes the reading performance of dyslexics. It is important first to stress the reliability of this result, which has been consistently reported across studies. In addition, this deficit is severe, since it is consistently observed in comparisons with younger children of the same reading level, thus suggesting that the developmental trajectory of dyslexics is deviant when it comes to sublexical reading skills (e.g., for English-speaking dyslexics, see reviews by Rack et al., 1992; Van Ijzendoorn & Bus, 1994; for French-speaking dyslexics, see Casalis, 1995; Grainger et al., 2003; for German-speaking dyslexics, see Landerl et al., 1997; Wimmer, 1993, 1995; Ziegler et al., 2003; for Spanish-speaking dyslexics, see Jimenez-Gonzalez & Valle, 2000).

This deficit is also more noticeable when spelling-to-sound relationships are more inconsistent; for instance, in English as compared to French or Italian (Paulesu et al., 2001) or to German (Landerl et al., 1997). In languages with a more transparent orthography, this phonological deficit mainly manifests itself in slow pseudoword reading (e.g., in German: Wimmer, 1993, 1995; Ziegler et al., 2003; in Spanish: Jimenez-Gonzalez & Valle, 2000).

However, some studies conducted in languages with a shallow orthography have reported visual deficits in dyslexics (in Italian: De Luca et al., 1999, 2002; Judica et al., 2002; in German: Hawelka & Wimmer, 2005; Hutzler & Wimmer, 2004). Nevertheless, it is not certain that dyslexics' atypical pattern of eye movements is the cause of their reading disabilities. This deficit might just be a consequence of those reading disabilities, especially since all of these studies relied on comparisons with average readers of the same chronological age, unlike those demonstrating the consistent presence of phonological deficits in developmental dyslexia. In addition, dyslexics' atypical pattern of eye movement was found more massively for pseudoword than for word reading. Therefore, this deficit cannot be definitively ascribed to a deficiency of their visual processing.

Some studies also indicate that dyslexics may rely on compensatory strategies. This point is illustrated by the studies which show how morphological information is used by dyslexics and by younger average readers of the same reading level (Colé et al., 2005; Elbro & Arnbak, 1996). The results suggest that dyslexics rely on a compensatory reading strategy based on identifying morphological units and, probably, on the meaning conveyed by morphemes. It may be by way of such compensatory strategies that some dyslexics have managed to partially overcome their phonological deficit. The strong lexicality effect found in most dyslexics is also likely to be no more than the result of a compensatory strategy. Dyslexics probably use the lexical information conveyed by words to supplement their poor phonological skills, which could explain why their performance on pseudowords is so poor.

SINGLE CASE STUDIES

The group studies just presented were based on the assumption that the population of dyslexics constitutes a homogeneous group. The main objective of single case studies, on the contrary, is to highlight contrasted profiles of dyslexia. These studies mainly rely on Coltheart's dual-route account of reading (Coltheart et al., 2001), which assumes that written words can be processed either by means of an orthographic procedure based on lexical units, or by means of a sublexical procedure based on grapheme–phoneme correspondences. Findings on acquired dyslexia played a crucial role in the elaboration of this model, for they suggest that these two reading procedures can be selectively impaired, the lexical procedure being deficient in so-called surface dyslexics (Coltheart, Masterson, Byng, Prior, & Riddoch, 1983) and the sublexical procedure, in so-called phonological dyslexics (Beauvois & Derouesné, 1979).

One important question is whether these two subtypes can be found in developmental dyslexics that are not suffering from a deficit due to brain damage, but from a problem that arises as the neurological bases of the cognitive architecture underlying reading acquisition is being set up. If we assume that a single procedure – the sublexical reading procedure – provides the basic mechanism for acquiring written-word knowledge (Ehri, 1998; Share, 1995), a deficit of the sublexical reading skills should necessarily lead to a deficit of the lexical reading skills. Thus, dissociated profiles should not be found in developmental dyslexia. However, studies based on single cases of developmental dyslexia have shown some instances of "purely" phonological dyslexics (e.g., Campbell & Butterworth, 1985; Snowling, Stackhouse, & Rack, 1986a; Temple & Marshall, 1983; Valdois et al., 2003) and of "purely" surface dyslexics (e.g., Castles & Coltheart, 1996; Coltheart et al., 1983; Hanley, Hastie, & Kay, 1992; Valdois et al., 2003).

Studies with English-speaking participants

The deficit of phonological dyslexics is assumed to involve the sublexical reading route, not the lexical reading route, because these children are thought to rely primarily on a reading procedure based on the activation of specific word knowledge. Accordingly, their performance on pseudowords is expected to be selectively impaired, and the effect of lexicality, but not regularity, is hypothesized to be strong. In addition, the errors produced by this type of dyslexic are assumed to be mainly lexicalization mistakes (a word replaces a pseudoword) or paralexic mistakes (*favor* is read *flavor*). This subtype in developmental dyslexia was first described by Temple and Marshall (1983). HM was a 17-year-old girl of above-average intelligence who had reached a reading age of 11 years according to her word-reading scores on the Schonell list. As expected, lexicality was found to have a strong negative impact on her performance. For instance, she was able to read all 25 words on a list but only 9 (36%) of the pseudowords, which differed from the words by only one letter (*streed* from *street, foom* from *room*). For pseudoword reading, her performance was negatively affected by item length (her lowest scores were on long pseudowords) and positively affected by homophony (pseudowords that sounded like real words were read better than non-homophone pseudowords). For word reading, her scores were affected by frequency but not by regularity (she read exception words well), and most of her mistakes were due to visual paralexia (*press* was read *pass*) or derivational errors (*imagine* was read *image*). HM thus exhibited most of the characteristics of phonological dyslexia. In addition, as noted by Bryant and Impey (1986), her scores on pseudoword reading were lower than those of younger children at the same reading level. However, her lexical reading route was far from being preserved, as indicated by her results on the Schonell test (59% correct responses).

Another case of phonological dyslexia was presented by Snowling et al. (1986a). JM was a boy who was followed starting at the age of 8. At that time, his IQ was above average (full IQ 123) but he was only able to read a few words, those he knew by heart (some regular, some irregular). On the other hand, he was totally unable to read even very simple pseudowords. JM was transferred to a special school for dyslexic children, where he was offered specialized teaching on an intensive basis in a small class. In spite of this, four years after the first assessment (at the age of 13) JM had progressed only by roughly half the average rate in reading, and his impairment had changed little (Hulme & Snowling, 1992). It was still very difficult for him to read pseudowords. On complex items (e.g., *ildpos*), his scores were lower than those of younger children of the same reading level. In word reading, JM produced paralexic responses (*favor* read as *flavor*). However, JM developed compensatory strategies, as suggested by the significant improvement in his performance when he was given a semantic prime (for instance, the pseudoword *sawce* presented after the word *tomato*).

The JM and HM cases thus exhibit most of the characteristics of phonological dyslexia, but they also have an above-average IQ. They may therefore be more likely than dyslexics with an average or low IQ to have developed compensatory strategies, as suggested by the positive effect of homophony on HM's performance and that of semantic priming on JM's performance. However, the lexical reading route of these phonological dyslexics remains far from efficient.

In contrast to phonological dyslexia, surface dyslexia is assumed to involve a deficit in the lexical reading route but not the sublexical route. Their performance on irregular words is thus hypothesized to be selectively impaired, and the regularity effect, to be strong. In contrast, their scores on pseudowords should be just as good as on regular frequent or infrequent words, and the effects of lexicality and frequency should be negligible. In addition, the errors produced by this type of dyslexic should be phonologically plausible. This profile was found in MI, a 10-year-old surface dyslexic (Castles & Coltheart, 1996). According to his accuracy scores, his performance on irregular words was very low, but he was within the normal range on pseudowords and regular words. However, as noted by Harm and Seidenberg (1999, footnote 5[3], p. 507): "His reading was very effortful and he often took several seconds to sound out a word, methodically working through letter by letter before producing the final pronunciation." Thus, MI seems to rely on a very slow sequential processing to read words.

Another case of surface dyslexia was presented by Coltheart et al. (1983), CD, a 15-year-old girl with a reading age of 11. As expected, her scores were affected by regularity – she performed quite well on regular words (90% correct responses) but not on irregular ones (67%), and she produced regularization errors on irregular words (*quay* was pronounced with a /kw/). Apart from the fact that only 4 of the 13 errors on irregular words were regularization errors, Bryant and Impey (1986) highlighted two other main problems in this case. First, CD's sublexical reading route was impaired, as suggested by her low scores on pseudoword reading (less than 25% correct responses), which were even lower than those of younger children at the same reading level. Second, the regularity effect was not stronger for CD than for same-reading-level controls. CD's phonological reading skills thus seem to be less well preserved than her orthographic skills, which is the opposite of what would be expected for a surface dyslexic.

Two other often-quoted cases of surface dyslexia have been published, JAS (Goulandris & Snowling, 1991) and Allan (Hanley et al., 1992). Both were older than MI and CD. Allan was a 22-year-old man with an above-average IQ (nonverbal IQ 131, verbal IQ 122). His sublexical reading route was spared whereas his lexical route was impaired, at least according to spelling scores. His word spelling was on a par with those of a 9-year-old child and his scores were affected by regularity (he spelled irregular words less well than regular ones and produced mainly phonologically acceptable spellings) but not by frequency. On the other hand, his word-reading scores reached the ceiling level. However, a deficit of the lexical procedure was observed in his homophone reading scores, since he had trouble defining homophone words and produced a significant number of erroneous choices of homophone pseudowords on a lexical decision task (11 errors out of 15).

Allan's performance was also poor on a task used to assess sequential processing in reading. A word and a pseudoword differing by only one letter were presented. They were four or five letters long, and the modified letter was at the beginning, in the middle, or at the end. For average readers, the best scores are obtained on this task when the target letter is either in the initial or final position (Friedrich, Walker, & Posner, 1985).[4] In contrast, Allan's scores decreased as the target letter moved away from the beginning of the word, making his performance very high for the initial position and very low for the final position. These results indicate that Allan relied on a highly sequential kind of processing, contrary to what is observed in average adult readers. However, even if Allan made more mistakes than average readers (11% versus 3.3%), there was no difference in processing speed (around one second). In addition, Allan's performance was higher for words than for pseudowords, thus suggesting the participation of lexical reading skills, as found for normal readers (Friedrich et al., 1985).

Like Allan, JAS (Goulandris & Snowling, 1991) was an adult developmental dyslexic with well-preserved sublexical reading skills and impaired lexical reading skills, at least according to his spelling scores which were equivalent to those of an average 10-year-old reader with a high proportion of phonologically plausible errors (80%). In reading, his performance was in the normal range, except on homophones. However, contrary to Allan, JAS's visual memory was impaired, on the processing of both alphabetic and non-alphabetic items (letters and abstract shapes). Goulandris and Snowling suggested that JAS's difficulties were due to a visual memory deficit thought to prevent him from remembering the orthographic characteristics of the words. Such a deficit was not observed in the other cases of surface dyslexia (e.g., for Allan: Hanley et al., 1992; for MI: Castles & Coltheart, 1996). These contradictory findings can be explained by the fact that some surface dyslexics may be phonological dyslexics who have good compensatory strategies for their phonological deficits, whereas others may suffer from a specific cognitive deficit related to their visual memory (e.g., JAS) or sequential processing (e.g., Allan).

In conclusion, it seems important to bear in mind that a surface profile has mainly been found in adolescent or adult dyslexics, who seem to have overcome the deficit affecting their sublexical reading route, at least as indicated by their accuracy scores.

Subtypes of dyslexia in languages other than English

Among the alphabetic writing systems, English and French are the primary ones with a significant number of irregular spellings. Therefore, cases of developmental phonological and surface dyslexia reported in languages other than English are mainly found in French studies (Casalis, 1995; Valdois, 1996; Valdois et al., 2003). In one of these studies (Valdois et al., 2003), the performance of two French dyslexics (Laurent and Nicolas) was compared with those of same-chronological-age and same-reading-level controls. Laurent was characterized as a phonological dyslexic and Nicolas as a surface dyslexic. Laurent was a 15-year-old boy with an average IQ (110) and a low reading level (8 years 6 months according to a standardized reading test, Lefavrais, 1967). Nicolas was younger (13 years old); his IQ was average (104), and his reading level similar to Laurent's (8 years 2 months, according to the same test).

Laurent's and Nicolas's profiles were based on their reading and spelling scores, with both accuracy and speed being taken into account on the reading tasks used. According to Valdois et al. (2003), Laurent displayed all but two of the characteristics of a phonological dyslexia profile. First, his pseudoword accuracy scores were on a par with those of same-age controls. Second, his irregular-word spelling scores were poor (48%)[5] and lower than his pseudoword spelling scores (65%). These results are the opposite of the main features of phonological dyslexia, characterized by a severe deficit in phonological skills accompanied by well-preserved orthographic skills. However, Laurent took three times as long as same-age controls to process pseudowords (2900 ms versus 900 ms), which he read even more slowly than younger children of the same reading level (1900 ms). Therefore, with respect to his pseudoword reading speed, Laurent's profile was found to be deviant.

Nicolas exhibited all but two of the characteristics of a surface profile. First, his pseudoword-processing speed was low (2200 ms), but did not differ significantly from that of reading-level controls (1900 ms). Second, his reading scores were affected by word frequency, with a difference of 15% on regular words (100% for high-frequency words; 85% for low-frequency words) and 35% on irregular words (75% and 40%, respectively). The frequency effect was less noticeable for Laurent: 5% for regular words (95% and 90%) and 15% for irregular words (95% and 80%). These unexpected results were not highlighted by Valdois et al. (2003), which is surprising, since the word-frequency effect is assumed to be found mainly in phonological dyslexia, not in surface dyslexia. However, Nicolas's surface profile emerged in spelling, since he was able to correctly spell 87.5% of pseudowords but only 43% of irregular words.

In addition, whereas Laurent's scores were lower than those of same-reading-age controls on three tests involving phoneme awareness, Nicolas reached the ceiling level on almost all phonological awareness tests. Also, Laurent's scores were below Nicolas's on phonological short-term memory tasks, especially on the backward digit span and long pseudoword repetition tasks. Conversely, the visual short-term memory of neither of these dyslexics was found to be impaired, at least according to the Corsi test.

The visual skills of the two boys were assessed by other tasks. First, an unpronounceable string of five letters was presented very briefly (200 ms). In one condition, they were required to identify the five letters; in another condition they had to name one of the letters, the one that had been marked during the presentation of the string. Laurent's scores were in the normal range, whatever the task and letter position. Conversely, Nicolas's scores were lower than those of same-reading-level controls when one of the last two letters was at stake. The other visual task involved the rapid reading of words of variable length (4, 6, or 9 letters). After the presentation of a word, the children had to name the item they had seen. The display time of each word was adjusted to each subject in such a way that he was able to correctly process 80% of the short items. This procedure set the display time at 150 ms for Laurent and at 250 ms for Nicolas. Control data was not available. Laurent's scores were not affected by item length, with performance ranging between 90% and 75%. Conversely, Nicolas's scores declined dramatically as the words got longer (80%, 25%, and 10%, for 4-, 6-, and 9-letter words, respectively).

According to Valdois et al. (2003), the fact that length had no effect on Laurent's scores indicates that he relied on whole-word processing. Given that high-frequency words are the ones most apt to be handled by this procedure, it is surprising that the word frequency effect was less noticeable in Laurent's performance than in Nicolas's. In contrast, Laurent's sublexical reading route was noticeably impaired, as pointed out by his slowness in pseudoword reading, even compared to younger children of the same reading level. This is indicative of a deviant developmental path. The impairment of his sublexical reading route could be due to his poor capacities in the areas of phonological awareness and phonological short-term memory, these deficits being assumed to hinder the acquisition of sublexical reading skills.

Nicolas's profile was somewhat different. Contrary to Laurent, first, his pseudoword-reading scores were similar to those of same-reading-level controls, which indicates delayed but non-deviant development. Second, his phonological skills outside of reading were well preserved, at least according to his accuracy scores. Third, he suffered from a sequential visual impairment when he had to process briefly presented strings of unpronounceable letters or words. However, Nicolas needed 250 ms to correctly read short words while Laurent needed only 150 ms to achieve the same results. To ensure that Nicolas's deficit in visual processing was no more than the result of his slowness, these skills should have been assessed with and without time limitations. Moreover, the time he took to correctly achieve the phonological awareness and phonological short-term memory tasks should have been taken into account as well.

Since Nicolas processed pseudowords very slowly, it is difficult to contend that his sublexical reading route was not impaired. It is also difficult to maintain that he relied mainly on this route, given the word-frequency effect on his reading scores. Therefore, it seems questionable to ascribe his lexical reading-route impairment to problems in visual sequential processing.

Similarities between anglophone and non-anglophone dyslexics

The deficit of the sublexical reading procedure of French dyslexics mainly shows up as slow processing, not as low accuracy. For instance, whereas Laurent (Valdois et al., 2003) read correctly 88% of the pseudowords that differed by only one letter from real words, HM (a slightly older English-speaking phonological dyslexic; see Temple & Marshall, 1983) had an accuracy level of 36% for pseudowords of the same type. These findings once again suggest that the deeper the orthographical system, the greater the dyslexics' reading deficit.

No matter what language is under investigation, evidence for unambiguously dissociated profiles in dyslexia is weak. On the one hand, all three phonological dyslexics examined here (HM, JM, Laurent) were found to suffer from an impairment of the sublexical reading route, even as compared to younger children of the same reading level. However, their lexical reading route was far from being intact. On the other hand, three of the surface dyslexics (MI, CD, Nicolas) were found to have deficient phonological reading skills, based on accuracy for CD and on processing time for MI and Nicolas. Contrary to what can be expected in surface dyslexia, the sublexical reading route of CD may be even more impaired than his lexical reading route. For the other two surface dyslexics (Allan and JAS), orthographic impairment was observed mainly in spelling, not in reading. Nonetheless, some of the surface dyslexics were found to suffer from disabilities not observed in the phonological dyslexics. For instance, JAS's visual memory was impaired, for letter strings and for abstract shapes as well. This was not the case for Allan or for Nicolas, who were found to have problems with visual sequential processing. As explained by Snowling (2000), it is possible that some surface dyslexics have compensated for their phonological deficit (or were only suffering from a mild phonological impairment), while others have a specific cognitive deficit linked to their visual memory (e.g., JAS) or to visual sequential processing (e.g., Allan and Nicolas). This issue will be re-examined in the next section.

MULTIPLE CASE STUDIES

Aside from the fact that the presumably typical profiles like those exhibited by the phonological dyslexics HM, JM, and Laurent or by the surface dyslexics MI, CD, Allan, JAS, and Nicolas turn out to be not very typical, single case studies do not tell us anything about the prevalence of these profiles. What is more, dyslexics who suffer from a double deficit are excluded, ipso facto, from studies that look only at typical dissociated cases. To avoid these two problems, it is necessary to rely on multiple case studies that include dyslexics not required to fit a certain profile. At least to our knowledge, the first investigator to have conducted such a study was Seymour (1986), who thoroughly examined a series of 21 cases of English-speaking dyslexics. More recently, in three English studies (Castles & Coltheart, 1993; Manis, Seidenberg, Doi, McBride-Chang, & Peterson, 1996; Stanovich, Siegel, & Gottardo, 1997) and two French studies (Génard, Mousty, Content, Alegria, Leybaert, & Morais, 1998; Sprenger-Charolles et al., 2000), 283 cases of dyslexia were assessed (175 English speakers and 108 French speakers).

We selected these two sets of multiple case studies for review because they both took a neuropsychological approach similar to the one used in single case studies. The Tayside sample (Seymour, 1986) was chosen because the investigations examined phonological and visual processing and took both accuracy and processing time into account. The other three English and two French studies were selected for their reliance on identical methodologies to compare dyslexics with controls of the same chronological age and same reading level, thereby allowing for cross-linguistic comparisons.[6]

Subtypes of dyslexia in English (Seymour, 1986)

In an attempt to avoid the bias induced by the selection of very special cases, Seymour examined 21 dyslexics whose problems in reading and spelling had been sufficient to trigger referral to official agencies or local voluntary organizations. These dyslexics came from the Tayside district of Scotland and were recruited with the help of the Tayside Dyslexia Association. Table 3.5

(see p. 115) presents the main descriptive data for each dyslexic, in decreasing order of age (chronological age, verbal and nonverbal IQs, reading level). If exclusionary criteria had been applied, two of these participants, LH and MP, would not have been eligible as dyslexics. LH came from a disadvantaged social background and had a low verbal IQ (VIQ 67; performance IQ 96) and MP had a low performance IQ (PIQ 73; VIQ 80). The reading level of 14 of the 21 dyslexics fell within the range of the younger controls. These dyslexics could thus be considered as matched to the controls on reading level.

The participants were given a large battery of tests including two reading aloud tasks and two visual tasks. The first reading task involved high-frequency irregular and regular words, the second, non-homophone and homophone pseudowords. The test items were between three and seven letters long. The reading tasks assessed the efficiency of the lexical and sublexical reading routes, and measured accuracy and vocal reaction time. The visual tasks were based on letter-string comparisons (same–different judgments, yes–no). One visual task (identity-matching task) included a 3-, 7-, or 11-letter array (*AAA* . . .) to be compared to another array of the same length that differed by the number of "different" letters present on "no" trials (all or one only) and by the location of the different letter (beginning, middle, or end of the array). In the other visual task (array-matching task), two arrays each containing five letters were also shown simultaneously one above the other. The legality of the sequence was manipulated (e.g., *RTBLJ* could never be a word, while *SLART* could). For the "no" trials, all letters could be different, or there could be only one difference that varied in position (1 to 5, e.g., *SLART-SPART, RTBLJ-RTBZJ*). The subjects were instructed to classify the display as "same" when the array contained the same letters in the same positions. With this experimental framework, it is possible to examine accuracy and speed in reading and visual tasks, and to compare the effect of length in the two types of tasks. Dyslexics with a selective deficiency of the visual processor were expected to be sensitive not only to length but also to position.

For the controls, the results presented in Seymour's book (range of the means and standard deviations) as well as those we were able to compute (means and standard deviations for the reading aloud tasks)[7] are reported in Tables 3.5 and 3.6 (see pp. 115–116). The means and standard deviations (SD) of each dyslexic are given in the same tables. The grey cells indicate efficient performance. Performance was said to be efficient when the score was less than one SD above the control mean (number of errors, processing speed, lexicality and regularity effects in reading tasks) or when they were defined to be so by Seymour (visual tasks). In the latter case, the mean reaction time had to fall within the normal range (690–1300 ms range and 0–8% error range on identity matching, and within the 1050–1850 ms and 2–18% ranges, respectively, on array matching).

Dyslexic reading skills and profiles

The reading scores are included in Table 3.5 (mean vocal reaction time and mean number of errors). The vocal reaction time was one standard deviation (SD) above that of the controls for 19 and 18 dyslexics in word and pseudoword reading respectively, and the number of errors was one SD above that of the controls for 10 and 14 dyslexics (word and pseudoword reading, respectively). As shown in Figures 3.7a (errors) and 3.7b (vocal reaction time), the dyslexics' pseudoword deficit appeared to be rather severe since the scores of all but four of them (RO, DP, MF, AR) were 1.65 SD above the mean of the controls on number of errors and/or processing time.

Two main variables were manipulated in the reading tasks: lexicality and regularity (see Table 3.5). As compared to controls, dyslexics exhibiting a stronger effect of lexicality without any effect of regularity are assumed to suffer from a specific phonological impairment. In contrast, the presence of a stronger regularity effect without a lexicality effect is taken as an indicator of a surface profile. The lexicality effect exceeded that of the controls for 17 of the dyslexics (for accuracy scores and/or vocal reaction time). Fourteen exhibited no regularity effect and thus could be considered as having a phonological profile (SS, SE, LT, AD, DT, MT, FM, JM, GS, SB, SM, CE, JB, PS). The regularity effect on high-frequency words was significant for five dyslexics but none of the controls. It would be possible to classify two of these five dyslexics as surface dyslexics (DP and AR) given their relatively well-preserved phonological reading skills; the other three (MP, LA, and LH) can be said to have a mixed profile given their poor pseudoword scores and significant word-regularity effect. The remaining two dyslexics seem to suffer from a mild form of dyslexia (RO and MF). Based on the same principles as in the single case studies examined above, there were 14 phonological dyslexics, 3 mixed profiles, 2 surface dyslexics, and 2 unspecified cases (see Table 3.6).

On the basis of his own classification method, Seymour found 18 dyslexics with a phonological impairment (see Table 3.6). This set included the above phonological dyslexics (14) and mixed profiles (3), plus DP, who was classified by us as a possible candidate for a surface profile. The remaining three cases were classified by Seymour as suffering only from a visual impairment. This set included our two unspecified profiles (RO and MF) plus one of our surface-profile candidates (AR).

Of the 21 dyslexics 14 had the same reading level as the younger controls on a standardized reading test. According to Seymour's classification, only three were found not to have impaired phonological skills (RO, MF, and AR). According to our re-examination of Seymour's data, there were two deviant surface profiles (DP and AR), two delayed profiles suffering from a mild form of dyslexia (RO and MF), and ten dyslexics with deviant phonological reading skills.

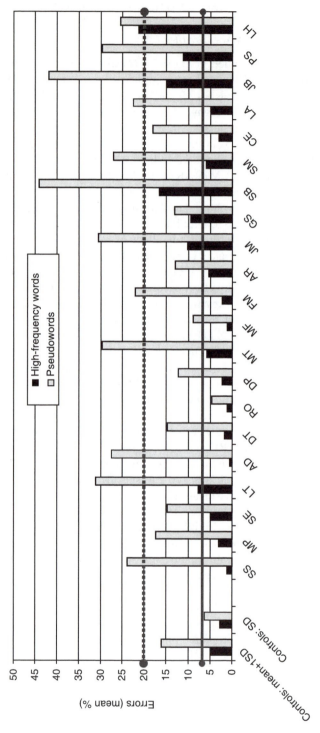

Figure 3.7(a). Word and pseudoword reading: accuracy scores (adapted from Seymour, 1986).
Solid and Dashed Lines: 1.65 SDs from the control means (6.7% for words and 20.2% for pseudowords).

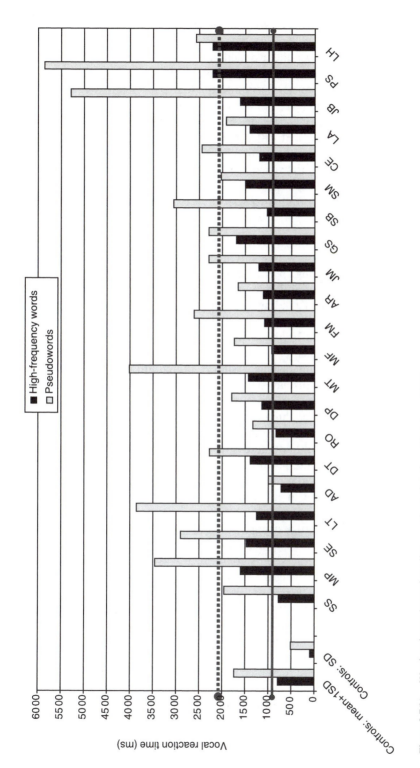

Figure 3.7(b). Word and pseudoword reading: vocal reaction times (Seymour, 1986).
Solid and Dashed Lines: 1.65 SDs from the control means (854 ms for words and 2060 ms for pseudowords).

The similarities between the two methods of classification thus seem larger than the differences, at least as far as phonological deficits are concerned. The most significant discrepancies pertain to the four participants we labelled as having a surface profile (DP and AR) or a mild form of dyslexia (RO and MF). Among them, three constituted Seymour's set of dyslexics with specific visual-processor impairment (RO, MF, and AR). To better understand these discrepancies, we need a comprehensive presentation of how Seymour assessed the efficiency of the visual processor.

Visual deficits: Accuracy and speed, length and position effects

A brief scan of Tables 3.5 (reading skills) and 3.6 (visual skills) clearly indicates that impaired scores were less frequent on visual tasks than on reading tasks. Based on processing speed, 9 dyslexics exhibited impaired visual skills (1 for identity matching and 9 for array matching) whereas most of these individuals had deficient reading skills (18 or 19 out of 21). For accuracy, only 3 dyslexics were out of the normal range (1 for the identity task, 3 for the array task) while 10 and 14 were found to have impaired word- and pseudoword-reading skills.

The identity-matching task is assumed to require parallel processing. Therefore, no effect of display size is expected on "yes" answers. In other words, reaction time on "yes" answers should not increase as a function of the number of letters. Also, high-frequency word reading can be achieved via the lexical route and is hypothesized to involve parallel processing. Hence, vocal reaction time should not increase as a function of high-frequency word length. On the other hand, given that pseudoword reading is assumed to be achieved via the sublexical route and the grapheme-to-phoneme translation is hypothesized to operate in a serial fashion, vocal reaction times should increase with pseudoword length.

The length effect on letter strings, words, and pseudowords was assessed in terms of the linear relationship between reaction time and length, expressed in milliseconds per letter.[8] When significant, it was concluded that reaction time was related to item length, and this was taken as an indicator of the possible involvement of serial processing. The position of the "different" letter in the array-matching task was analyzed in a similar manner. Reaction times were expressed as a function of left-to-right position of the single different letter. A significant linear trend was taken as evidence of the involvement of serial processing operating in the left-to-right across the array. The results of each dyslexic are presented in Table 3.6, along with the range of the control means and standard deviations.

Processing speed was very fast on the identity-matching task. The length effect of 11 control children ranged from −8 ms per letter to 16 ms per letter.

Table 3.5

Chronological age, reading age, IQ (verbal and performance) and reading performance, errors and processing time (adapted from Seymour, 1986). Grey: reading performance in the normal range.

	Chronological age	IQ V-IQ	IQ P-IQ	Reading age Schonell	High-frequency words (regular-irregular) Errors %	Time	Pseudowords Errors %	Time	Lexicality effect Errors %	Time	Homophony effect (pseudowords) Errors %	Time	Regularity effect (high-frequency words) Errors %	Time
Average Readers														
Mean	11.7			12.3	2.2	685.5	9.8	1223	7.6	258	5.9	258	1.1	3.9
SD	0.6			0.4	2.7	102	6.3	507	5.7	310	5.1	310	2.7	66
Range	10.9–12.3			11.4–12.6										
+1SD					<4.9	<787.5	<16.1	<1730	<11.0	<568	<11.0	<568	<3.8	<70
+1.65SD					<6.7	853.8	<20.2	<2060	<13.2	<770	<14.3	<770	<5.5	<113
Dyslexics							Grey: Reading Performance in the Normal Range; *: Significant Effect; NO: No Effect							
SS	25.03	125	130	+12.06	1.2	783 (0179)	23.8	1953 (1056)	22.6	1170	NO	NO	NO	NO
MP	22.06	80	73	11.08	3.0	1594 (0962)	17.4	3453 (1434)	14.4	1859	*20	?	NO	*380
SE	21.07	108	99	+12.06	4.8	1466 (1805)	14.8	2903 (1889)	10.0	1437	?	*600	NO	NO
LT	19.00	99	123	11.05	7.7	1247 (1362)	31.1	3858 (2467)	23.4	2611	?	*1200	NO	NO
AD	17.07	106	132	+12.06	0.6	723 (0150)	27.5	1004 (0395)	26.9	281	?	?	NO	NO
DT	17.03	105	147	+12.06	1.8	1383 (0493)	14.8	2279 (1012)	13.0	896	NO	*457	NO	NO
RO	16.10	126	?	+12.06	1.2	838 (0142)	4.7	1336 (0580)	3.5	498	NO	NO	NO	NO
DP	16.01	104	114	12.02	2.4	1132 (0398)	12.3	1795 (1007)	9.9	663	NO	*1400	NO	*+300
MT	14.11	100	107	12.02	5.9	1437 (0770)	29.7	4018 (2721)	23.8	2581	?	NO	NO	NO
MF	14.08	106	126	12.03	1.2	932 (0337)	8.9	1743 (1063)	7.7	811	NO	NO	NO	NO
FM	14.07	102	117	10.07	2.4	1087 (0484)	22.1	2607 (1594)	19.7	1520	*?	NO	NO	NO
AR	14.06	117	121	11.00	5.4	1117 (0540)	13.0	1653 (0748)	7.6	536	NO	NO	*8?	?
JM	14.02	112	90	11.04	10.2	1209 (0743)	30.5	2288 (1275)	20.3	1079	?	*600	NO	NO
GS	13.05	121	83	09.09	9.5	1695 (0782)	13.1	2292 (1063)	3.6	597	*12	*400	NO	NO
SB	13.04	113	132	10.00	16.7	1031 (0648)	44.1	3055 (3107)	27.4	2024	*20	?	NO	NO
SM	13.02	94	117	10.05	6.0	1490 (0775)	27.1	2023 (0819)	21.1	533	NO	NO	NO	NO
CE	13.00	114	106	11.10	3.0	1194 (0520)	18.2	2440 (1707)	15.2	1246	*15	*1000	NO	NO
LA	12.11	122	118	11.06	4.8	1399 (1200)	22.5	1910 (2700)	17.7	511	NO	NO	*36	NO
JB	12.06	94	102	09.00	14.9	1612 (0874)	41.9	5298 (3027)	27.0	3686	*18	*2700	NO	NO
PS	12.03	94	103	09.06	11.3	2209 (2098)	29.7	5856 (4043)	18.4	3647	NO	NO	NO	NO
LH	11.02	67	96	08.07	21.4	2205 (2206)	25.4	2566 (1411)	4.0	361	NO	NO	*25	NO

? = These data either were not presented in the book or were ambiguous (for example, it is not clear whether the regularity effect for AR was found only for high-frequency regular words).

Table 3.6

Visual tasks: errors and time, length and position effects (adapted from Seymour, 1986). Grey–visual performance in the normal range

Nature of the deficit or of the profile
- phonological deficit or phonological dyslexia
- visual deficit or surface dyslexia
- mixed: phonological and visual deficit or phonological and surface dyslexia

	Identity matching		Array matching		Length effects ms/letter (ms)			Position & legality ms/position		Nature of the deficit (according to Seymour, 1986)		Type of profile (according to the neuropsychological approach)
	Errors %	Time	Errors %	Time	Identity task	Frequent word	Pseudo word	Array position	Array legality			
Average readers: efficient performance characteristics												
Mean range	0 to 8	690 to 1300	2 to 18	1050 to 1850	-8 to 16[1]	-2 to 23[2]	28 to 42[3]	16 to 245				
SD range		130 to 360		290 to 580								
Dyslexics: grey–visual performance in the normal range					*: significant effect; NO: no effect							
SS	1.7	978 (222)	3	1610 (0415)	12	*35	*169	68	*260	Phonological		Phonological
MP	0.8	961 (308)	4	2613 (0849)	*19	*196	*340	*331	*300	Phonological	Visual	Phonological	Surface
SE	0.8	857 (205)	3	1912 (0639)	*27	*362	*413	*166	NO	Phonological	Visual	Phonological
LT	5.0	543 (116)	13	760 (0180)	*7	*196	*288	27	NO	Phonological		Phonological
AD	2.5	657 (126)	6	1006 (0297)	*13	*20	*73	*100	*200	Phonological		Phonological
DT	0.8	851 (302)	1	1299 (0507)	*11	*113	*299	53	NO	Phonological		Phonological
RO	2.5	1281 (388)	2	2545 (0736)	*54	*26	*221	103	600	Phonological	Visual	Phonological	Mild[4]
DP	1.7	735 (256)	4	1099 (0427)	6	*70	*328	*165	NO	Phonological	Visual	Phonological	Surface
MT	6.7	1160 (676)	26	2801 (1683)	-5	*81	*785	159	1500	Phonological	Visual	Phonological
MF	0.8	1107 (367)	0	2139 (0667)	*28	*55	*266	*153	300	Phonological	Visual	Phonological	Mild[4]
FM	1.7	826 (238)	2	1321 (0406)	*20	*136	*621	77	NO	Phonological		Phonological
AR	1.7	1004 (460)	4	2261 (1019)	*32	*133	*191	127	NO	Phonological	Visual	Phonological	Surface
JM	2.5	739 (191)	10	1388 (0375)	10	*164	*474	36	300	Phonological		Phonological
GS	0.8	825 (248)	10	1735 (0489)	*15	*264	*389	*229	300	Phonological	Visual	Phonological
SB	13.3	573 (104)	25	778 (0238)	4	*131	*707	-2	NO	Phonological		Phonological
SM	2.5	812 (228)	8	1499 (0453)	*18	*243	*361	*287	200	Phonological	Visual	Phonological
CE	0.0	1648 (890)	5	3597 (2838)	*38	*68	*427	289	NO	Phonological	Visual	Phonological
LA	8.3	606 (126)	23	1011 (0320)	1	*96	278	*100	NO	Phonological		Phonological
JB	0.8	918 (263)	7	1255 (0378)	12	*161	*548	49	NO	Phonological		Phonological	Surface
PS	0.0	1038 (260)	4	2148 (0481)	*21	*206	*951	95	*360	Phonological	Visual	Phonological
LH	0.0	1131 (365)	2	3163 (1182)	*21	*539	*368	-93	*700	Phonological	Visual	Phonological	Surface

1. Discarding the results of two subjects whose length effects were 18–28 ms/letter (Seymour, 1986); 2. Discarding the results of 2 subjects whose length effects were 31 and 48 ms/letter (Seymour, 1986); 3. Discarding 5 subjects whose length effects were 48 to 396 ms/letter (Seymour, 1986); 4. Mild form of dyslexia.

No linear trend was observed for these children, but the length effect was significant for the other two (18 and 29 ms/letter). In contrast, 12 dyslexics exhibited a significant linear trend, although the magnitude of the difference between their scores and those of the average readers was small, and in most cases the length effect fell within the normal range (−5 to 15 ms/letter) or just above it (18 to 21 ms/letter). Only 5 dyslexics obtained a strong length effect (27–32 ms/letter for SE, MF and AR, 38 ms/letter for CE, and 54 ms/letter for RO). Three of these 5 were classified by Seymour as having only an impairment of the visual processor (RO, MF, and AR), the other two being assumed to also suffer from a phonological deficit (CE and SE).

The length effect obtained by the controls on high-frequency words was between −2 ms/letter and 23 ms/letter (discarding the results of two subjects whose length effects were 31 and 48 ms/letter). The effect of item length was statistically negligible for most of the average readers, while it was significant for most of the dyslexics. The length effect of only two dyslexics was within or just above the normal range (20–26 ms/letter for AD and RO). The increase as the words lengthened was five times greater than the upper bound of the controls for 13 dyslexics (more than 110 ms/letter). Everyone but AR here was phonologically impaired.

For pseudoword reading, the controls' length effect ranged between 28 and 42 ms/letter (discarding the results of 5 controls whose length effects were 48, 74, 107, 148, and 396 ms/letter). The linear trend was significant for all but two of the controls and for almost all of the dyslexics. The scores of all dyslexics were outside the normal range. In addition, every dyslexic except SS, AD, and AR exhibited a very large length effect that was five times greater than the upper bound of the average readers (more than 210 ms per letter). This group included all but one (AR) of the 13 dyslexics above-mentioned as having a strong length effect on high-frequency words. The fact that for most of the dyslexics the item-length effect was greater in pseudoword reading than in word reading, and greater in word reading than in the identity-matching task, suggests that this effect is not due simply to an impairment of the visual processor in dyslexics. This remark applies to all three dyslexics presumably suffering from a selective impairment of their visual processor. Their scores were more strongly influenced by length in pseudoword reading than in high-frequency word reading or identity matching (221, 26, and 54 ms/letter, respectively, for RO; 266, 55, and 28 ms/letter for MF; 191, 133, and 32 ms/letter for AR).

For the array-matching task, the position effect of the control group ranged from 16 to 245 ms/position, except for one child with a very slow serial procedure (445 ms/position). Seven of the controls displayed evidence of left-to-right serial processing, but no evidence of this type of processing was found for the other six children. The results of the dyslexics were very close to the controls' and only three dyslexics exhibited very slow left-to-right serial processing (287 to 331 ms/position, SM, CE, and MP). Finally, the effect of letter-string legality, taken to be indicative of the availability of an orthographic model of spelling patterns, was somewhat inconsistent, both for the average readers and for the dyslexics. However, one can note a facilitative legality effect of more than a quarter of a second for 9 dyslexics, 2 with no phonological deficit (RO and MF) and 7 with an impaired phonological processor (SS, MP, MT, JM, GS, PS, and LH).

Conclusion

A large majority of the 21 dyslexics were found to suffer from a phonological deficit, the same 17 participants according to Seymour's classification and to our own re-examination of the data. These results indicate the high prevalence of a phonological deficit in developmental dyslexia. In addition, in the comparison between the 14 dyslexics that had the same reading level as the younger controls, most of the dyslexics (10–11) had deviant phonological skills, and the proportion of dyslexics assumed to have a specific visual deficit (according to Seymour) or a surface profile (our classification) was small (2 or 3 children). Therefore, no matter what criteria are used to classify dyslexics, the developmental trajectory in the area of phonological reading skills is deviant in most cases.

Three dyslexics were classified by Seymour as having a selective impairment of the visual processor (RO, MF, and AR). All three were, nonetheless, found to be more negatively influenced by the length of the items in the pseudoword-reading task than in the word-reading task, and more in the word-reading task than in the identity-matching task. In addition, their scores were within the normal range in the array-matching task. The evidence of a clear-cut selective visual-processing impairment thus seems inconclusive. Furthermore, the strong effect of item length observed on pseudoword reading for all dyslexics suggests that the slow serial processing on which they relied when reading pseudowords cannot be definitively ascribed to deficient visual skills.

As noted by Seymour himself (1986), all dyslexics in the sample displayed some evidence of phonological dyslexia defined in terms of inaccuracy, slow reaction times, and a length effect on pseudoword reading. This dominant pattern was accompanied by some signs of impaired visual skills. In addition, indicators of reliance on compensatory strategies were also observed. For instance, RO and MF strongly benefited from legality in the array-position task, perhaps to supplement their weak visual skills. In contrast, their performance was not better on homophone pseudowords than on non-homophones. This was the case for eleven dyslexics classified as having a phonological impairment who benefited from homophony in the pseudoword-reading task, perhaps to supplement their weak phonological skills.

One can assume that these compensatory strategies are probably what enabled some of these dyslexics to partially overcome their phonological deficit. Support for this hypothesis is found in some data reported by Seymour (1986) about the early spoken- or written-language development of the three dyslexics he classified as suffering from a specific visual-skill impairment: RO's language development was considered to have been delayed and his early speech to be very indistinct; MF's onset of speech was delayed and confusion over the order of sounds in words was noted; AR's reading performance when he was about 10 years old appeared indicative of a mixed profile with a phonological deficit (Seymour & Porpodas, 1980). Therefore, these three dyslexics could be phonological dyslexics who have well compensated their phonological deficit.

Finally, note that MP and LH should not have been included in the cohort given their IQ. Yet their profiles did not turn out to be atypical in any respect. This finding is consistent with Vellutino et al.'s (2000) results suggesting that there are no great differences between IQ-discrepant and non-discrepant poor readers on measures of recoding skills (see also the review by Stuebing et al., 2002), which casts doubt on the validity of the discrepancy criterion.

Subtypes of dyslexia: English-speaking vs. non-English-speaking dyslexics

More recently, in three studies with English-speaking children (Castles & Coltheart, 1993; Manis et al., 1996; Stanovich et al., 1997) and two with French-speaking children (Génard et al., 1998; Sprenger-Charolles et al., 2000), 283 dyslexics (175 anglophones and 108 francophones) were compared to 401 same-chronological-age controls (151 anglophones and 250 francophones) and 342 same-reading-level controls (67 anglophones and 275 francophones). This data set should allow us to reliably estimate the prevalence of the various dyslexic profiles in each language.

Two methods were used to analyze the results: the classical method and the regression method. In the former, children are classified as dyslexics when their reading scores are at least one standard deviation (SD) below the mean of average readers. They are labeled as phonological dyslexics when only their sublexical reading route (assessed via pseudoword reading) is impaired, and surface dyslexics when only their lexical reading route (assessed via high-frequency irregular-word reading) is impaired. When both routes are deficient, they are said to have a mixed profile or a double deficit. In contrast to the classical method, the regression method points out a *relative* deficit, either in the orthographic skills of dyslexics as compared to their phonological reading skills, or in their phonological reading skills as compared to their orthographic skills. Stanovich et al. (1997) characterized the subtypes defined in this manner as "soft", as opposed to the "hard" subtypes defined using the classical method. More precisely, soft subtypes are defined by plotting pseudoword performance against irregular-word performance (and vice versa) and then examining the 90% (or 95%) confidence intervals around the regression lines determined from the control group. A phonological dyslexic is a child who is an outlier when pseudowords are plotted against irregular words but who is in the normal range when irregular words are plotted against pseudowords. Surface dyslexics are defined in the opposite fashion. Dyslexics whose scores are outside the confidence intervals in both cases have a mixed profile. In the five studies we examined, the sole indicator of reading efficiency was accuracy, except in one study in which latency was also assessed (Sprenger-Charolles et al., 2000). The descriptive data are presented in Table 3.7.

Prevalence of phonological, surface, and mixed profiles

The results for the hard subtypes are presented in Figure 3.8, which shows the proportion of dyslexics whose reading scores were one standard deviation below (for accuracy) or above (for speed) the mean of the chronological-age controls on pseudowords only (hard phonological profile), high-frequency irregular words only (hard surface profile), pseudowords and irregular words (mixed profile), as well as those with no deficit on either assessment. According to the accuracy scores, mixed profiles predominate, since both pseudoword and irregular-word reading are deficient in most dyslexics (69%). The overall number of hard dissociated profiles is rather small (25%), although the prevalence of the phonological and surface subtypes is not very consistent across languages and measures. Indeed, as many hard phonological dyslexics

Table 3.7
Sample size, sex ratio, chronological age (CAC) and reading level (RLC) controls

	Castles & Coltheart, 1993	Manis et al., 1996	Stanovich et al., 1997	Génard et al., 1998	Sprenger-Charolles et al., 2000
Number of dyslexics	56	51	68	75	31
Sex ratio (male/female)	56–0	37–14	29–39	50–25	20–11
Mean chronological age	11	12	9	10	10
Range	8½–15	9–15	11 months	9–12	11 months
Number of CAC	56	51	44	231	19
Sex ratio (male/female)	56–0	35–16	16–28	99–132	11–8
Number of RLC	17*	27	23	256	19
Sex ratio (male/female)		18–9	13–10	109–147	11–8

* Analyses reported in Stanovich et al. (1997) including 40 of the 56 dyslexics.

as surface dyslexics were found in the accuracy-based English studies (15% and 17%, respectively, in Castles & Coltheart, 1993; 10% and 10% in Manis et al., 1996; 9% and 12% in Stanovich et al., 1997). In contrast, the percentage of hard phonological dyslexics was lower in the accuracy-based French studies (3% versus 23% surface dyslexics in Génard et al., 1998; 10% versus 19% in Sprenger-Charolles et al., 2000), but not when latency was examined (16% and 19%, respectively, in Sprenger-Charolles et al., 2000). However, when both measurements were taken into account, almost all of the francophone dyslexics exhibited a mixed profile (Sprenger-Charolles et al., 2000). Finally, a small number of dyslexics were found to behave as chronological-age controls for high-frequency irregular-word and pseudoword reading alike, at least when only accuracy was examined (6%). When both accuracy and speed were considered (Sprenger-Charolles et al., 2000), the irregular word and/or the pseudoword reading scores of all the dyslexics were found to deviate from the norms.

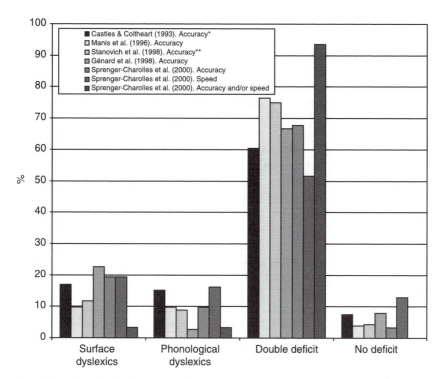

Figure 3.8 Chronological age comparison: mean percentage of each profile, according to the classical method (scores at least 1 SD away from the control group mean for irregular and pseudoword reading).

  * = From Manis et al. (1996)
** = Personal communication from Stanovich

The distribution of the different profiles obtained using the regression method is presented in Table 3.8 The soft subtypes were determined via accuracy scores in four of the five studies. In Sprenger-Charolles et al.'s study, because of ceiling effects on irregular-word accuracy in chronological-age controls, this method was used only for correct-response latencies. The results pointed out a low proportion of mixed profiles (9%) and a high proportion of soft dissociated profiles (70%). Thus, they are in sharp contrast to those found using the classical method. However, the proportions of the two soft dissociated profiles varied strongly across studies. Soft phonological dyslexics were more prevalent than soft surface dyslexics in two studies (55% versus 30% in Castles & Coltheart, 1993; 52% versus 32% in Sprenger-Charolles et al., 2000), equally prevalent in two others (33% versus 29% in Manis et al., 1996; 25% versus 22% in Stanovich et al., 1997), and much less prevalent in another (4% versus 56% in Génard et al., 1998). More surprisingly, a large number of dyslexics without any reading deficits were found (21%), with strong variations across studies (25% in Stanovich et al., 1997; 28% in Manis et al., 1996; 37% in Génard et al., 1998, but only 9% in Castles & Coltheart, 1993, and 13% in Sprenger-Charolles et al., 2000).

In sum, in comparisons with chronological-age controls, the percentage of dyslexics with a dissociated profile varies according to the analysis method, the measure, and the language. However, the results obtained with the classical method are more consistent than those obtained with the regression method and reveal a low percentage of hard dissociated profiles and a high percentage of mixed profiles.

The outcomes of comparisons with reading-level controls are presented in Table 3.9. Only the data from the regression method were usable because the number of hard dissociated profiles found via the classical method was too low. The most striking finding was that in four of five studies, the number of soft phonological dyslexics remained high (nearly 40% in Castles & Coltheart

Table 3.8

Chronological age comparison: mean percentage of each profile, according to the regression-based method (confidence interval: 90% or 95%)

Confidence interval	90%	95%	90%	95%	95%
	Castles & Coltheart (1993) Accuracy	Manis et al. (1996) Accuracy	Stanovich et al. (1997) Accuracy	Génard et al. (1998) Accuracy	Sprenger-Charolles et al. (2000) Time latency
Phonological dyslexics	54.7	33.3	25.0	4.0	51.6
Surface dyslexics	30.2	29.4	22.1	56.0	32.3
Double deficit	5.7	9.8	27.9	2.7	3.2
No deficit	9.4	27.5	25.0	37.3	12.9

according to Stanovich et al.'s 1997 reanalyses, and in Sprenger-Charolles et al., 2000; 25–30% in Manis et al., 1996, and in Stanovich et al., 1997), whereas the soft surface profiles almost disappeared. Soft phonological dyslexics only amounted to 8%, and there was not a single soft surface profile in the other study (Génard et al., 1998).

On the whole, among the 265 dyslexics involved in the reading-level comparison, the proportion of soft deviant phonological profiles was fairly high (24.5% or 65 cases) and the proportion of soft deviant surface profiles was very low (3% or 7 cases), with a delayed developmental reading trajectory for most of these dyslexics (79% or 193 cases). However, these assessments were based on either accuracy or processing speed alone. If it had been possible to take both measures into account, the number of delayed profiles would probably have been lower and the number of phonological dyslexics higher.

Robustness of the soft phonological, soft surface, and soft mixed profiles

Other evaluations of dyslexics' phonological and orthographic skills were carried out by Manis et al. (1996), Stanovich et al. (1997), and Sprenger-Charolles et al. (2000) in order to assess the robustness of the soft subtypes found using the regression method, especially those based on a reading-level comparison. The most significant findings were that the phonological reading skills of soft phonological dyslexics were always markedly inferior to those of controls, but the orthographic skills of soft surface dyslexics were not.

For instance, the phonological reading skills of the soft phonological dyslexics in Stanovich et al.'s (1997) study were always below those of the reading-level controls, not only on the experimental pseudoword-reading task used to define the groups, but also on another assessment of their

Table 3.9

Reading-age comparison: mean percentage of each profile, according to the regression-based method (confidence interval: 90% or 95%)

Confidence interval	90%	95%	90%	95%	95%
	Castles & Coltheart (1993) Accuracy*	Manis et al. (1996) Accuracy	Stanovich et al. (1997) Accuracy	Génard et al. (1998) Accuracy	Sprenger-Charolles et al. (2000) Time latency
Phonological dyslexics	37.5	29.4	25.0	8.0	38.7
Surface dyslexics	5.0	2.0	1.5	0.0	9.7
Double deficit	0.0	0.0	0.0	0.0	0.0
No deficit	57.5	68.6	73.5	92.0	51.6

* Analyses reported in Stanovich et al. (1997) including 40 of the 56 dyslexics.

phonological reading skills that was not used for the group assignment. In contrast, the orthographic reading skills of the soft surface dyslexics were not below those of the reading-level controls, once again not only on the experimental task used to define the groups, but also on another assessment of their orthographic reading skills. Similar trends were observed in Manis et al.'s study (1996).

In the Sprenger-Charolles et al. study (2000), two groups of dyslexics were found to have a soft dissociated profile based on the comparison of their scores to those of same-chronological-age controls on pseudoword and irregular-word latencies. It should be noted that because of ceiling effects on irregular-word accuracy in the chronological-age controls, accuracy scores could not be used in this comparison. Each of these two groups of dyslexics was compared to younger same-reading-level controls on the same measures as well as on irregular word and pseudoword accuracy scores. The results are presented in Figure 3.9, which shows accuracy scores and vocal response times for the soft phonological and surface dyslexics, and for the two control groups, made up of the same children tested when they were 8 (reading-level controls) and 10 (chronological-age controls) years old.[9] An important trade-off was observed for the reading skills of the controls between the ages of 8 and 10. These children read pseudowords more accurately than words when they were 8, but no longer did so two years later. This means that the chronological age comparison and the reading-level comparison were not based on the same thing at all, and points out the relevance of reading-age comparisons, especially since according to this match, the dyslexics shared the same overall reading level with the controls.

Based on the reading-level comparison, the high-frequency irregular-word scores of the soft phonological and surface dyslexics did not fall significantly below those of the reading-level controls, whether on accuracy or speed. In contrast, both groups of dyslexics were found to be deficient in pseudoword reading, either in terms of processing speed (for the soft phonological dyslexics) or accuracy (for the soft surface dyslexics).

Whatever study we consider (Manis et al., 1996; Sprenger-Charolles et al., 2000; Stanovich et al., 1997), the orthographic skills of soft surface dyslexics are never found to lag behind those of younger children at the same reading level. In contrast, the phonological reading skills of soft phonological dyslexics are always lower than those of reading-level controls (Sprenger-Charolles et al., 2000; Stanovich et al., 1997). In addition, according to the sole study in which both accuracy and speed were assessed, it seems that even the phonological skills of the soft surface dyslexics were far from being spared (Sprenger-Charolles et al., 2000). Finally, the mixed profiles actually turned out to be phonological dyslexics with poorly compensated orthographic skills. Indeed, according the Stanovich et al. (1997) study, the phonological reading skills of the soft mixed profiles did not differ significantly from those of the

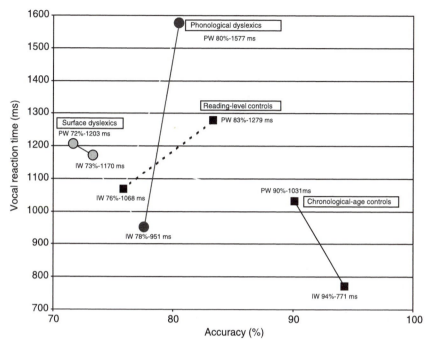

Figure 3.9   Accuracy and latency for reading-level controls, and for dyslexics classified according to the regression method as phonological or surface dyslexics based on their pseudoword (PW) and irregular-word (IW) latencies as compared to chronological-age controls (adapted from Sprenger-Charolles et al., 2000).

soft phonological dyslexics. However, the orthographic skills of these mixed profiles lagged behind those of soft phonological dyslexics.

Summary and conclusion

Two significant but contradictory findings emerged concerning the prevalence of the subtypes. First, for the comparisons with chronological-age controls, the classical method based on accuracy revealed a low percentage of hard dissociated profiles (25%) and a high percentage of mixed profiles (69%); the opposite was found using the regression method, which indicated 70% soft dissociated profiles and 9% mixed profiles. Second, in the comparison with younger children of the same reading level, the percentage of soft deviant phonological profiles is clearly higher (24.5%) than that of soft deviant surface profiles (3%), with the developmental reading trajectory being delayed for most dyslexics (73%), at least when only accuracy or only speed are considered. However, the proportions of hard and soft phonological dyslexics are far below those of hard and soft surface dyslexics in the accuracy-based francophone studies (Génard et al., 1998; Sprenger-Charolles et al., 2000) but not in the accuracy-based anglophone studies (Castles & Coltheart, 1993; Manis et al., 1996; Stanovich et al., 1997) or in the speed-based French study (Sprenger-Charolles et al., 2000).

The discrepancies between the anglophone and francophone studies may be due to linguistic factors and to the measures used. Because grapho-phonemic correspondences are more regular in French than in English, French-speaking dyslexics may manage to use the sublexical reading route with less difficulty than English-speaking dyslexics. This could explain why fewer hard and soft phonological dyslexics were found in French than in English when accuracy scores were taken into account. However, as many soft phonological dyslexics were found in the latency-based francophone study as in the accuracy-based anglophone studies, suggesting that the phonological deficit of French-speaking dyslexics mainly shows up as slow processing.

The fact that, in the chronological age comparison, the proportion of dyslexics found to have unimpaired reading skills was very large according to the regression method and very small according to the classical method may be due to difference in the balance between sublexical and lexical reading skills according to reading level. For this reason, the regression method, which is based on the relative discrepancy between these two skills, is prob-ably not the best method for evaluating dyslexic profiles in a comparison to chronological-age controls (see discussions of the trade-off between sublexical and lexical reading skills, chapter 2, pp. 52–55).

Finally, differences in the dyslexics' chronological age may also account for some of the discrepancies in the results of the regression-based anglo-phone studies. The proportion of dyslexics exhibiting a mixed profile was larger in Stanovich et al. (1997, 28%) than in Castles and Coltheart (1993, 6%) and Manis et al. (1996, 10%). These differences could be due to the fact that the dyslexics enrolled in the Stanovich et al. (1997) study were younger (age 9) than those in the other two English studies (age 11 in Castles & Coltheart, 1993; age 12 in Manis et al., 1996). As argued by Stanovich et al. (1997, p. 124), some of the young dyslexics "in both the deviant groups might continue to practice reading and to receive considerable exposure to print. . . . This print exposure may result in these children having relatively less seriously impaired orthographic processing mechanisms. . . . However, their more ser-iously impaired phonological processing abilities will probably not develop at the same rate . . ., thus resulting in greater dissociation between phonological coding ability and exception word fluency with development". This could cause a greater number of dissociated profiles, especially the phonological profile, among older dyslexics than among younger ones.

Regarding the reliability of the different profiles, the orthographic skills of soft surface dyslexics are consistently found not to differ from those of younger same-reading-level children (Castles & Coltheart, 1993; Génard et al., 1998; Manis et al., 1996; Sprenger-Charolles et al., 2000; Stanovich et al., 1997). In contrast, the phonological reading skills of soft phonological dyslexics systematically fall below those of reading-level controls (Manis et al., 1996; Sprenger-Charolles et al., 2000; Stanovich et al., 1997). In addition, mixed profiles in fact behave like phonological dyslexics (Stanovich et al., 1997). The results concerning the phonological skills of soft surface dyslexics are less clear-cut. They appear to be comparable to those of reading-level controls in some studies (Manis et al., 1996) but not in others (Sprenger-Charolles et al., 2000).

These results replicated those found in single case studies (e.g., Snowling et al., 1986a; Temple & Marshall, 1983, according to Bryant & Impey's re-analyses, 1986; Valdois, et al., 2003) and suggest that the developmental trajectory of phonological dyslexics is deviant, but that the surface dyslexic trajectory is not. However, phonological deficits have very often been reported in single cases of surface dyslexia (e.g., Coltheart et al., 1983, according to Bryant & Impey's reanalyses, 1986; Valdois et al., 2003), as well as in some multiple case studies (e.g., Zabell & Everatt, 2002). Nonetheless, discrepant results have been observed in some studies (e.g., Bailey, Manis, Pedersen, & Seidenberg, 2003). But even then, some of the "discrepancies" do not seem to be so discrepant. For instance, in the Bailey et al. (2003) study, it was reported that surface dyslexics exhibited a tendency to score lower than reading-level controls on pseudoword reading.

Together with the results of the single case studies and Seymour's case series studies (1986; see pp. 109–119), the findings of the other multiple case anglophone studies (Castles & Coltheart, 1993; Manis et al., 1996; Stanovich et al., 1997; Zabell & Everatt, 2002), and multiple case francophone studies (Génard et al., 2000; Sprenger-Charolles et al., 2000) seem more in line with the hypothesis that a phonological deficit is at the core of developmental dyslexia, than with the claim that clear-cut subtypes like those found in acquired dyslexia can be discerned in developmental dyslexia. However, even the so-called dissociated profiles found in acquired dyslexia do not seem to be "pure" forms of either surface or phonological dyslexia (Harm & Seidenberg, 2001; Van Orden, Pennington, & Stone, 2001).

INVARIABILITY AND VARIABILITY IN THE EXPRESSION OF DEVELOPMENTAL DYSLEXIA

In the present chapter, we have examined different types of studies (group studies, single case studies, and multiple case studies) conducted in various languages, for the purposes of evaluating the reliability and prevalence of the dyslexic performance pattern. In this section, we would like to highlight the main results of the studies examined, and give some possible explanations.

Summary of the main results

Group studies indicate that a specific phonological impairment characterizes the reading performance of dyslexics (see pp. 78–102). It is important to first stress the reliability of this result, which has been consistently reported across studies. In addition, this deficit is severe, since it is consistently observed in comparisons with younger children of the same reading level, thus suggesting that the developmental trajectory of dyslexics is deviant when it comes to sublexical reading skills (e.g., for English-speaking participants, see reviews by Rack et al., 1992; Van Ijzendoorn & Bus, 1994; for French-speaking dyslexics, see Casalis, 1995; Grainger et al., 2003; for German-speaking dyslexics, see Landerl et al., 1997; Wimmer, 1993, 1995; Ziegler et al., 2003; for Spanish-speaking dyslexics, see Jimenez-Gonzalez & Valle, 2000). This deficit is also more noticeable when spelling-to-sound relationships are more inconsistent; for instance, in English as compared to French or Italian (Paulesu et al., 2001) or to German (Landerl et al., 1997). In languages with a more transparent orthography, the sublexical reading deficit of dyslexics mainly shows up as slow pseudoword reading (e.g., in German: Wimmer, 1993, 1995; Ziegler et al., 2003; in Spanish: Jimenez-Gonzalez & Valle, 2000).

Regarding single case and multiple case studies, both indicate that the phonological reading deficit of phonological dyslexics emerges even in comparisons with younger children of the same reading level (single case studies: Hulme & Snowling, 1992; Temple & Marshall, 1983, reanalysis by Bryant & Impey, 1996; Valdois et al., 2003; multiple case studies: Castles & Coltheart, 1993; Manis et al., 1996; Seymour, 1986; Sprenger-Charolles et al., 2000; Stanovich et al., 1997). These results point out a deviant developmental trajectory for phonological dyslexics. However, their lexical reading route is far from being preserved. This result is easy to understand if we agree that the building of the orthographic lexicon depends on the efficiency of the sublexical reading procedure (see chapter 2). Consequently, most dyslexics exhibit a mixed profile, although their phonological reading deficit is the most severe, emerging even in comparisons with younger children of the same reading level.

Compared to phonological profiles, surface profiles are rare and not very robust. In addition, the lexical reading route of these dyslexics is not found to be less efficient than that of younger children who read at the same level. The developmental trajectory of surface dyslexics can thus be seen as merely delayed (Manis et al., 1996; Sprenger-Charolles et al., 2000; Stanovich et al., 1997; Valdois et al., 2003). However, phonological deficits are often reported in cases of surface dyslexia, compared to chronological-age controls (Sprenger-Charolles et al., 2000; Valdois et al., 2003; Zabell & Everatt, 2002) or even to reading-level controls (e.g., reanalyses of Coltheart et al., 1983, by Bryant & Impey, 1986). Therefore, it seems difficult to contend that the phonological skills of surface dyslexics are well preserved, especially since their phonological deficit may be masked when only accuracy is taken into account.

Surface profiles and visual deficits in developmental dyslexia

There is a plethora of explanations for the surface dyslexia pattern. Some researchers postulate that this profile may be due to both a slight phonological impairment and aggravating environmental factors (Stanovich et al., 1997). Children from a disadvantaged social background may not only be less exposed to written material but may also be given less help in overcoming their reading deficiency than children from a social environment likely to motivate them to learn to read despite their difficulties. This account could explain why the phonological deficit of surface dyslexics is generally less noticeable than their orthographic deficit, the acquisition of well-defined orthographic representations needing frequent exposure to print. Support for this interpretation has been found in twin studies, which suggest that this type of dyslexia is more related to environmental factors than is phonological dyslexia, where the genetic contribution to the group reading deficit is much greater (Castles, Datta, Gayan, & Olson, 1999).

Another account of a specific cognitive impairment in surface dyslexia is rooted in the idea that in the same way as phonological short-term memory may be highly critical for using the sublexical reading procedure, visual short-term memory may be crucial to the lexical reading procedure. In this view, surface dyslexics are assumed to suffer from a visual short-term memory deficit that prevents orthographic word-pattern acquisition. However, this attractive explanation has not been corroborated so far. Except in some studies (e.g., Goulandris & Snowling, 1991), deficits in visual short-term memory have not been observed in cases of surface dyslexia (e.g., Castles & Coltheart, 1996; Hanley et al., 1992; Valdois et al., 2003).

Another candidate for a specific cognitive impairment in surface dyslexia is visual sequential processing. Such a deficit has been found in some cases of surface dyslexia (Allan: Hanley et al., 1992); Nicolas: Valdois et al., 2003); RO, MF, and AR: Seymour, 1986). In addition, a number of group studies in languages with a shallow orthography have reported visual sequential processing deficits in dyslexics (in Italian: De Luca et al., 1999, 2002; Judica et al., 2002; in German: Hawelka & Wimmer, 2005; Hutzler & Wimmer, 2004).

As regards group studies, we have already noted that it is difficult to imagine how the dyslexic phenotypic pattern of performance could differ markedly across largely similar alphabetic writing systems. Moreover, it is not obvious that the atypical pattern of eye movements observed in the dyslexics enrolled in these group studies is the cause of their reading disabilities. As a matter of fact, this deficit may be just a mere consequence of those reading disabilities (Rayner, 1998), especially since these studies relied on comparisons with average readers of the same chronological age, unlike those demonstrating the consistent presence and high prevalence of phonological deficits in developmental dyslexia. In addition, the results of these studies do not allow a straightforward interpretation as surface dyslexia. Indeed, the atypical pattern of eye movement was found not only for word reading (as expected from the surface dyslexic account, but also for pseudoword reading, and even more massively for pseudowords than for words).

The same finding was obtained in the study by Hanley et al. (1992), where Allan's visual performance was higher for words than for pseudowords. A greater impairment of visual sequential processing on pseudowords than on high-frequency words or letter strings was also noted in the study by Seymour (1986), where the sequential processing of dyslexics was assessed by means of both accuracy and speed. However, even the three dyslexics said to suffer from a severe and specific visual impairment (RO, MF, AR) were found to be negatively influenced by item length, especially in pseudoword reading, thus suggesting that the poor serial processing on which they relied to read these items cannot be definitely attributed to a defective visual processor.

Finally, in most studies showing specific visual deficits in developmental dyslexia, the children's phonological skills were assessed without taking processing speed into account, on tasks with no time constraints, whereas visual skills were examined with time-constrained tasks (very short stimulus display duration; e.g., Valdois et al., 2003). A similar criticism applies to the study by Wimmer and Mayringer (2002). It is therefore not possible to rule out the hypothesis that these dyslexics were only suffering from a processing speed deficit.

Compensatory strategies

In skilled readers, written-word identification processing seems to be context free, to the point of being dubbed a "reading reflex" (Perfetti & Zhang, 1995; see chapter 1, pp. 3–7). Indeed, context-based processing in written-word identification decreases as age and reading ability increase (Perfetti et al., 1979; Raduege & Schwantes, 1987; West & Stanovich, 1978), less-skilled readers and dyslexics making greater use of the written context than good readers do (Bruck, 1990). This point is illustrated by the studies presented in the present chapter (pp. 92–101), which shows how morphological information is used by dyslexics and average same-reading-level readers. The results suggest that dyslexics rely on a compensatory strategy based on the identification of morphological units, and probably on the meaning conveyed by morphemes.

It is probably by way of such compensatory strategies that some dyslexics have managed to partially overcome their phonological deficit. Support for this hypothesis is found in single case studies. For instance, JM (Hulme & Snowling, 1992) was shown to gradually develop compensatory strategies, as suggested by the positive effect of semantic priming on his reading performance. Also, in Seymour's multiple case study (1986), the performance of most of the dyslexics suffering from a severe phonological impairment was better on homophone pseudowords than on non-homophone pseudowords. A similar effect of homophony was reported for HM (Temple & Marshall, 1983). The strong lexicality effect found in most developmental dyslexics is also likely to be no more than the result of a compensatory strategy. Dyslexics probably use the lexical information conveyed by words to supplement their poor phonological skills, which could explain why their performance on pseudowords is so poor.

Indirect evidence for the use of compensatory strategies to counteract inadequate phonological skills is provided by three cases of adolescent dyslexics (RO, MF, AR; Seymour, 1986), all assumed to be highly deficient only in visual skills (Seymour, 1986). In fact, early language development was considered to be delayed in two of these dyslexics (RO and MF), whereas AR's reading performance when he was aged about 10 seemed indicative of a mixed profile with a phonological deficit (Seymour & Porpodas, 1980). Therefore, these three dyslexics could be phonological dyslexics who have well compensated their phonological deficit.

Compensatory strategies may also account for the finding that the phonological deficits of some surface dyslexics seem to simply disappear, due to the effects of age and/or special training. This explanation helps us understand why the most robust cases of surface dyslexia have been found in adults (Goulandris & Snowling, 1991; Hanley et al., 1992). Furthermore, the results of some training studies (see Olson, Wise, Ring, & Johnson, 1997) suggest that most dyslexics found to have a phonological deficit, even as compared to reading-level controls at the onset of a remedial training in phoneme awareness and phonological decoding, shifted to a surface profile by the end, and still exhibited that profile on a follow-up test one year later.

Conclusion

The main outcome of the studies reviewed here is that a deficit of the sublexical reading procedure is the key characteristic of developmental dyslexia, for this deficit is consistently found in group studies, and is systematically observed in most dyslexic participants in single and multiple case studies. As expected, given that the building of the orthographic lexicon depends on the efficiency of sublexical reading procedure (chapter 2), the lexical reading procedure of dyslexics is also found to be impaired. The deficit of their

CHAPTER FOUR

Phonological and sensori-motor explanations of dyslexia

According to the data presented in the previous chapters, there is an impressive amount of evidence indicating that phonological factors play a decisive role in the acquisition of normal reading and that phonological processes are impaired in dyslexic children. Basic evidence in support of the primary role of phonological factors in reading comes from studies on pseudoword reading. The fact that early performance in pseudoword reading is the best predictor of later reading achievement shows that phonology plays a crucial role in the build-up of lexical templates for written words (see chapter 2). Furthermore, problems in pseudoword reading have been shown to be closely associated with dyslexia. Such a deficit is prevalent in the dyslexic population and emerges even in comparisons with younger children of the same reading level, thus suggesting a deviance in the development of the dyslexics' phonological reading route (see chapter 3).

In the present chapter we will look for the possible origin of the dyslexics' reading deficit by examining the classical phonological explanation that ascribes dyslexics' reading deficit to a specific cognitive deficiency in phonological processing, primarily, in phonemic awareness and in phonological short-term memory. We also examine the current non-phonological explanations according to which dyslexics' phonological deficit is secondary to more basic sensori-motor impairments: a deficiency in either rapid auditory processing (Tallal, 1980), or in the visual magnocellular pathway (Livingstone, Rosen, Drislane, & Galaburda, 1991; Stein & Walsh, 1997), or in motor skills (Nicolson, Fawcett & Dean, 2001). We conclude that the non-phonological explanations are rather weak, and we propose a new phonological explanation of dyslexia, in which a specific mode of speech perception is a possible determinant of developmental dyslexia.

THE CLASSICAL PHONOLOGICAL EXPLANATION OF DYSLEXIA

The difficulties experienced by dyslexics in reading new words are generally explained in terms of their poor phonological skills, especially phonemic awareness and phonological short-term memory. In this section we will examine the evidence supporting this "classical" phonological explanation. The studies reviewed in chapter 2 (pp. 56–67) indicated that, among the pre-reading abilities linked to reading acquisition, phonemic awareness is the best predictor of future reading level. Evidence for a unique contribution of syllabic awareness and rhyme awareness remains quite limited, even in English. Furthermore, phonemic awareness helped improve reading.

Likewise, the classical phonological explanation of developmental dyslexia is based on the fact that deficits in phonemic awareness, as well as in phonological short-term memory, can explain the reading deficit of dyslexics. These deficiencies may constitute a hindrance to the proper acquisition of the sublexical reading procedure. Indeed, this procedure requires the ability to connect sublexical writing units (graphemes) with their corresponding sublexical speaking units (phonemes), and then to bring together the units that result from the phonemic decoding process. The first operation requires fully-established phonemic categories; the second, adequate phonological short-term memory. A child who is unable to correctly handle phonemes, and on top of that suffers from a deficit in phonological short-term memory, will hardly be able to use a sublexical reading procedure. Thus, developmental dyslexia may be rooted in a specific cognitive deficit that is phonological in nature.

In addition, as we have already emphasized in chapter 3 (pp. 77, 91), deficits in the speed of access to the spoken lexicon have been observed in dyslexic children more recently (Wolf & Bowers, 1999; Wolf et al., 2000, 2002). More precisely, it has been assumed that there are two independent sources of reading dysfunction, one related to phonological processing (usually assessed by accuracy scores in phonological awareness and in phonological short-term memory tasks), the other related to lexical access (usually assessed by processing speed in the rapid automatic naming of highly frequent items: RAN). Two types of evidence have been presented in support of the double deficit hypothesis. First, naming tasks have been found to explain unique variance in reading beyond that explained by phonological awareness. Second, phonological awareness and rapid naming appear to be differentially related to reading skills, the former to accuracy scores and the latter to processing speed.

However, this evidence has been challenged. On the one hand, the relationships between RAN task scores and reading were stronger for letters and digits than for objects or colors. As suggested by Wagner et al. (1997), it is possible that including alphanumeric stimuli makes some RAN tasks mere proxies for individual differences in early literacy and print exposure, which explains why the predictive power of these skills vanishes when early reading skills are taken into account. On the other hand, non-timed measures (of phonological awareness and short-term memory) were compared to timed measures on RAN tasks. To ensure that there were two entirely different deficits in dyslexia, one related to phonological skills and the other related to naming speed, it would be necessary to use timed measures in both cases.

In the following section the studies of undifferentiated groups of dyslexics are first examined, and then those dealing with dyslexics exhibiting a dissociated profile, either a phonological profile or a surface profile, as well as those with a mixed profile.

Studies with groups of undifferentiated dyslexics

Two studies quoted in chapter 3 (Lindgren et al., 1985; Paulesu et al., 2001) have highlighted that most of the differences between dyslexics and average readers were found in verbal processing, for instance, in phonemic segmentation. In the cross-linguistic study by Lindgren et al. (1985) in which Italian and English dyslexics were compared to same-chronological-age average readers, no difference in visual abilities (visuo-spatial and visuo-motor skills) was found. Also, whatever their native language (English, French or Italian), the adult dyslexics of the study by Paulesu et al. (2001) were found to have weaker skills than the same-chronological-age controls on tasks requiring phonological processing (phonemic awareness, short-term phonological memory and rapid naming).

In these two studies, dyslexics were compared to average readers of the same chronological age. If the reading level exerts a strong influence on phonological skills outside the reading domain, these results could therefore be due to the weakness of the dyslexics' reading level (Bryant & Impey, 1986). This does not seem to be the case since similar trends have been reported when dyslexics have been compared to same-reading-level controls.

Furthermore, among the various phonological skills, deficits in phonemic skills seem to be the most important. For instance, in the study by Pennington, Cardoso-Martins, Green, and Lefly (2001), the scores in phonemic awareness, phonological short-term memory and rapid naming of 70 dyslexics (children from age 7 to 12 years and teenagers from age 12 to 18 years) were compared to those of controls having the same reading level. For both age groups the scores of the dyslexics were lower than those of the controls on tasks that required handling phonemes. On the other hand, only the most severely impaired teenage dyslexics were found to have weaker scores than the same-reading-level controls on phonological short-term memory. Finally, the scores of the dyslexic teenagers and children were found to be no weaker than that of the same-reading-level controls on rapid naming tasks. Similar trends have been reported by Chiappe, Stringer, Siegel, and Stanovich (2002) in a study in which adult dyslexics were also compared to same-reading-level controls. As in the previous study, the major part of the variance in reading (more than 50%) was explained by phonemic awareness skills.

Deficits in phonemic awareness were also reported in other studies comparing reading-level controls to English-speaking dyslexics (e.g., Joanisse, Manis, Keating, & Seidenberg, 2000; Swan & Goswami, 1997a), and non-anglophone dyslexics (e.g., in German, Landerl et al., 1997). However, some results suggest that when grapheme–phoneme correspondences are transparent, deficits in phonemic awareness are only found in the very beginning of reading acquisition (e.g., in German: Landerl & Wimmer, 2000).

Other studies suggest that dyslexics do less well on phonological tasks when they cannot rely on their lexical knowledge, i.e., when the tasks involve pseudowords or rare words (see for instance, for phonemic awareness: Bruck, 1992; Bruck & Treiman, 1990; Swan & Goswami, 1997a; for phonological short-term memory: Snowling, Goulandris, Bowlby, Howel, 1986b; for naming tasks: Swan & Goswami, 1997b). In the study by Swan and Goswami (1997b), the vocabulary level was assessed by a naming task involving pictures of short and long words which were either frequent or rare. The same items were presented in a task where the subjects had to point to the picture which best represented a given word; out of four pictures one represented the word, and the three other pictures offered either a visual foil, phonological foil or semantic foil. The children were also submitted to a classical vocabulary test in which they had to designate the picture that corresponded to a given name. In the naming test, the scores of the dyslexics were weaker than those of the younger average readers of the same reading level for the rare words, but not for the frequent words. Moreover, the dyslexics produced many phonological errors and were the only participants who were negatively affected by the length of the items, whatever their frequency. On the other hand, in the two vocabulary tests that only required the subjects to designate the picture that corresponded to a given word, the scores of the dyslexics did not differ from those of the controls.

The dyslexics thus have difficulty recovering the phonological codes of words as evidenced by: (1) the fact that their scores were lower than those of the controls only in the lexical task that required to sound out a word; (2) the production of many phonological errors in this task; (3) the negative incidence of item length on their scores. Finally, group studies have also highlighted deficits in the phonological domain before reading acquisition in future dyslexics. This was the case for phonological awareness (especially phonemic awareness), phonological short-term memory, and rapid naming (e.g., Hawelka & Wimmer, 2005; Wimmer, 1996).

To summarize, studies with undifferentiated groups of dyslexics indicate that even same-reading-level controls outperformed dyslexics on tasks that imply phonological processing (phonemic awareness, phonological short-term memory and rapid naming). This suggests once again that the developmental trajectory of dyslexics is deviant. Other results also indicate that dyslexics do less well on these phonological tasks when they cannot rely on their lexical knowledge, e.g., when pseudowords or rare words were used to assess phonemic awareness, phonological short-term memory or naming skills. Finally, competence in phonemic awareness, phonological short-term memory and rapid naming is the most reliable predictor of the future reading level of reading of children (see also chapter 2).

Dyslexics with a phonological, surface or mixed profile

The results of studies involving dyslexics with different profiles (phonological, surface or mixed profiles) are contradictory. In some studies only phonological dyslexics were found to suffer from phonological deficits (Bailey et al., 2003; Manis et al., 1996; Stanovich et al., 1997), but not in others (Jimenez-Gonzalez & Ramirez-Santana, 2002; Sprenger-Charolles et al., 2000; Zabell & Everatt, 2002).

A specific deficit in phonological awareness, and more specifically in phonemic awareness, is expected for phonological dyslexics. A task involving deleting the first or last segment of a word, either a syllable or a phoneme, was used in a study by Stanovich et al. (1997). Whereas the scores of the phonological and mixed profile dyslexics were found to lag behind those of the reading-level controls, those of the surface dyslexics were comparable to the scores of the reading-level controls. Similar results were observed in a study by Manis et al. (1996) for phonemic awareness tasks where the scores of the phonological dyslexics were consistently lower than those of reading-level controls while those of the surface dyslexics were not.

However, in other studies no difference was observed between phonological and surface dyslexics in reading-related skills. For instance, in the study by Zabell and Everatt (2002), phonological dyslexics were found to behave in the same way as surface dyslexics on four tasks requiring phonological processing (in addition to a pseudoword-reading task, a spoonerism task, an alliteration task, and a rhyme fluency task), both in accuracy and speed. Furthermore, no statistical difference between phonological and surface dyslexics was found in the rapid naming of pictures or digits, again, no matter what measure was used (accuracy or speed). Also, in the study by

Jimenez-Gonzalez and Ramirez-Santana (2002), there was no difference between phonological and surface dyslexics in phonological awareness.

In the study by Sprenger-Charolles et al. (2000), phonological and visual short-term memory skills were also assessed. A specific deficit in phonological memory was expected for the phonological dyslexics; a specific deficit in visual memory that would prevent the memorization of the visual shape of words was expected for the surface dyslexics. Visual memory was assessed using the Corsi test. The experimenter defined a path by pointing in succession to various dots (2 to 7) located in a two-dimensional space. The children were required to reproduce each of the paths. A similar task was used to assess phonological short-term memory. Here, the children were asked to repeat three- to six-syllable pseudowords. Contrary to the hypotheses, phonological dyslexics were not significantly worse off than surface dyslexics in phonological short-term memory and surface dyslexics were not significantly worse off than phonological dyslexics in visual short-term memory. On the other hand, both phonological and surface dyslexics lagged behind reading-level controls on phonological short-term memory, thus suggesting, once again, the presence of a phonological impairment in surface dyslexics.

The children were also given a phonemic awareness test when they were 5 years old.[1] At that time, all the children were unable to read. They were asked to delete the first segment of ten two-phoneme and ten three-phoneme pseudowords (such as *zu, na, gur, saf*). The scores of the future phonological dyslexics were not lower than those of the future surface dyslexics; the performance of both was inferior to that of the future average readers (Sprenger-Charolles et al., 2000).

Moreover, a large majority of the future dyslexics was totally unable to achieve this task before learning to read (score 0 for 23 of the 33 future dyslexics, i.e., 70%), whatever their future profile of dyslexia. This was the case for only 3 of the future average readers (16%). However, the scores of 3 of them were very weak (1 or 2 out of 20). It was considered that children whose phonemic awareness scores were between 0 and 2 before learning to read were "at risk" for reading acquisition; 73% of the future dyslexics and 32% of the future average readers had such scores (unpublished data from the study by Sprenger-Charolles et al., 2000).

In summary, phonological dyslexics have consistently been found to lag behind reading-level controls regarding phonemic awareness, phonological short-term memory or rapid naming; this has also been noted for mixed profiles, but not for soft surface profiles. However, according to at least some studies, the phonological skills of surface dyslexics do not appear to be intact, even before reading acquisition.

Dyslexics are thus suffering from deficiencies in phonological processing that can explain their reading deficit. However, the origin of their phonological deficits is open to debate. In the following section, we will show why perceptual explanations of dyslexia should be based on alternative perceptual modes rather than on deficits, and we will situate the perceptual explanations in the framework of a three-stage model of speech perception We will then argue that dyslexics' phonological deficits are secondary to more basic sensori-motor impairments. This point can allow us to put forward some new hypotheses about the possible origin of the dyslexics' phonological deficits.

DYSLEXIA AS A SPECIFIC MODE OF SPEECH PERCEPTION

As explained here above, there is a fairly large consensus for ascribing dyslexia to a phonological dysfunction. However, the precise nature and origin of the phonological deficits remain in debate. The phonological deficits might arise from a specific problem in conscious access to phonemic representations. Phonemic awareness is weaker for dyslexics vs. average readers matched for chronological and lexical age and longitudinal studies indicate that the phonemic awareness deficit can be observed in future dyslexics, even before they learn to read. This last finding has special importance for conclusions on the effect of phonemic awareness on reading because we know that reading in turn affects phonemic awareness as evidenced by comparisons between illiterate and literate people (Morais et al., 1979). However, in longitudinal studies aimed at evidencing the role of phonemic awareness in pre-readers on later reading performances, the effect of phonemic awareness was still significant when pre-reading skills were controlled (see pp. 61–62, 63–65, 138).

While dyslexics' deficits in pseudoword reading and mastering letter-sound correspondences are related to a of lack phonemic awareness, the origin of the deficit remains unspecified in the classic phonological explanation of dyslexia. Here research points to three possible directions: attention, memory, and perception.

Three possible directions: Attention, memory, and perception

Attention problems affect analytic behavior and might therefore disturb the phonological analysis of words. However, only some part of the dyslexic population is affected by such problems (Shaywitz, Fletcher, & Shaywitz, 1994). Rather than being an intrinsic feature of dyslexia, the attention deficit is only found in some dyslexic children and it arises from co-morbidity with attention deficit/hyperactivity disorder (ADHD). There is, therefore, no way by which attention failures might explain dyslexia as a whole.

What about deficits in memory and perception then? Dyslexics' problems in phonological short-term memory (e.g., Liberman, Mann, & Werfelman, 1982) might affect phonological analyses by imposing limitations on the storage of grapheme-to-phoneme conversions. However, limitations in the short-term storage of phonological units should not only affect the identification of written words but also that of spoken words. If phonological short-term memory were the culprit, not only written language but spoken language as well would be seriously affected in dyslexic children. Much the same criticism can be addressed to the possible implications of the perceptual problems evidenced in dyslexic children. Errors in the discrimination of phonological contrasts (e.g., as between /ba/ and /da/: Mody, Studdert-Kennedy, & Brady, 1997) should not only affect the perception of letters but also that of speech sounds.

We are thus faced with the paradox that deficits in perception and memory might well be at the origin of reading problems but would not be specific enough to leave speech perception almost unaffected. A possible solution to this paradox is that dyslexia does not arise from a perceptual *deficit* but from a specific *mode* of perception, different from the one found in the general population. Perceptual explanations of dyslexia have made some progress in this direction with basically two different options. One line of research, which culminates in the magnocellular theory, seeks to define the origin of dyslexia as a different mode of sensory processing, characterized by a lesser amount of temporal precision and a larger amount of spatial precision. Another line of research assigns dyslexia to a specific mode of phonological perception characterized by the use of allophonic rather than phonemic units.

Before examining the evidence in support of the different explanations of dyslexia, we will first plug them into the framework of different models of speech perception and language development. We then proceed to a critical review of sensory theories of dyslexia, either visual or auditory, and examine the evidence in support of a specific mode of speech perception in dyslexia. Finally, the different explanations of dyslexia are compared in terms of reliability and causality and future challenges for perceptual explanations are presented.

Speech perception in dyslexics: A developmental perspective

Dyslexics have a deficit in speech perception. A fair proportion of dyslexic children show a weakness in phoneme discrimination; they make a greater number of errors than do average readers when presented with pairs of syllables which differ only by a single phonemic feature (Adlard & Hazan, 1998). This might indicate a weakness in the very representation of speech sounds and the problem then is to understand the specific nature of speech perception in developmental dyslexics. Is there a difference of degree or of type? And how can this difference be important enough to impair reading acquisition while leaving only the barest traces in spoken language?

Speech perception can be conceived of as the end product of three successive stages. The first consists of the extraction of acoustic cues, the second of analog-to-digital transformation of acoustic cues into phonetic categories, and the third of the grouping of phonetic categories into phonological categories (Serniclaes, 2000; Werker & Logan, 1985; Werker & Tees, 1984b). While both the auditory and phonetic processing stages are largely innate, the phonological stage crucially depends on exposure to spoken language. Human infants are born with predispositions for perceiving all the possible phonetic contrasts, which are then selectively activated as a function of the presence versus absence of the corresponding contrast in the linguistic environment. This fairly classical view on speech development (Werker & Tees, 1999) is based on a considerable amount of empirical evidence. Neonates can already discriminate between a range of phonetic categories (Eimas, Siqueland, Jusczyk, & Vigorito, 1971), even between those which are not present in their ambient language (e.g., Lasky, Syrdal-Lasky, & Klein, 1975). Adult listeners keep some ability for encoding non-native phonetic contrasts, but with a shorter memory decay period than for native contrasts, thereby indicating that the decline of the initial ability to discriminate the universal set of phonetic contrasts within the first year of life involves a change in processing rather than a sensorineural loss (Werker & Tees, 1984b). This reveals a "phonetic" level of processing, corresponding to natural phonetic contrasts, intermediate between acoustic processing and a "phonological" level, corresponding to phonemic contrasts.

Possible explanations for developmental dyslexia have been sought at each of the processing stages evidenced in studies on speech perception: auditory, phonetic, and phonological. Classical explanations of dyslexia locate the core deficit either at the sensory (auditory-visual) or the phonetic level, with cascading effects on phonological representations. However, a simpler explanation is that dyslexia arises directly from differences in phonological perception, without afferent deficiencies at earlier processing levels.

The auditory explanation (Tallal, 1980) posits a deficit in the temporal processing of fast spectral changes such as formant transitions in stop consonants, while the perception of slowly varying spectral changes are preserved. More recently, the auditory temporal deficit has been reformulated within the framework of the duality of sensory processing (Stein, 2001). Due to intrinsic limitations in the analysis of physical events, by either man or machine, any stimulus can be apprehended with different degrees of spectral versus temporal precision (e.g., Joos, 1948).

The trade-off between *spectral* and *temporal* analysis for auditory stimuli, or equivalently between *spatial* and *temporal* analysis for visual stimuli, is found in the neural system where it corresponds more or less to the difference between parvocellular and magnocellular systems (Breitmeyer & Ganz, 1976). A specific "magno" deficit in the analysis of stimuli requiring high temporal precision, such as phonemes in speech perception and individual letters in reading, might explain dyslexia without severely affecting auditory and visual perception in general. The magno deficit has an evident interest for the explanation of dyslexia because it is grounded in the basic characteristics of stimulus analysis and has specific consequences for reading. However, the problem with this explanation is that the magno deficit is not reliable (see p. 148), and that the perceptual deficit in dyslexia does not seem to be related to sensory analysis in general but rather restricted to speech perception (see p. 150).

Deficits in speech perception can arise either at the phonetic or the phonological processing stage. A basic property of speech perception is that speakers do not discriminate between variations of the acoustic stimuli which are not relevant for linguistic categorization. "Categorical perception" (CP) filters out a huge amount of irrelevant acoustic details and, therefore, is of crucial importance to processing the rapid information about phonemes in the speech signal (Liberman, Cooper, Shankweiler, & Studdert-Kennedy, 1967). Now, there is a CP deficit in dyslexia (first evidenced by Godfrey, Syrdal-Lasky, Millay, & Knox, 1981) and this deficit is quite reliable (Serniclaes, Bogliotti, Messaoud-Galusi, & Sprenger-Charolles, submitted).

The next question then is to understand how such a deficit might selectively impair reading acquisition. A possible solution would be that the CP deficit is phonological rather than phonetic in nature. CP is already present in the predispositions of the prelinguistic child for perceiving the universal set of phonetic contrasts. However, categorical predispositions are not organized around the same boundaries as those evidenced in adults. The former are universal and phonetic in nature whereas the latter are language specific and phonological in nature. It is therefore possible for an individual to be endowed with phonetic CP without having acquired phonological CP. Indeed, there is evidence for suggesting that dyslexics selectively lack phonological CP.

SENSORI-MOTOR DEFICITS

Temporal versus spatial and spectral coding

Any stimulus can be apprehended with different degrees of temporal versus spatial (or spectral) precision due to the intrinsic limitations in the analysis of physical events (Gabor, 1947; Joos, 1948). The higher the spectral precision, the lower the amount of available temporal precision – a trade-off which makes that a wide range of different procedures is potentially available for stimulus analysis. Rapid spectral transitions are better depicted when stimuli are analyzed with a higher degree of temporal precision, at the expense of spectral resolution. This is evident for the analysis of speech segments (see Figure 4.1), especially those carrying the information on stop consonants which are short and transitional in nature even when produced at a fairly slow rate (consonants are indicated by triangles in Figure 4.1).[2]

Spectral transitions play an important role in speech perception (Liberman et al., 1967), suggesting that the auditory system proceeds with high temporal precision when listening to speech. However, an alternative hypothesis is that speech perception is achieved by a specialized subsystem, specific to the processing of linguistic sounds produced by a human vocal tract (Liberman & Mattingly, 1985). While the auditory versus speech specific alternative has an interest in its own, let us keep in mind for the moment that in any case speech perception has to proceed with high temporal velocity rather than with spectral acuity. In other words, speech perception has to "think" in spectral movements rather than in spectral templates.

The trade-off between spectral and temporal precision in audition is paralleled by a similar trade-off between spatial and temporal precision in vision. Interestingly, investigations on visual perception in normal-reading adults suggest that the perception of words requires a fairly high degree of temporal precision, at the expense of a loss in spatial definition. Though we are dealing with words, the evidence is mainly based on letter identification because words are not processed holistically. Data on word identification with visual noise indicate that words are unreadable unless letters are separately identifiable (Pelli, Farell, & Moore, 2003). This means that spatial precision for word identification can be measured with individual letters. Much the same is true

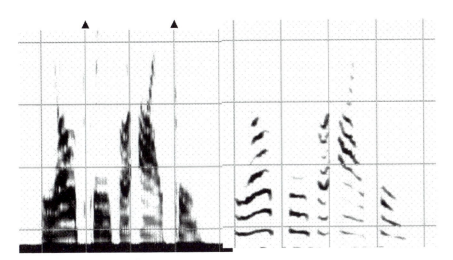

Figure 4.1. Trade-off between temporal and spectral precision.
Spectrograms (by Winpitch®) of the spoken sentence "We all scream for ice cream". The temporal window used for left-side representation (23 ms) is narrower than the one used for the right-side one (92 ms). Triangles indicate consonants.

for temporal precision. As the time required for word identification is directly related to that required for its constituent letters, rate of word identification depends on the rate of letter identification. Gauging the share-out between spatial versus temporal precision in word reading can therefore rely on the evidence collected with letters.

Data collected with spatially frequency filtered letters indicate that they are processed with a single visual channel (Solomon & Pelli, 1994; for similar evidence with words see: Legge, Pelli, Rubin, & Schleske, 1985). Use of single spatial channel for letter identification means low spatial precision in absolute terms, as the output of that single channel does not have to compete with other channels. Further, the precision is also low in relative terms when the human is compared to an artificial observer using an optimal strategy (i.e., an "ideal" observer, see Solomon & Pelli, 1994). No wonder then if low spatial precision for letter identification by the human might seem counter-intuitive (Skottun, 2000).

As to temporal precision, other studies show that letter and word identification performance remains fairly constant for durations beyond 60 ms (letters) or 200 ms (5-letter words; Pelli, Burns, Farell, & Moore, accepted). This represents a fairly high rate of temporal processing, not very far from the one prevailing in speech recognition which, as we have seen, is known to place high demands on temporal resolution. Indeed, the minimal duration for recognizing isolated vowels or consonants (around some 40 ms: Tekieli & Cullinan, 1979) is slightly below the durational range evidenced for individual letters. Obviously, the expert reader trades low spatial resolution with high temporal resolution, comparable to that prevailing in speech perception.

The physiological basis for spatio-temporal trade-offs in vision seems to reside in anatomical and functional differences between two different perceptual systems. The sensory analysis of visual stimuli is achieved through different pathways, beginning in the retina and ending in the cortex, with differing relative temporal versus spatial precision. The magnocellular pathway responds to high temporal and low spatial frequencies, whereas the parvocellular pathway responds to high spatial and low temporal frequencies (Breitmeyer & Ganz, 1976). When compared to parvo retina ganglia, magno ganglia are larger and have a greater dendritic area, therefore responding to lower spatial frequencies. They also have more rapidly conducting axons, and hence a higher temporal resolution. The magno and parvo systems extend through different layers of the lateral geniculate nucleus and from there to different parts of the cortex. A dorso-medial stream receives input from the magno pathway and projects into the posterior parietal cortex, with visual guidance of attention and movements as its main function (Newsome, Britten, & Movshon, 1989). A ventro-lateral stream receives input from both the magno and parvo pathways, projects into the infero-temporal cortex and has object recognition as its main function (Milner & Goodale, 1995).

The anatomical differences between the magno and parvo pathways suggest that the former has crucial importance for attaining normal reading rates. The magno system is endowed with high temporal precision which is necessary for controlling rapid saccadic movements between fixations. Conversely, the parvo system can proceed with high spatial precision and the input to the parvo (the fovea) is essential for reading letters during fixations. One might think that the high spatial precision potential of the parvo is fully used for recognizing letters. However, as already explained, letter perception is achieved with low spatial precision, i.e., the "details" of letters are not taken into account. Proceeding with low spatial precision means reducing fixation time which contributes to fasten the whole reading process. This tends to indicate that the fairly high processing rates found in normal reading, close to those prevailing in speech perception, arise from the conjunction of rapid control of saccadic movements by the magno system with rapid decoding of letter information by the parvo system, the latter at the price of a reduction in spatial precision.

The balance between *spatial* and *temporal* processing channels in visual perception is paralleled by a similar balance between *spectral* and *temporal* processing in the sensory analysis of auditory signals. There is probably an auditory magnocellular system whose function is to process auditory transients although without clear anatomical separation from other auditory pathways (Stein, 2001).

Magnocellular deficit in vision

Suppose that for genetic and/or environmental reasons, a child cannot afford high temporal resolution. Letter identification would then be slower and word identification would require longer fixation time. Words would be readable but at a slower pace, which might constitute a severe handicap for acquiring reading automatisms. However, that problem would arise from temporal constraints in letter decoding and would therefore be specific to reading. The temporal deficit would not affect the perception of visual stimuli in general, as weak temporal resolution can be compensated by enhanced spectral resolution.

The hypothesis of a specific temporal deficit is central to the magnocellular explanation of dyslexia. The magnocellular theory of dyslexia explains the reading deficit as a dysfunction in the sensory analysis of visual stimuli which would specifically arise from the magnocellular system, not from the parvocellular system. This is the main assertion of the magnocellular theory since its initial formulation (Lovegrove, Bowling, Badcock, & Blackwood, 1980). Though since then, it has been modified in some aspects (Stein, 2003; Stein & Walsh, 1997).

Magnocellular theory is supported by both neurological and behavioral evidence. Post-mortem examinations of dyslexics' brains have revealed dis-orders in the magnocellular layers of the lateral geniculate nucleus as well as smaller magno cells than in controls (Galaburda & Livingstone, 1993) without concomitant differences in parvocellular layers (Livingstone et al., 1991).

Psychophysical experiments have indicated that developmental dyslexics have reduced contrast sensitivity at low spatial frequencies, especially for flickering stimuli, whereas at high spatial frequencies their contrast sensitivity is normal and might even be superior to that of normal readers (Lovegrove et al., 1980). Poor readers also have more difficulty than good readers in detect-ing a blank inter-stimulus interval (ISI) at low spatial frequencies, suggesting they have longer lasting visible persistence at these frequencies (Martin & Lovegrove, 1987; Slaghuis & Davidson, 1993; Slaghuis & Lovegrove, 1985).

However, other aspects of these results suggest that poor readers also have shorter lasting visible persistence at high spatial frequencies. Further behavioral evidence in support of the magnocellular theory was found in a series of investigations with the "Ternus" Apparent Movement Display (Ternus, 1938). When three horizontally aligned equidistant squares are shortly presented and then presented again moved to the left by one between-square distance, then again to the right, the squares appear to move forward and backward as a group for inter-stimulus intervals (ISI) of 50 ms or more (i.e., temporal frequencies of 20 Hz or less). However, when the ISI was less than 50 ms (frequencies higher than 20 Hz), the perception of group move-ment is prevented by visible persistence of the squares in their previous position. Poor readers experience less group movement than controls, again suggesting a magnocellular deficit (Slaghuis, Twell, & Kingston, 1996). Still another source of evidence in support of a magno deficit is that dyslexics have impaired visual motion sensitivity (e.g., Cornelissen, Richardson, Mason, Fowler, & Stein, 1995).

While several different dysfunctions suggest a magnocellular deficit in dyslexia, the implications of these dysfunctions for reading are not always clear. Magno-related dysfunctions involving persistence effects were initially interpreted as arising from inadequate inhibition of the parvo responses by the magno pathway. This was supposed to be the common origin of both reduced contrast sensitivity at high temporal frequencies (Slaghuis & Lovegrove, 1985), longer lasting persistence at these frequencies (Cestnick & Coltheart, 1999), and lesser sensitivity to group movement with the Ternus task (Breitmeyer & Ritter, 1986). It later appeared that saccadic inhibition from the magno system does not reduce parvo activity but selectively affects previous magno activity (Burr, Morrone, & Ross, 1994). However, the main problem with the saccadic deficit explanation is that it is difficult to relate to reading problems in dyslexics because dyslexics confuse neighboring letters whereas reading saccades cover more largely spaced letters (Stein & Walsh, 1997). While deficiencies in temporal processing still suggest a magno deficit, its implications for reading should not be sought in saccadic inhibition.

Magno activity itself, rather than its inhibitory effects during saccades, seems to be disturbed in people affected by developmental dyslexia. Specifically, both eye movement control and direction of visual attention, two different functions managed by the magno system, might be deficient in dyslexia (Stein, 2003). Arguments in support of a deficient control of eye movement are that some proportion of children with dyslexia have unstable eye dominance, unsteady fixation and poor vergence control (Stein & Fowler, 1982; Stein, Riddell, & Fowler, 1988), as well as difficulties in letter ordering (Cornelissen, Bradley, & Stein, 1991; Cornelissen, Hansen, Hutton, Evangelinou, & Stein, 1997). The magno system controls "bottom-up" direction of attention rather than "top-down" guidance of attention by post-perceptual contextual factors. Bottom-up processing is driven by stimulus factors which direct vision towards specific locations inside words.

The "optimal viewing position" is approximately located on the centre of the word with a slight bias towards the left in left-to-right writing systems (O'Regan & Jacobs, 1992) and a slight bias towards the right in right-to-left systems (Vitu, O'Regan, & Mittau, 1990). In a target detecting task, good readers were more accurate when the target appeared on the right side of a fixation point while poor readers were equally accurate on both sides, suggesting the absence of the characteristic left–right asymmetry (Brannan & Williams, 1987). Similar results were obtained with a letter report task (Ducrot, Lété, Sprenger-Charolles, Pynte, & Billard, 2003). The absence of the characteristic left–right asymmetry suggests different scanning strategies, though it might also arise from a narrower perceptual span (Aghababian & Nazir, 2000).

With the "visual motion" version of the magnocellular theory (Stein, 2003), the temporal processing deficit in dyslexia is ascribed to inappropriate sequencing of groups of letters rather than to longer visual persistence of letters. Visual motion disturbances readily account for letter blurring and they might also be at the origin of other temporal deficiencies such as reduced contrast sensitivity with flickering and lack of blank interval detection. However, what remains unexplained is that dyslexics' performances tend to be better than those of controls for stimuli with low temporal definition and high spatial definition. The primary interest of the double dissociation between temporal versus spatial processing and reading status is to demonstrate the specificity of the magnocellular deficit. But there is more than that. If dyslexics were reliably better for stimuli with low temporal/high spatial definition, this would mean that their better functioning parvo pathway compensates for their magno deficit. As sensory analysis is based on the integration of temporal and spatial processing channels, enhanced spatial information might compensate for the temporal information-processing deficit, up to a point. While the imbalance between temporal and spatial processing has severe consequences for reading acquisition, it might only marginally affect visual perception in general. The potential interest of the magnocellular deficit is then to explain dyslexia with a specific mode of visual perception.

Deficits in the magno-visual system represent an interesting suggestion for explaining dyslexia. However, the robustness (i.e., the reliability across studies) of such deficits is fairly low. In a review of the visual deficit in dyslexic children, Skottun (2000) found that the effect was only significant in 4 studies out of 22, i.e., in about 20% of the cases. Furthermore, in 11 of the 18 studies in which the magno deficit was not found, the reverse effect was significant, i.e., magno-visual performances were better in dyslexics vs. controls. This puts the magnocellular model of dyslexia into serious doubt. A further reason for questioning this model is that the magno deficit is also poorly reliable across individuals. The prevalence of the magnocellular deficit among dyslexics is 20–25%, to summarize the outcomes of different studies (Amitay, Ben, Banai, & Ahissar, 2002; Cornelissen et al., 1995; Ramus, Pidgeon, & Frith, 2003a; Ramus, Rosen, Dakin, Day, Castellote, White, & Frith, 2003b; White et al., in press; Witton et al., 1998).

While the prevalence of the deficit among dyslexics is currently used as a reliability criterion in studies on dyslexia, it does not take account of the cut-off point chosen in the distribution of controls (i.e., 1 SD or 1.65 SD) for classifying children as deficient, thus introducing a potential source of bias between studies. This problem can be solved by using percent correct classification, the mean of correct assignment of each individual in the study as either dyslexic or control (see Molfese, 2000 for an example in studies on dyslexia). Correct classification of dyslexics corresponds to the prevalence of the deficit, i.e., the proportion of dyslexics with a deficit, whereas correct classification of controls corresponds to the proportion of controls without a deficit (83% with 1 SD cut-off point, 95% with 1.65 SD). With a 1.65 SD cut-off in the distribution of controls for deciding whether the deficit is present and some 23% estimated prevalence, correct classification with magno-visual deficits amounts to 59%. This is a fairly low value given that chance classification would give 50% correct classification.

If vision problems contribute independently to some form of dyslexia, they should occur in subjects who are not affected by phonological troubles. However, in studies where phonological troubles were controlled visual deficits were more often present in children who also had severe phonological deficits (Borsting, Ridder, Dudeck, Kelley, Matsui, & Motoyama, 1996; Cestnick & Coltheart, 1999; Ramus et al., 2003a; Slaghuis & Ryan, 1999). Furthermore, vision problems seem to explain only a small part of the variance in reading performances (Chiappe et al., 2002; Kronbichler, Hutzler, & Wimmer, 2002; Ramus et al., 2003b; White et al., 2006). Magnocellular sensitivity does not explain more than 20% of the variance in people's reading, though the relationship between motion perception and reading might be stronger (Stein, 2003).

Different studies have tried to use visual remediation to improve reading performances in dyslexics. Monocular occlusion was used to stabilize eye movement control, a procedure which helped some dyslexic children to improve their reading performances. However, only children with binocular instability benefited from monocular occlusion (Cornelissen, Bradley, Fowler, & Stein, 1992; Stein, Richardson, & Fowler, 2000).

Temporal deficits in audition

The claim that dyslexics suffer from a specific dysfunction of temporal information processing by the auditory system was initially based on the fact that they had difficulty with temporal order judgment (TOJ) for brief or rapidly changing stimuli as well as with long stimuli at short interstimulus intervals (ISIs) (Tallal, 1980). Temporal and visual processing deficits were later merged into the same theoretical framework and assigned to a common magnocellular deficit (Stein, 2001; see, however, Heim, Freeman, Eulitz, & Elbert, 2001).

However, several other studies failed to duplicate these results (e.g., Chiappe et al., 2002). In a review on the possible role of auditory processing in dyslexia, Rosen (2003) reports manifold evidence against the auditory temporal deficit. The most straightforward argument is that auditory deficits are not restricted to short ISIs. The problem with the initial evidence in Tallal's studies was that performance at long ISIs had reached the ceiling, leaving possible group differences out of reach. In a longitudinal study (Share, Jorm, MacLean, & Matthews, 2002), no difference in TOJ of nonspeech stimuli was found between future dyslexics and controls for at short ISIs before learning to read (at about 5 years old). However, a significant difference in TOJ was found for long ISIs, in contradiction with the temporal deficit model. Furthermore, later comparisons between the dyslexic children from the same study, at 9 years old, with reading level (RL) controls failed to reveal any significant difference between groups, for either at long or short ISIs. Other studies show that the dyslexics' deficit in TOJ is not restricted to short ISIs (Marshall, Snowling, & Bailey, 2001; Nittrouer, 1999; Reed, 1989).

Deficits in the detection of amplitude modulation of speech stimuli might give alternative support to the temporal deficit model (Lorenzi, Dumont, & Füllgrabe, 2000; McAnally & Stein, 1996; Rocheron, Lorenzi, Füllgrabe, & Dumont, 2002). Dyslexic children need higher amplitudes to detect and discriminate between amplitude modulations at different frequencies. However, the deficit does not seem to be specifically located at high modulation rates. Finally, mixed results were obtained in studies where temporal and spectral performances were compared. While one study showed reading-disabled, middle-school children to be impaired in the detection of temporal differences between tones (Watson, 1992), another study showed adult dyslexics to be more impaired for frequency versus temporal discrimination of sounds (McAnally & Stein, 1996).

We saw in the previous section that the magnocellular deficit in vision is not robust; only 20% of the studies display results in the expected direction. The temporal deficit in audition, which is considered by some authors (Stein, 2001) as the auditory counterpart of the magno deficit in vision, also lacks robustness, as we have seen, though no quantification is available. The reliability of auditory deficits is also fairly low with a prevalence of about 40% according to a review of 10 studies by Ramus (2003), yielding about 68% correct classification (with an assumed 1.65 cut-off). While the reliability of auditory deficits as a whole seems larger than the one of visual deficits (59% correct classification), the former often do not tap rapid auditory processing (Ramus, 2003; Rosen, 2003). Accordingly, deficits in both auditory and visual processing of stimuli requiring high temporal precision seem to be weakly reliable. Only one-third of the dyslexics have both auditory and visual deficits (Ramus, 2001), yielding 64% correct classification with a classical 1.65 SD cut-off. Finally, the contribution of auditory capacities to reading performances is weaker (some 43% explained variance, Ramus et al., 2003b) and sometimes nonsignificant (Chiappe et al., 2002; White et al., 2006).

Concerning remediation assays, sensory training with auditory stimuli fails to be conclusive. Training with lengthened consonant–vowel transitions does not always improve speech perception abilities (McAnally, Hansen, Cornelissen, & Stein, 1997) and when it does there is no generalization to reading (Agnew, Dorn, & Eden, 2004; Bradlow et al., 1999). Failure to improve reading performances remains present for training with lengthened C–V transitions even if this leads to improvements in phonemic awareness (Habib et al., 2002).

In addition to the rapid auditory deficit hypothesis, there have been several other attempts to identify deficits at the sensory level. Other auditory dimensions have been explored with some success: "Perceptual centers" (P-centers: Goswami et al., 2002; Muneaux, Ziegler, Truc, Thomson, & Goswami, 2004) and auditory stream segregation (Helenius, Uutela, & Hari, 1999). Many of these attempts remain to be more thoroughly tested. Others, such as backward masking (Wright, Lombardino, King, Puranik, Leonard, & Merzenich, 1997), though present in audition, fail to generalize to speech perception (Rosen & Manganari, 2001).

Sensori-motor deficits

Different studies suggest that dyslexics also have motor problems. Problems of equilibrium and motor coordination were reported (Wolff, Cohen, &

Drake, 1984). Automatization deficits were also observed in dyslexics as their performance in a task executed routinely decreases sharply when they also have to achieve another interfering task at the same time (Nicolson & Fawcett, 1990). In addition to behavioral evidence, neuroimagery data revealed a reduction of cerebellar activity in tasks involving a motor activity (Brunswick, McCrory, Price, Frith, & Frith, 1999; McCrory, Frith, Brunswick, & Price, 2000; Nicolson, Fawcett, Berry, Jenkins, Deans, & Brooks, 1999). The magnocellular theory accounts for the cerebellar deficit because of the relationship between the magnocellular system and the cerebellum (Stein, 2001). The cerebellar hypothesis would explain why reading automatisms are not properly acquired by dyslexics. It would also explain their phonological deficit as a motor deficit affecting articulatory coding (Nicolson et al., 2001).

One problem raised by the cerebellar hypothesis is that it violates the selectivity principle. If automatization deficits are severe enough to affect reading processes they should also affect a wide range of other skills. Why should reading exert demands on automatization greater than those required for walking, for example? Similarly, if problems in the control of articulatory gestures are involved in dyslexia, they should also affect speech production. Though some studies claimed to evidence articulatory deficits in dyslexic children, the basis of the evidence is fairly low. Differences between dyslexic children and chronological age controls in naming speed of pictured objects, repetition of polysyllabic words and repetition of phrases might be taken as arguments for speech production difficulties, though they might also be a reflection of various other deficits in phonological processing (Catts, 1986, 1993). Specifically, a rapid naming deficit might reflect difficulties in lexical access while repetition tasks involve perceptual processing as well. In another study, evaluation of children's production of French intervocalic /b/ or /p/ stop consonants by trained phoneticians revealed no differences in production errors between dyslexic children and chronological age controls, though quality assessments indicate differences in the production of /p/ between the two groups (Lalain, Nguyen, & Habib, 2002). This gives some support to the hypothesis of a deficit in motor timing control (Wolff, Michel, & Ovrut, 1990), as the production of the voiceless /p/ stop in a vocalic (i.e., voiced) surrounding requires precise control of the timing between laryngeal and supra-laryngeal articulators.

Another problem with the cerebellar theory is that the prevalence of motor deficits among dyslexic children is variable, sometimes strong sometimes weak. Depending on the task, the motor performances of 40 to 100% of the dyslexic children are more than one standard deviation below those of controls (Nicolson et al., 2001). However, regression analyses indicate that motor capacities do not predict reading level (Chiappe et al., 2002; Ramus et al., 2003b; White et al., 2006).

SPEECH PERCEPTION DEFICITS

Categorical perception (CP) versus precision

A good deal of the studies on speech perception deficits in dyslexia claim to investigate "categorical perception" differences between dyslexics and controls. However, these studies used different criteria: magnitude of the discrimination peak on a stimulus continuum, slope of the identification function, difference between observed discrimination scores and those expected from identification. It is important to realize that these criteria tap into different aspects of categorization. In this section, the difference between categorical *perception* (CP) and categorical *precision* is illustrated with examples taken from our work.

Difference between observed and predicted discrimination scores: The classic CP criterion

By definition, perception is strictly categorical when only the stimuli belonging to different categories can be discriminated, not those belonging to the same category (Liberman, Harris, Hoffman, & Griffith, 1957). Perception is perfectly categorical if stimuli can be discriminated only insofar as they are labeled differently, i.e., for stimuli varying on a /ba/-/da/ continuum, discrimination between any two stimuli should increase with the difference between the percentages of /ba/ or /da/ labels assigned to each stimulus. The degree of CP can then be measured by comparing the observed discrimination scores to those expected from the labeling differences between two stimuli, the latter being derived from the labeling data with elementary probability formulas (Pollack & Pisoni, 1971). The smaller the difference between observed and expected discrimination score, the higher the degree of CP, as illustrated in Figure 4.2 in a comparison between normal-reading children and adults (Medina, Geron, & Serniclaes, 2006). Labeling and discrimination data were collected on a synthetic "de"–"te" voice onset time (VOT) continuum (where "e" stands for the neutral schwa vowel here). The labeling curves (Figure 4.2, left panel; percent /d/ responses) are fairly similar for both groups suggesting similar precision. However, discrimination data (Figure 4.2, right panel; percent correct discrimination of pairs of stimuli) indicate that CP largely differs between groups. For the mothers (circles), the observed scores (white symbols) are close to those predicted from labeling (black symbols) indicating almost perfect CP. For the children (squares), observed discrimination scores differ from the predicted ones, indicating a weaker degree of CP.

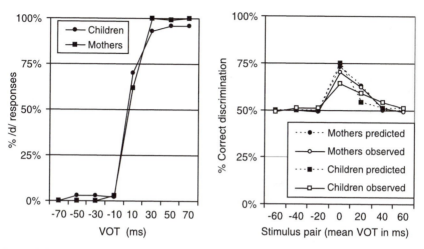

Figure 4.2. Same categorical precision, different categorical perception.
Example with two groups of subjects – here 9-year-old normal-reading French children and their mothers (adapted from Medina et al., 2006).

Slope of the labeling curve: An index of boundary precision

In the classical conception of CP (Liberman et al., 1957), labeling data are used to calculate the expected discrimination scores, which give a baseline for measuring the amount of discrimination between stimuli which is not explainable from differences in their labeling. While labeling scores are used as a baseline for assessing CP in the classical approach, they can also have an intrinsic interest. The *slope* of the labeling curve can be used as an index of categorical *precision*, considering that a steeper slope reflects a higher degree of precision (Hazan & Barrett, 2000; Simon & Fourcin, 1978). Distinguishing categorical perception from precision is not a purely formal exercise. There are instances in which groups only differ in *precision* and not in CP, as illustrated in Figure 4.3 with a comparison between illiterate and literate adults (Serniclaes, Ventura, Morais, & Kolinski, 2005).

Labeling and discrimination data were collected on a synthetic /ba-da/ place of articulation continuum, generated by modifying the onset frequencies of F2 and F3 formant transitions. The labeling curves (Figure 4.3a; percent /b/ responses) differ between groups; the slope is steeper for literates (circles) than for illiterates, which indicates higher precision for literates versus illiterates. However, discrimination data (Figure 4.3b; percent correct discrimination of pairs of stimuli) indicate that the observed scores (white symbols) are close to expected ones (black symbols) for both groups, which

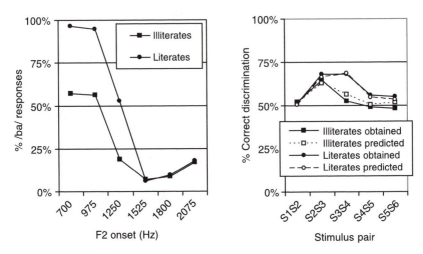

Figure 4.3(a) and (b).   Same categorical perception: (a) different categorical precision; (b) differences in discrimination peak at the phoneme boundary between illiterates and literates: plain lines correspond to observed discrimination scores and dashed lines correspond to the expected scores, calculated from the labeling responses. (Adapted from Serniclaes et al., 2005.)

illustrates how CP can remain constant and even near perfect irrespective of categorical precision.

Discrimination peak at the labeling boundary: A cumulative index of categorical perception and categorical precision

The difference in discrimination between stimuli which lie across a category boundary and those located within a category, i.e., the discrimination peak at the point of the stimulus continuum corresponding to the phoneme boundary (or "phoneme boundary effect": Wood, 1976), has also been used as a criterion for assessing categorical perception. The boundary peak provides a global assessment of both categorical perception and categorical precision. This is illustrated in Figure 4.4 where the boundary peak corresponds to the size of the difference between *observed* across- and within-category scores. With no difference in precision between groups, as in the child vs. adult comparison, the boundary peak only depends on CP (see Figure 4.4a, plain lines). With no CP differences between groups, as in the illiterate versus literate comparison, observed and expected discrimination scores coincide and the boundary peak only depends on the amount of categorical precision (see Figure 4.4b, plain lines and dashed lines). There are also instances where

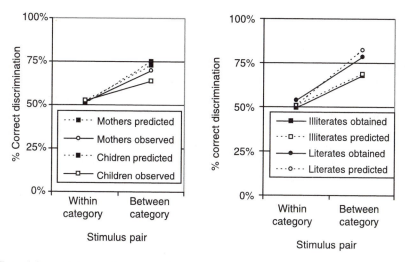

Figure 4.4(a) and (b).   Differences in discrimination peak at the phoneme boundary between children and adults (4.4a, adapted from Medina et al., 2006), and between illiterates and literates (4.4b, adapted from Serniclaes et al., 2005).

groups differ in both CP and precision. This is the situation which prevails between dyslexics and chronological-age (CA) controls.

Categorical perception deficit in dyslexia

Both differences in categorical perception (CP) and in categorical precision were evidenced in studies on developmental dyslexia. Evidence supporting a CP deficit in dyslexia is mainly based on differences in discrimination peak at the phoneme boundary. While the boundary peak depends both on CP and categorical precision, CP contributes most to boundary peak differences between dyslexics and controls, as explained below. So, as many authors have done in the interpretation of their data, we will consider that boundary peak differences approximate CP differences.

We recently reviewed the literature on the differences between dyslexic children and chronological-age controls in the discrimination and labeling of speech continua (Serniclaes, 2006; Serniclaes et al., submitted). In studies with discrimination data, significant differences in *categorical perception* between dyslexics and chronological-age controls were found in about 75% of the tests in different studies (Bogliotti, 2003; Godfrey et al., 1981; Maassen, Groenen, Crul, Assman-Hulsmans, & Gabreëls, 2001; Manis & Keating, 2004; Messaoud-Galusi, Carré, Bogliotti, & Serniclaes, 2002; Serniclaes, Sprenger-Charolles, Carré, & Démonet, 2001; Serniclaes, Van

Heghe, Mousty, Carré, & Sprenger-Charolles, 2004; Werker & Tees, 1987). Significant differences arose either from a lower boundary peak, from higher within-category discrimination, or from both a lower boundary peak and higher within-category discrimination for dyslexics vs. controls. An example is presented in Figure 4.5. The discrimination peak across the phoneme boundary (S3–S4 stimulus pair) is lower for the dyslexics while their within-category discrimination scores (other pairs) are noticeably larger.

Other differences, in categorical *precision*, were made evident by comparing the slopes of the labeling curves of dyslexics vs. chronological-age controls in studies with labeling data. Significant differences between groups were found in about 40% of the tests in 12 different studies (Blomert & Mitterer, 2003; Bogliotti, 2003, 2005; Breier et al., 2001; Chiappe et al., 2002; De Gelder & Vroomen, 1998; Godfrey et al., 1981; Joanisse et al., 2000; Maassen et al., 2001; Manis et al., 1997; Reed, 1989; Werker & Tees, 1987).

A typical example taken from a study by Breier et al. (2001) is presented in Figure 4.6. In that study, the relationship between categorical precision and dyslexia was examined while controlling for attention deficit/hyperactivity disorder (ADHD). The results showed that the slope of the labeling curve was significantly shallower for dyslexic children including those also affected by ADHD, thereby indicating a lesser degree of categorical precision, but not for those only affected by ADHD.

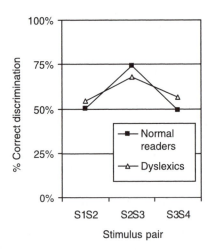

Figure 4.5. Categorical perception deficit in dyslexic children.
Reduced boundary peak and increased within-category discrimination for 13-year-old dyslexics vs. CA controls, collected along a synthetic /ba-da/ place of articulation continuum (adapted from Serniclaes et al., 2001).

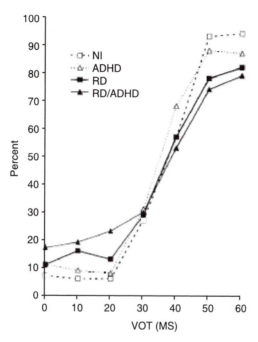

Figure 4.6. Categorical precision deficit in dyslexic children.
Shallower slope of the labeling function for different subgroups of children between 10 and
11 years of age, dyslexics (RD & RD/ADHD) vs. controls (NI & ADHD) along a /ga/-/ka/
voicing continuum (adapted from Breier et al., 2001).

Differences in categorical precision between dyslexics and chronological-
age controls are much less robust than boundary peak differences. However,
though the latter have often been taken as evidence for CP differences
between groups, they might reflect both categorical perception and categorical
precision differences. Part of the robustness of boundary peak differences
between dyslexics and controls arises from the fact that it is a global indicator
of a categorization deficit, including both categorical perception and precision. However, given the low robustness of the categorical precision deficit
this factor contributes very little to the reliability of boundary peak differences between groups. A rough estimation of CP reliability after deducting
the contribution of categorical precision, and supposing the two deficits are
independent, leads to an estimated CP robustness of about 65%. The
assumption of independence is supported by the comparison between illiterate versus literate adults (see Figures 4.3, 4.4; Serniclaes et al., 2005). Only
precision is weaker for illiterates, indicating that it probably depends on read-

ing experience while categorical perception is independent of reading. This indicates a difference in nature between the two deficits.

Different results suggest that the categorical precision deficit in dyslexia is also not very reliable across individuals either (Joanisse et al., 2000; Manis et al., 1997). However, an examination of individual differences in boundary peaks between dyslexics and controls suggest that CP, or at least some mixture of categorical perception and precision, is fairly reliable. Information on individual differences was only found in two studies. Maassen et al. (2001), in a study on the discrimination of voicing and place of articulation continua in 9-year-old Dutch children, found that discrimination scores allowed for correct classification of about 75% of the participants as dyslexics or normal readers (chronological-age controls). Much the same result was found by Bogliotti (2005) in a study on the discrimination of a voicing continuum in 10-year-old French dyslexic children.

While the CP deficit is fairly robust and reliable when dyslexic children are compared to chronological-age controls, what about comparisons with reading-age controls? The evidence on this topic is scarce and, to our knowledge, only available from unpublished theses and reports. However, available data point to reduction in categorical perception deficit when dyslexics are compared to reading-level controls (in French: Boissel-Dombreval & Bouteilly, 2003; in Dutch: Foqué, 2004). As reading-level controls are younger than dyslexics of the same reading age, the reduction of the CP deficit cannot be attributed to reading experience. Rather, the reduced difference between dyslexics and reading-level controls, compared to the one prevailing between dyslexics and chronological-age controls, seems to be the consequence of the effect of age on CP, as suggested by the mother–child comparison presented above (Figures 4.2, 4.4).

Now, as both age and reading level affect CP, does the CP deficit in dyslexia result from a developmental delay or is there a permanent underlying dysfunction in categorization processes? Though we cannot answer this question with a high degree of confidence for the moment, adult studies suggest a permanent deficit. Behavioral studies suggest that the CP deficit in either late adolescent or adult developmental dyslexics is weak and such studies have failed to find significant differences between dyslexics and controls up to now (adults: Leloup, 2002; 17-year-old adolescents: Bogliotti, 2005). However, a recent study shows that 9-year-old dyslexic children have significantly weaker CP compared to reading-age controls (Bogliotti, Serniclaes, Messaoud-Galusi, & Sprenger-Charolles, in prep).

Furthermore, neuroimagery data indicate that CP is processed in different cerebral areas in dyslexics vs. controls (Ruff, Cardebat, Marie, & Démonet, 2002). What is more, examination of individual data indicated that the degree of activation in Broca's area is positively correlated to CP performances in controls but negatively correlated to CP in dyslexics (Dufor, Serniclaes,

Balduyck, Sprenger-Charolles, & Démonet, 2005; Dufor, Serniclaes, Sprenger-Charolles, & Démonet, submitted). This indicates that when dyslexics exhibit categorical perception, it is obtained through different neural circuits than in normal-reading subjects, suggesting compensatory strategies.

CP deficit as allophonic perception

Auditory versus speech-specific processing

While visual deficits necessarily affect visual stimuli in general, including written symbols, auditory deficits might be unrelated to speech perception deficits. According to the motor theory (Liberman & Mattingly, 1985), speech perception is achieved by a specific module, distinct from general auditory processing, and connected with motor representations of the vocal tract. The contention that direct links exist between perception and motor commands is supported by the existence of mirror neurons (Fadiga, Fogassi, Paresi, & Rizolatti, 1995; Rizolatti, Fadiga, Gallese, & Fogassi, 1996; Studdert-Kennedy, 2005). In further support of this conception, fRMI results show that, with exactly the same acoustical stimuli, a change in perceptual mode from nonspeech to speech affects the locus of brain activity (Dehaene-Lambertz, Pallier, Serniclaes, Sprenger-Charolles, Jobert, & Dehaene, 2005).

The existence of a speech-specific perceptual subsystem opens the possibility that the perceptual deficit in dyslexia is unrelated to auditory processing (Studdert-Kennedy, 2002). Comparisons between matched speech and nonspeech stimuli only showed a deficit for speech in the discrimination of syllables or syllable-like sounds differing in the direction of formant transitions for poor readers vs. chronological-age controls (Mody et al., 1997).

Similarly, when using exactly the same stimuli (sinewave analogues of speech sounds), first presented as nonspeech whistles and later as syllables, the deficit in categorical perception was only clearly present in the speech mode (Serniclaes et al., 2001). Backward masking provides another example of dissociation between auditory dysfunction and speech perception. Backward masking corresponds to the decreased perceptibility of an auditory event induced by a later occurring event, e.g., a frequency transition signalling a stop consonant is masked by a following vocalic segment as in consonant–vowel syllables. Wright et al. (1997) showed that a backward masking deficiency is somehow correlated with dyslexia. However, when comparing the backward masking deficit for nonspeech versus speech stimuli, Rosen and Manganari (2001) showed that in a group of dyslexics for which the deficit was indeed present for nonspeech, it was nevertheless absent for speech, i.e.,

the degree of backward vowel to consonant masking in the perception of /ba/
-/da/ syllables was no less normal than the one of forward masking in the
perception of /ab/-/ad/ syllables. The backward masking deficit having no
impact on speech perception, it cannot possibly affect phonological representations involved in reading acquisition. This is in accordance with a longitudinal study indicating that auditory capacities at school entry do not predict later reading deficits (Share et al., 2002).

Electrophysiological investigations with event-related evoked potentials
(ERPs) also point to speech-specific deficits, though with some mixed findings according to a review by Lyytinen and coworkers (Lyytinen, Guttorm,
Huttunen, Hämäläinen, Leppänen, & Vestiren, 2005). "Mismatch negativity" (MMN), i.e., the first deflection of negative polarity associated to a
stimulus contrast, was less for adult dyslexics vs. normal readers in response
to a speech contrast (/da/ vs. /ga/) whereas no difference was found for a
pure tone frequency change (Schulte-Körne, Deimel, Bartling, & Remschmidt, 1998). However, Lyytinen et al. (2005) report several studies in
which MMN differences between dyslexics and controls were found for
nonspeech contrasts, with some results indicating that such differences are
more salient with complex sound patterns. Differences in both MMN amplitude and cerebral lateralization were found, with MMN to speech contrasts being less lateralized to left in children at familial risk for dyslexia
(e.g., Maurer, Bucher, Brem, & Brandeis, 2003). Similarly, a MMN investigation with the sinewave analogues of speech sounds revealed a difference
in hemispheric polarity when dyslexic children were compared to chronological-age controls (Dehaene-Lambertz, Sprenger-Charolles, & Serniclaes,
in preparation). A left-hemisphere orientation was obtained for controls,
similar to that of adult normal readers in the speech mode. However, for
dyslexics the orientation was shifted towards the right hemisphere, similar
to what is found for nonspeech processing in normal adults (Dehaene-
Lambertz et al., 2005). The involvement of the right hemisphere in categorical perception by dyslexics suggests that speech contrasts are processed by
neural circuits which are not specialized for processing linguistic stimuli.
This hypothesis is supported by the results of the Dufor et al. (2005) tomo-
graphic study which showed that while CP performances of adult normal
readers are positively correlated with an increase in activity in Broca's area
for the change in processing mode, from nonspeech to speech, the CP performances of adult dyslexics are negatively related to the change in activity
in Broca's area.

To summarize the outcome of the studies dealing with the speech versus
nonspeech issue in dyslexia, two general considerations emerge. First,
differences in the perception of speech contrast between dyslexics and controls are more "robust" in the sense that they are more consistently found
across studies than are perception differences with nonspeech contrasts.

Second, the difference between neural processing of speech and nonspeech contrasts seems to be fuzzier in dyslexics.

Phonetic versus phonological processing

According to a fairly standard model of speech perception, the extraction of phonological segments from speech sounds takes place in three major processing steps: psychoacoustic, phonetic, and phonological (see p. 141). If the perceptual deficit in dyslexia is specific to speech, as suggested by the studies examined at the beginning of this section (pp. 159–160), it might occur at either the phonetic or phonological processing level.

Newborns are endowed with predispositions for discriminating phonetic predispositions and they adapt to the lack of a given contrast in the language by deactivating the corresponding predisposition (p. 141). However, while some phonetic contrasts can be completely absent from the language, others occur in combination, creating phonemic contrasts as evidenced by allophonic variations (Figure 4.7).

Allophones are contextual variants of phonemes along some phonetic dimension. For instance, the /d/ phoneme in English (received pronunciation) has [d] and [t] as allophones on the voice onset time dimension (VOT: the temporal relationship between onset of "voice", i.e. laryngeal vibrations and release of the mouth closure; Lisker & Abramson, 1964). The /d/ phoneme is pronounced as a voiced stop in medial unstressed position (e.g., pronounced as [d] in "leader") where it contrasts with the /t/ phoneme which is pronounced as a voiceless unaspirated stop in that context (e.g., pronounced as [t] in "litter"). However, the same /d/ phoneme is generally pronounced as a voiceless unaspirated stop in initial position (e.g., pronounced as [t] in "dear") where it contrasts with the /t/ phoneme which is pronounced as a

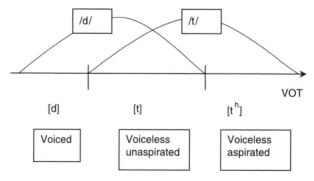

Figure 4.7. Phonemes and allophones.
Allophonic variations of English /d/ and /t/ phoneme categories along the voice onset time (VOT) dimension.

voiceless aspirated stop in that context (e.g., pronounced as [tʰ] in "tear"). It follows that the [t] phonetic segment is not only an allophone of /d/ but also an allophone of /t/ as the latter is pronounced as [tʰ] in initial stressed position but as [t] in medial unstressed position. When present in a given language, the same phonetic segment (or "phone") is generally the allophone of two different phonemes. Similar allophonic variations are found for voicing in French stops though they depend on other contextual factors than in English. In French, allophonic variations of voiced and voiceless phonemes occur within each position (initial or medial).

As the prelinguistic child naturally discriminates between phonetic distinctions, the phonetic overlap between phonemes means that the acquisition of phoneme percepts involves in-depth restructuring of the categorization process. After exposure to the sounds of their native language, children not only lose their sensitivity to the boundaries which are not relevant in their language (Werker & Tees, 1984a) but they acquire new boundaries. For example, up to about six months of age, infants discriminate three voicing categories, separated by two VOT boundaries: a negative VOT boundary and a positive VOT boundary (Aslin, Pisoni, Hennessy, & Perrey, 1981; Lasky et al., 1975). However, the French VOT boundary is located at 0 ms (Serniclaes, 1987), a value which is not included in the infant's predispositions (Lasky et al., 1975), although it appears fairly early in the course of language development (Eilers, Gavin, & Wilson, 1979; Hoonhorst, Colin, Deltenre, Radeau, & Serniclaes, 2006). This means that a new boundary, irreducible to one of the two natural phonetic boundaries, because it falls right between these two boundaries, has to be acquired. The fact that the boundary is located around 0 ms VOT in French means that negative and positive VOT are equally important for voicing identification, and therefore that the categorical predispositions for the perception of negative and positive VOT are both activated and coupled in the course of perceptual development (Figure 4.8). The perceptual apparatus adapts to allophonic variations in speech production by proceeding to *couplings* between the predispositions for perceiving the phonetic features engaged in these variations. Couplings create new functional entities inside which features are integrated. These are fairly sophisticated processes as they generate new perceptual boundaries and typically replace categories with boundaries.

Different studies show that the categorical perception deficit in dyslexic children is not only due to reduced between-category discrimination but also to better within-category discrimination (e.g., Godfrey et al., 1981; Manis & Keating, 2004; Serniclaes et al., 2001; Werker & Tees, 1987). If this was due to a better discrimination of *acoustic* variants of the same phonetic category, dyslexics would lack categorical perception of phonetic features. However, other data suggest that dyslexics' enhanced within-category discrimination is not due to a higher sensitivity to *acoustic* details. Rather, they are more sensi-

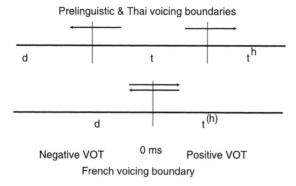

Figure 4.8. Couplings between predispositions along the VOT dimension (adapted from Serniclaes et al., 2004).

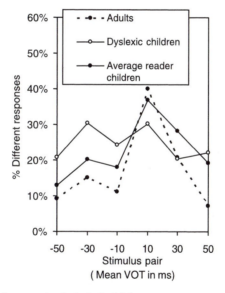

Figure 4.9. Allophonic perception in dyslexic children.
Discrimination ("different" responses; ordinate) between stimuli varying along a voice onset time (VOT) continuum (abscissa) for three groups of French-speaking subjects: adult average readers, 9-year-old dyslexics and same chronological age average readers (adapted from Serniclaes et al., 2004).

tive to *allophonic* variants of the same phoneme category. Discrimination data collected along the VOT continuum revealed two different discrimination peaks for French-speaking dyslexic children (Serniclaes et al., 2004; see Figure 4.9), one corresponding to the phoneme boundary and the other to an allophonic boundary, i.e., the voiced-voiceless which is phonemic in three-category languages such as Thai.

The discrimination peak at the phoneme boundary (at 10 ms VOT) is stronger for the average readers vs. dyslexics. The latter display a second peak around an allophonic boundary (this boundary, –30 ms VOT, is also found in pre-linguistic children as a well as for speakers of Thai, a language with three voicing categories). This peak also appears for the normal speakers but is much weaker. Enhanced sensitivity to allophonic contrasts was observed for another group of French dyslexic children, also by comparison with chronological-age controls (Bogliotti, 2003). In another study where a group of Australian English-speaking children in the first grade were compared to children of the same age but without reading experience, the latter exhibited enhanced sensitivity to the Thai voiced-voiceless boundary (Burnham, 2003). This study was possible because parents have the choice to send their child to school at two different ages in Australia and the results suggest that allophonic sensitivity depends on reading experience. However, this inter-pretation is contradicted by the absence of categorical perception differences between illiterate adults and controls (Serniclaes et al., 2005; see Figures 4.3, 4.4). The apparent effect of reading experience in the Australian study might be due to a selection bias as children who go to school later might be those with slower cognitive development.

The discrimination between allophonic distinctions by dyslexic children suggests that they perceive speech using allophonic rather than phonemic units. The origin of allophonic perception might arise from a *lack of coupling* between predispositions in the course of perceptual development. As explained above, voicing perception in French, and several other two-category languages, is based on a coupling between predispositions for per-ceiving phonetic contrasts. The coupling is not specific to voicing and might be fairly common in speech perception. Although we are only at the begin-ning of the investigations on this topic, a further instance of coupling has already been shown for the perception of place of articulation in languages with three place categories instead of the four potential ones (Bogliotti, 2005; Geng, Mády, Bogliotti, Messaoud-Galusi, Medina, & Serniclaes, 2005; Serniclaes, Bogliotti, & Carré, 2003). Though couplings probably are used widely in the acquisition of phonological perception in human languages, they constitute intrinsically complex processes. It would therefore not be sur-prising that the unfolding of the developmental processes conducive to the couplings might fail in part of the population, for genetic and/or environ-mental reasons.

The possibility that dyslexic children already differ in the way they per-ceive speech at an early age is supported by long-term longitudinal studies. Auditory event-related potentials (ERPs) to speech and nonspeech syllables recorded at birth reveal several differences between children who, eight years later, would be characterized as dyslexic, poor or normal readers (Molfese, 2000). A review of physiological studies of developmental dyslexia confirms that ERPs to speech sounds reliably predict later language development and reading acquisition (Lyytinen et al., 2005). Prospective studies reveal that newborns with familial risk for dyslexia differ from those without familial risk in ERPs for speech contrasts (Guttorm, Leppänen, Richardson, & Lyytinen, 2001) and that these differences predict later language development at 2.5 years of age (Guttorm, Leppänen, Poikkeus, Eklund, Lyytinen, & Lyytinen, 2005). According to Lyytinen and co-workers (2005), these findings, together with those of several other electrophysiological investigations, support the hypothesis of a very early speech perception problem that contributes to difficulties in phonological processing. Finally, a longitudinal study with French children (Kipffer-Piquard, 2003), indicates that minimal pair discrimination at the beginning of kindergarten (at age 5) can predict some 25% of the variance in reading level at the end of Grade 2 (at age 8). As minimal pair discrimination gives a rough estimation of categorical perception, this result presents the possibility that early assessment of CP performances might contribute to both the prediction of later reading performances and the early detection of dyslexic children.

While a lack of coupling between phonetic predispositions in early perceptual development affects the emergence of a pre-lexical stage of phonological processing, it should not have important implications for speech perception. Understanding speech with allophonic rather than phonemic categories should not raise major problems. With allophonic perception, words with the same phonemes but with different allophonic realizations will have separate lexical representations, i.e., they will behave like synonyms in normal phonemic processing. Speech perception should then be fairly efficient with allophonic representations although it will be more demanding in terms of information processing. The situation will be quite different for understanding written language which, at least in alphabetic systems, requires well-defined phonemic representations.

In normal development, allophonic differences are usually not perceived which makes associating different allophones with the same letter (e.g., associating medial [d] and initial [t] with "d") fairly natural. But suppose a child does not learn to group allophones into phonemic categories. She or he might then still recognize spoken words perfectly, though with different percepts: "leader" will be perceived as [lider], and "dear" will be perceived as [tir], but still differ from "tear" which is pronounced as [t^{h}ir]. However, with allophones instead of phonemes, a child will encounter serious problems for understanding letter–sound correspondences.

Indeed, as illustrated in Figure 4.10, with an allophonic mode of speech perception there will be the same letter for different sounds (e.g., the "d" letter for either [d] in medial position or [t] in initial position) and different

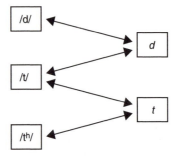

Figure 4.10. Implications of allophonic perception for reading.
Decoding speech in allophonic rather than phonemic units implies that perceptual segments are not in a one-to-one relationship with graphemes even with a perfect alphabetic transcription.

letters for the same sound (e.g., either the "d" letter in initial position or the "t" letter in medial position for the [t] sound). A child who perceives allophones instead of phonemes (e.g., /d/, /t/ and /tʰ/ in a language where only /d/ and /tʰ/ are phonemic) would have difficulty attributing the same written symbol (e.g., "t") to sounds belonging to different categories in his or her oral repertoire (e.g., /t/ or /tʰ/). The mismatch between spoken categories and phonemes might raise important problems for learning to read, even with fairly transparent orthographic systems.

If people affected by developmental dyslexia perceived speech in allophonic rather than phonemic units, this should open the way to explaining their specific reading deficit with a specific mode of perception. Indeed, decoding speech in allophonic units has evident implications for reading acquisition. One-to-one correspondence between spoken units and graphemes would not be possible even with a perfectly transparent orthography, which constitutes a major obstacle for learning the alphabetic code. While the problem raised by allophonic perception will be present even in a perfectly transparent orthography, i.e., with a one-to-one correspondence between phonemes and graphemes, it will increase exponentially with the adjunction of many-to-one correspondences between letters and sounds (see the cross-linguistic studies presented in chapters 2 and 3), not to mention the groupings of several letters into grapheme units. Interestingly, a cross-linguistic investigation found a common neural basis for dyslexia in spite of functional differences in its implications for reading, which also depends on the transparency of the grapheme–phoneme correspondence (Paulesu et al., 2001).

Computer simulations support the hypothesis of a causal relationship between the CP deficit and dyslexia by showing that the suppression of "phonological attractions" between phonetic features, conceptually similar to the "phonological couplings" defined above, has important negative effects on the reading performance of a connectionist network (Harm & Seidenberg,

1999). This supports the argument that allophonic perception severely affects reading performances in the human.

Perception versus attention and memory

One recurrent question in the study of dyslexia is whether the perceptual deficits observed in dyslexic children are genuinely perceptual in nature. An alternative explanation would be that these deficits are the side effect of attention disorders. Behavioral evidence for perceptual deficits is collected through the repetitive presentation of stimuli which require sustained attention from the participants. Furthermore, the stimuli are often quite artificial in the sense that they are presented out of their usual context: syllables or isolated words instead of sentences, single tones instead of melodies, elementary visual layouts instead of landscapes. Repeated exposure to such artificial stimuli is potentially boring and sustained attention might therefore be difficult to maintain. A portion of the dyslexic population suffers from ADHD, about 30 to 70% depending on how the disorder is defined (Shaywitz et al., 1994). Thus, it is possible that the perceptual deficits observed in dyslexics as a group are in fact due to the lack of coherent responses from the subgroup of dyslexics who also suffer from ADHD.

While computer simulations were first advanced in support of the possible confounding effect of attention in the demonstration of visual deficits with the Ternus task (Roach, Edwards, & Hogben, 2004), counter-evidence against a possible confounding effect of attention deficits was later collected with real subjects. Lower Ternus performances were indeed confirmed in a modified task with the effects of inattention controlled (Davis, Castles, McAnally, & Gray, 2001). Evidence against a possible side effect of an attention disorder was also provided in an experiment on categorical perception (CP). Comparisons between ADHD children and two subgroups of dyslexic children, either with or without ADHD, and controls showed that the CP deficit was only present for dyslexics, either with or without ADHD (Breier et al., 2001; see Figure 4.6).

While attentional problems associated with dyslexia do not explain perceptual deficits, memory problems might be the consequence of allophonic perception. The number of syllables correctly retrieved shortly after their presentation is smaller for children with dyslexia as compared to average readers (see pp. 135–137; see also Brady, Shankweiler, & Mann, 1983; Liberman et al., 1982; Mann & Liberman, 1984; Wagner et al., 1994) although results for visual memory tasks with nonverbal material are equivalent to those of average readers (see p. 138; see also McDougall, Hulme, Ellis, and Monk, 1994; Sprenger-Charolles et al., 2000). Limitations in phonological short-term memory might be a side effect of allophonic rather than phonemic representations of speech sounds. The number of parameters required for storing words is larger with allophones as they are more numerous than phonemes. While this possibility remains to be investigated, it would imply that problems in verbal memory associated with dyslexia arise from a larger size of memory repertoire rather than from intrinsic differences in processing.

Finally, problems in rapid automatic naming (RAN) have also been taken as an argument in support of the classic phonological explanation (see pp. 134–135). RAN depends on both quick retrieval in the mental lexicon and rapid articulatory processing, whereby each of these two factors include phonological components involved in reading. However, according to some researchers (Wolf et al., 2002) RAN is a better predictor of written-word identification, thus suggesting that it taps into lexical rather than pre-lexical phonology. Nonetheless, as lexical processes derive from pre-lexical processes in the course of reading acquisition (see chapter 2), these processes are related rather than being independent components of written-word processing. The same developmental sequence is true for spoken language acquisition (Werker, 2003), so early problems in phonological perception – such as those arising from a lack of coupling between phonetic predispositions – will later affect word perception.

ROBUSTNESS AND RELIABILITY OF PHONOLOGICAL AND NON-PHONOLOGICAL DEFICITS

Table 4.1 compares the different factors associated with dyslexia in terms of different criteria: causal status, robustness of group differences across studies and reliability (or prevalence) of individual differences. Causal relationship is inferred from studies with illiterate people. Robustness and reliability are taken from comparisons of dyslexic children with chronological-age controls, unless otherwise specified. Robustness is assessed according to the proportion of studies showing significant differences between groups. Assessments of the phonological deficit are based on phonemic awareness, plus other criteria such as RAN and phonological short-term memory, depending on the study.

As reported in Chapter 3, meta-analytic studies show that even when dyslexics are compared to reading-level controls, i.e., younger children with the same reading age, the deficit in pseudoword reading was significant in 10 studies out of a total of 16 (Rack et al., 1992). What is more, the meta-analytic combination of the studies that, individually, do not find a significant phonological deficit in pseudoword reading, shows this deficit to be present (Van Ijzendoorn & Bus, 1994). As perceptual studies with reading-level controls are not common, the summary presented in Table 4.1 is based on comparisons with chronological-age controls.

Pseudoword reading is the "golden standard" for assessing the deficit of the dyslexics' phonological reading route. It has 100% robustness, on

Table 4.1

Factors associated with dyslexia: causal status, robustness of group differences across studies and reliability of individual differences

	Pseudoword reading	Phonological deficit	Temporal deficit	Categorical precision	Categorical perception
Causal relationship	Criterion	Partially depends on reading		Depends on reading	Does not depend on reading
Robustness across studies	ref. 1 100 % (Meta-analysis)	ref. 2 Almost 100 %	ref. 3 20 % (Visual)	ref. 4 40 %	ref. 4 75 %
Reliability across individuals	ref. 5 100 % (Accuracy + RT)	ref. 6 100 % (Adults) 75 % (Children) (Ph.A. + STM + RAN)	ref. 7 64 % (Visual & auditory)		ref. 4 77 %

Ref. 1. Rack et al. (1992); Van Ijzendoorn & Bus (1994) / Reading-level controls. Ref. 2. Snowling (2000). Ref. 3. Skottun (2000). Ref. 4. Serniclaes et al. (2004). Serniclaes et al. (in prep.). Ref. 5. Sprenger-Charolles et al. (2000). Ref. 6. Ramus et al. (2003a, 2003b). White et al. (in press). Ref. 7. Cornelissen et al. (1995). Witton et al. 1998. Amitay et al. (2002). Ramus, et al. (2003a). Ramus et al. (2003b). White et al. (2006).

meta-analytic grounds (see chapter 3). Robustness across studies is probably also maximal for phonemic awareness, which as far as is known is 100% robust, followed by the categorical perception deficit (85%) and well above sensori-motor deficits (40% or less). Much the same pattern of results emerges if we consider the reliability between individuals. Pseudoword reading has 100% reliability when measured by either response accuracy or latency (see chapter 3). Reliability of deficits in phonemic awareness across individuals seems also maximal.[3]

When phonological performances of adult dyslexics were assessed with several different tasks, including phonemic awareness, phonological short-term memory and rapid auditory naming, all of the dyslexics were deficient relative to average readers (Ramus et al., 2003b). However, the prevalence of phonological deficits is less in two studies with dyslexic children. With much the same tasks, 77% (17 out of 22) of the children were deficient relative to age controls in one study (Ramus et al., 2003a) and only 52% (12 out of 23) were deficient in another study (White et al., 2006). The discrepancy between the outcomes of the studies using children seems to be due to a methodological bias; as the deficiency cut-off point was more severe in the White et al., study, where it was placed at 1.65 SD below the mean of controls, than in the Ramus et al., study, where it was placed at 1 SD below the mean. When assessed with percent correct classification, which takes account of cut-off point differences, the discrepancy between the two studies is much smaller with 80% and 74% correct classification yielding a mean of about 77%.

The reliability of the categorical perception deficit is similar to that of phonemic awareness and well above sensory deficits in terms of robustness and reliability, at least with children. It should also be noted that categorical *precision* is much less robust and less reliable than categorical *perception*, a perceptual factor which is sometimes confused with it. Furthermore, contrary to categorical perception, which is not deficient in illiterates, categorical precision depends on literacy.

CONCLUSION

Among the various correlates of developmental dyslexia, the categorical perception deficit is of special interest for the following reasons. First, the categorical perception deficit is phonological in nature and is therefore compatible with the prevalent theory of reading which attributes a decisive role to grapheme–phoneme conversions in reading acquisition (see chapter 2) and dyslexia (see chapter 3). Second, this deficit compares fairly well to other phonological deficits in terms of reliability between individuals and robustness across studies. Third, it seems not to depend on reading. Fourth, it might explain dyslexia as a specific mode of speech perception based on allophones rather than on phonemes.

Compared to other theories on dyslexia, allophonic perception explains specific reading impairment with a specific *mode* of perception rather than with a perceptual *deficit*, thereby resolving the selectivity issue in theories on dyslexia. While we might possibly explain dyslexia by a different mode of processing sensory input, this possibility remains largely unexplored though there have been some attempts in this direction in the framework of the magnocellular theory. Furthermore, allophonic perception makes specific predictions as to the origin of dyslexia and on its main phonological correlates. Allophonic perception postulates that: (1) dyslexia arises from a lack of coupling between phonetic predispositions in the course of perceptual development; (2) the lack of coupling between predispositions might also be at the origin of phonological awareness, short-term memory and rapid auditory naming deficits; (3) the lack of coupling may also explain the huge difficulties encountered by dyslexics when they have to map grapheme to phoneme without the help of their lexical knowledge (pseudoword reading).

The allophonic mode of perception provides a straightforward explanation of dyslexia and is fairly robust across studies and reliable across individuals. This suggests that with the allophonic theory we are not very far from the core deficit in dyslexia. However, three important questions remain to be solved before using this theory for remediation. First, we have to understand why allophonic discrimination does not show up in some studies. A possible answer to this question arises from the fact that categorical perception is achieved through different neural pathways in some developmental dyslexics, notably adult ones (Dufor et al., 2005, and submitted). While this suggests a change in procedure for attaining a categorical behaviour, we still do not know how this is made possible. However, given that lexical biases in phonological perception are greater for dyslexics (Reed, 1989; see also p. 136) some dyslexics might attain categorical perception by using lexical channels. This would at least be a logically possible solution to allophonic perception: word stimuli with different allophones are synonyms and therefore equivalent after lexical processing. Some dyslexics might then opt for a lexical procedure to solve their categorical perception problem. Compensatory procedures do not seem to call on phonological processes since they do not depend on the complexity of grapheme–phoneme correspondences in orthography. As noticed by Lyytinen et al. (2005) approximately one-fifth of adult dyslexics attain relatively normal reading, that proportion being independent of the orthographic regularity of the language, as comparable results of compensation have been reported in English and Finnish readers (Lefly & Pennington, 1991; Lyytinen, Leinonen, Nikula, Aro, & Leiwo, 1995; see also chapter 3).

Here we come to the second problem to be solved before we can develop efficient remediation: how can subjects learn to be categorical at a pre-lexical phonological processing stage? This is a very difficult point. Attempts to teach CP to second-language learners, i.e., to teach Japanese speakers to categorically perceive the English /r/ vs. /l/ contrast have regularly failed (Strange & Dittmann, 1984). A new methodology developed by Guenther and co-workers (Guenther, Husain, Cohen, & Shinn-Cunningham, 1999; Guenther, Nieto-Castanon, Ghosh, & Tourville, 2004) teaches CP along an arbitrary acoustic dimension. However, a recent attempt to use Guenther's method to remove allophonic perception in dyslexic children was not successful (Bogliotti, 2005). Only when we have a method to remediate to allophonic perception will we be able fully to assess its implications for dyslexia.

A third question that remains to be solved is to understand exactly how allophonic perception interferes with the acquisition of the "reading reflex". While it seems evident that allophonic units should disturb learning of grapheme–phoneme associations, to remediate this problem will probably not be sufficient even if children are taken at an early age. Complete automatization of grapheme–phoneme, such that they become instrumental in reading, takes much longer than simply having a passive knowledge of them (Blomert, 2005). However, automatization unfolds from knowledge with age (see chapter 1) and learning in normal readers but not in dyslexics (Snowling, 2000). The question then is to identify the incentives towards instrumentation of the knowledge about grapheme–phoneme correspondences. Here, the parallelism between reading and speech perception might again provide some hints. Speech perception calls on highly automatic processes, anterior to reading in both phylogenetic and ontogenetic terms. Yet reading affects speech perception. Several studies show that printed letters affects perception speech sounds when presented simultaneously (Dijkstra, Schreuder, & Frauenfelder, 1989). Further, fRMI investigations show that these interactions take place in brain areas also involved in the audiovisual integration of speech sounds with lip movements (in the planum temporale and superior temporal gyrus: van Atteveldt, Formisano, Goebel, & Blomert, 2004), and within a time window comparable to the one used for natural cross-modal associations between single neurones in animals (van Atteveldt, Formisano, Blomert, & Goebel, submitted). This suggests that fairly ancient phylogenetic circuits are recycled for the sake of audiovisual integration of lip movements and speech sounds, and then also for integration of letters and speech sounds. From there it is evident that further investigations on the connexions between perception of speech and print should provide deeper insights into the acquisition of reading skills.

As a conclusion, while allophonic perception offers a new perspective for the study of dyslexia, future research is faced with several challenges. Most importantly, we need to know the age limits of effective remediation. We also need to gain a better understanding of the way dyslexics perceive speech, and especially how they segment the speech stream. While allophonic theory constitutes a first step in this direction, it still has to be articulated with other dimensions of language processing.

CHAPTER FIVE

Explaining normal and impaired reading acquisition

In this chapter we first review the most notable results presented in the book, and then propose a plausible framework for explaining reading acquisition (chapter 2) and developmental dyslexia (chapters 3 and 4) based on the results of studies on skilled reading (chapter 1) and behavioral and neuroimaging data (chapter 1, pp. 14–17, and chapter 4, pp. 185–189).

SUMMARY OF THE MAIN RESULTS PRESENTED IN THE PRECEDING CHAPTERS

In skilled readers, the seemingly effortless understanding of a text is based on the very rapid identification of written words. Written-word processing is largely independent of context effects and becomes increasingly autonomous as reading expertise develops (chapter 1, pp. 3–7). Another essential property is its automaticity: written words are processed without the mobilization of attentional resources (chapter 1, pp. 7–10). In addition, the written-word identification "reflex" (Perfetti & Zhang, 1995) includes very rapid access to both the orthographic and phonological codes of words, before their semantic codes are retrieved (chapter 1, pp. 10–14). Moreover, skilled readers activate phonological codes earlier and more automatically than do less-skilled readers. Finally, dyslexics have trouble activating the phonological codes of written words (chapter 1, p. 14).

The primary challenge facing the beginning reader, then, is to acquire automatic written-word processing that requires no attentional resources and is rapid and irrepressible. The development of this kind of automatic processing will enable beginners to attain a reading comprehension level comparable to their aural level, by freeing the reading comprehension process of the explicit decoding effort needed in the initial stages of learning to read (chapters 1 and 2). It is in fact this written-word identification reflex that dyslexics do not manage to acquire (chapter 3).

We have seen in chapter 4 that a number of sensory-motor explanations of dyslexia have been proposed, but only the phonological explanation has proven to hold so far. The main argument in support of this explanation, developed in chapters 2 to 4, is that grapheme–phoneme consistency is the major factor that determines how easy or difficult it is to learn to read: learning to read is easier in shallow orthographies than in deeper ones (chapter 2). However, to be able to correctly map graphemes to phonemes, children need well-specified phonemic representations. When phonemic representations are not well specified, the connections between graphemes and phonemes are difficult to establish. Dyslexics have considerable trouble mapping graphemes to phonemes (chapter 3). These difficulties might be the consequence of a failure of their phonemic representations, based on allophonic rather than on phonemic units (chapter 4). It is this body of findings that will supply the basic elements of our comprehensive model of reading acquisition and developmental dyslexia.

EXPLAINING READING ACQUISITION AND DEVELOPMENTAL DYSLEXIA

Role of the sublexical reading procedure in learning to read

The many research findings presented in this book clearly indicate that the sublexical reading procedure plays a crucial role in reading acquisition. The data in support of these statements was obtained by comparing the development of regular- and irregular-word reading for words with a high or low lexical frequency. If it is the lexical reading procedure that governs reading acquisition, high-frequency words should be memorized more easily than low-frequency words, whether or not their grapheme–phoneme correspondences are regular. Conversely, if it is the sublexical reading procedure that governs reading acquisition, the opposite result is expected, namely, regular words should be learned more rapidly than irregular ones, regardless of their lexical frequency.

In fact, both word frequency and word regularity enhance reading acquisition, and the combination of the two has a strong facilitatory effect. However, regularity has a noticeably greater impact than frequency at the beginning of reading acquisition, probably because word-frequency effects are item specific, unlike regularity effects which depend on generalizations based on associations between frequent grapheme–phoneme correspondences. Thus, during the early stages, word frequency does not contribute much to the reading of regular words, but regularity is critical. This explains why, at first, reading acquisition is easier in shallow orthographies than in deep ones (chapter 2, pp. 29–35).

The results presented in chapter 2 also indicate that acquisition of the orthographic lexicon depends on the efficiency of the sublexical reading procedure. The most impressive argument in support of this assumption is that, even in languages with a deep orthography such as English, effective early use of sublexical reading procedure predicts later reading achievement (chapter 2, pp. 35–41). If acquiring sublexical reading skills is a necessary step in building the orthographic lexicon, then whenever these skills are not yet in place, lexical skills should also be insufficient. Studies on developmental dyslexia clearly support this assumption. A deficient sublexical reading procedure is consistently observed in group studies involving non-selected samples of dyslexics (chapter 3, pp. 75–85, 92) and is highly prevalent according to single and multiple case studies (chapter 3, pp. 100, 109–127). But dyslexics' lexical skills are nevertheless far from being preserved. Accordingly, most dyslexics are found to suffer from a double deficit, with the sublexical reading procedure being more severely impaired, a deficiency of this procedure emerging even in comparisons with younger children of the same reading level. This is indicative of the deviant developmental path of dyslexics' sublexical reading skills.

The importance of sublexical reading skills in learning to read and in reading disabilities stems from the fact that, in alphabetic writing systems, reliance on a small set of grapheme–phoneme correspondences gives children access to thousands of words they have heard but never seen before. When most words are regular, as in shallow orthographies, the learning process is very easy. However, even the highly irregular words found in deep orthographies contain some regular grapheme–phoneme correspondences. For example, the use of grapheme–phoneme correspondences in French causes the high-frequency irregular word *sept* (seven) to be pronounced /sept/, i.e., with three correct grapheme–phoneme mappings and one incorrect one (the *p* is not pronounced). Knowing that the word /sept/ does not exist but the word /set/ does, children can infer that the "p" is silent in this word, contrary to the word *septembre* (September) where it is not.

Children may learn most of the relationships between orthography and phonology through this implicit procedure. In this way, strong associations between orthographic and phonological units based on grapheme–phoneme correspondences and word frequencies enable children gradually to construct their orthographic lexicon. However, even when the lexical reading route is functional, children may still use the sublexical reading route, which becomes more and more efficient as the various associations between sublexical orthographic and phonological units are consolidated.

The fact that grapheme–phoneme consistency is the major factor in learning to read helps us understand the strong negative impact of orthographic opacity on the learning process (chapter 2). As to the origin of dyslexic children's failure to establish proper connections between graphemes and phonemes (chapter 3), studies on speech perception suggest that they decode speech with allophonic rather than phonemic units (chapter 4). Without phonemic representations, making the connection between speech units and graphemes poses tremendous problems, even with a perfect alphabetic transcription. When the respective effects of orthographic opacity and allophonic perception are simultaneously at play, the negative impact on reading acquisition is very strong. This seems to be the case for English-speaking dyslexics. The deficit of their sublexical reading skills is usually manifest in their accuracy scores, whereas in a language where the orthography is not so deep, dyslexics appear to be able to correctly map each grapheme to the appropriate phoneme, so their phonological deficit only shows up as slow pseudoword reading (chapter 3, pp. 76, 87, 101, 108, 126, 128). However, as repeatedly stressed by Shaywitz and Shaywitz (2005), some English-speaking dyslexics are able to read pseudowords accurately when the measures are untimed, but they continue to suffer from a phonological deficit that makes their pseudoword reading effortful and slow, thus reflecting the lingering effects of phonological impairment. Thus, when processing time is not taken into account, dyslexics may be mistakenly assumed to have outgrown their dyslexia.[1]

The grain size of processing units

In the preceding section, we did not look at the exact size of the processing units used to read, or at whether the same units are used by all beginning readers irrespective of language and reading ability. Concerning these issues, Ziegler and Goswami (2005) pointed out three main problems confronting beginning readers: the availability, consistency, and granularity of spelling-to-sound units.

The availability problem is primarily due to the fact that, before learning to read, orthographic representations are not available, apart from a few words that children may have learned by heart. Also, not all phonological units are consciously accessible prior to reading (chapter 2, pp. 56–62). The consistency problem comes from the multiple pronunciations of some orthographic units and the multiple spellings of some phonological units, both of which slow down reading acquisition. In addition, the amount of inconsistency varies across languages and across different types of orthographic units (chapter 2, pp. 22–29), which accounts for cross-language differences in reading development (chapter 2, pp. 29–46). Granularity refers to the size of the processing unit. The problem here is that there are many more ortho-graphic units to learn when access to the phonological system is based on larger grain sizes as opposed to smaller ones. In addition, the smaller grain-size units are meaningless (phoneme, onset rhyme, syllable) while the larger ones are meaningful (words) or are at the interface between the semantic and formal aspects of the language (morphemes). These units also differ in availability. For instance, the smallest meaningless phonological units (phon-emes) are less available than the larger sized meaningful phonological ones (words).

These considerations help us understand differences in the cost of learning to read using small *versus* large units. The use of a small number of graph-emes and their corresponding phonemes gives children the opportunity to gain access to thousands of words they have heard but never seen before. The memory load is not great in this case, but children have to use small-size phonological units that are not readily accessible. In contrast, when word breakdown at the grapheme–phoneme correspondence level is hindered by inconsistencies in the language (chapter 2), or by allophonic rather than phonemic representations (chapter 4), children have to learn a very large number of words by rote memory. The memory load is tremendous in this case, although the large-grain phonological units that children have to use are available, at least when the words are in their phonological lexicon. Reliance on these different types of units can have an impact on the sublexical reading procedure at different levels: first, in decoding from spelling to sound; second, in blending the resulting sound units; and for reading aloud tasks, in pro-gramming and producing the vocal response. They also probably have an impact on the access to the phonological lexicon. Achieving reading proficiency requires solving these three problems.

Concerning the availability of meaningless phonological units before read-ing acquisition, there seems to be a developmental trend from syllabic to infra-syllabic units, with conscious access to phonemes as the last stage in the process (chapter 2, pp. 56–62). However, the availability of processing units is not the only thing that counts; it is also their importance in the learning process. Phonemic awareness is the best predictor of future reading level, and evidence for the unique contribution of syllabic awareness and rhyme aware-ness is very limited, even in English (chapter 2, pp. 58–62, 63–65). Moreover, longitudinal studies indicate that the availability of phonemic units is low in future dyslexics before they learn to read (pp. 62, 93, 138). Finally, phonemic training programs can reduce the reading deficit of children at risk for read-ing disabilities (chapter 2, p. 63). These results may be due to the fact that even English-speaking children are confronted with an alphabetic writing system when learning to read, the main principle of such systems being that graphemes represent phonemes. Thus, it is not surprising to find that the early availability of phonemic units, and the early enhancement of this availability provided by specific phonemic training, facilitates reading acquisition. Nor is it surprising to find that poor phonemic skills impede reading acquisition.

Furthermore, while the predictive power of phonemic awareness decreases as reading acquisition progresses, that of morphological awareness increases (chapter 2, pp. 65–67). These findings can be explained by the fact that phonemic awareness is crucial for understanding the principle of the alphabet, and is thus more significant than morphological awareness at the onset of reading acquisition than in the subsequent steps. On the other hand, because of its linguistic properties, morphological knowledge may be more involved in the reading comprehension process, and probably also in the development of the lexical reading route.

Concerning the consistency problem, we have already noted that grapheme–phoneme inconsistencies have both a quantitative and a qualitative impact on normal reading acquisition (chapter 2, pp. 30–35, 35–46), and that the reading skills of dyslexics who are learning in a deep orthography appear to be more impaired than those of dyslexics learning in a shallow orthography (chapter 3, pp. 85–90, 108–109, 119–125), probably because of the combined negative effects of orthographic deepness and phonological skill inadequacy. In addition, phoneme–grapheme correspondences are less consistent than grapheme–phoneme correspondences in most alphabetic writing systems (chapter 2, p. 29). Thus, it is normal to find that learning to spell is more difficult than learning to read (chapter 2, Note 16, pp. 193–194).

Developmental changes offer a possible explanation for the granularity problem. Depending on what language they speak and how well they read, children seem to move rapidly from reliance on surface units (letters) to reliance on more abstract units (graphemes) and larger sublexical units such as onset-rhymes and/or syllables. Also, morphological chunks seem to gradually become the processing units of reading.

The use of graphemic units may facilitate grapheme-to-phoneme mapping, especially in languages where there are many multiple-letter units that always correspond to a single phoneme, as in French and Dutch, for example. Indeed, if the basic unit of the sublexical reading procedure is the grapheme rather than the letter, readers have fewer units to decode when the words contain multiple-letter graphemes than when they are composed of one-letter graphemes only. In English, the decoding process can also be facilitated by rhyme units, because taking word rhymes into account reduces the inconsistencies of vowel grapheme–phoneme correspondences in this language. Reliance on larger meaningless units may also facilitate the blending procedure because this lessens the memory load, no matter what type of unit is involved. For instance, children have fewer phonemic units to assemble in words containing multiple-letter graphemes than in words with one-letter graphemes. Thus, the presence of multiple-letter graphemes can have a facilitatory impact in silent reading tasks. This effect will be more noticeable on reading aloud tasks, since there are also fewer phonemic units to program in producing the vocal response. Moreover, children have fewer units to blend for accessing the phonological lexicon when they rely on larger meaningless units such as syllables. The use of larger grain sublexical units could therefore be helpful during an intermediate stage of reading acquisition, when access to the phonological codes of words is not yet fully automatized.

As already noted for morphological awareness, because of their linguistic properties, morphological units may be involved in the acquisition of the lexical reading procedure. However, given that until a relatively advanced school grade, the processing of these units continues to be affected by phonological factors, irrespective of the language's orthographic transparency (chapter 2, pp. 46–52), recourse to morphological units may be conceived of as a sort of compensatory strategy that supplements poor sublexical reading skills in the early stages of reading. This interpretation is supported by the fact that morphemic units appear to be utilized in this way by dyslexics (see chapter 3, pp. 97–101).

The nature of the units used by children also depends on their importance and their consistency in the language. For instance, syllable-based processing seems to play a more important role in languages where syllable boundaries are clear as they are in French and Spanish, for example, unlike English which is often ambisyllabic (chapter 2, pp. 42–46). In English, it is also because taking word rhymes into account reduces the inconsistencies of grapheme–phoneme vowel correspondences that beginning English readers make greater use of rhyme units, unlike beginners in languages with a shallower orthography who rely on grapheme–phoneme correspondences (chapter 2, pp. 38–41). This is true of Spanish, Greek, and French, for example, probably also because of the high frequency of open syllables in these languages where a word rhyme usually corresponds to a single phoneme. It is also true of German, despite the fact that in German, as in English, there are a greater number of closed than open syllables and thus more opportunity to process rhyme units. Reliance on rhyme units can therefore be regarded as a compensatory strategy.

Further cross-linguistic studies are needed in these areas, since studies on processing units in reading have focused mostly on grapheme–phoneme correspondences *versus* rhyme units, probably because of the characteristics of English orthography. It would also be worthwhile to further examine the facilitatory impact that taking units such as graphemes, onset-rhymes, syllables, and morphemes into account might have on the word-reading performance of children with impaired reading skills. The use of these units could help dyslexics develop a reading strategy that includes mechanisms that are more like the intrinsic mechanisms of the written-word identification reflex than the mechanisms underlying top-down compensatory strategies based on large meaningful unit. Relying on the syntactic context, for example, leads to a guessing strategy that strongly differs from the word-reading procedures utilized by skilled readers (chapter 1, pp. 5–7).

Categorical perception of speech sounds, reading acquisition, and developmental dyslexia

Most research on the phonemic abilities that account for the success or failure of reading acquisition has focused on explicit phonemic awareness (see chapter 2, pp. 56–65; chapter 4, pp. 134–139). Some studies presented in chapter 4 are in sharp contrast with this dominant field of research, since they have tapped more implicit phonemic abilities. Moreover, as already underlined, to map a grapheme to a phoneme, one has to be able to isolate the phoneme in the speech stream and also to have well-defined phonemic categories. The former skill has been widely investigated in studies using different types of tasks (deletion, counting, etc.; see chapter 2, pp. 56–65; chapter 4, pp. 134–139), but the latter, which can be assessed by phonemic-discrimination or phonemic-categorization tasks (chapter 4, pp. 152–167), has been largely neglected.

The categorical perception of speech sounds is based on the degree to which acoustic differences between variants of the same phoneme are less perceptible than differences of the same acoustic magnitude between two different phonemes. Various sources of evidence suggest that children with dyslexia are less categorical than average readers in the way they perceive phonetic contrasts, and that this deficit has a speech-specific component (chapter 4, pp. 155–167). A striking common point of the studies reviewed is that they all show that dyslexics do *poorly* when discriminating between phonemes and do *better* when discriminating acoustic variants of the same phoneme (i.e., allophones), which are in fact irrelevant to lexical processing in their language.

This suggests that dyslexics have a specific mode of speech perception, characterized by the use of allophonic rather than phonemic categories. Allophonic perception might arise from the weakness of phonological couplings among phonetic features during early perceptual development, and has specific implications for the establishment of grapheme–phoneme correspondences. In particular, it could explain why dyslexics have trouble using phonology-based reading procedure (chapter 3) without experiencing similar difficulties in speech perception. Understanding speech with allophonic rather than phonemic categories probably does not cause any major problems. Access to the mental lexicon by means of allophonic representations is conceivable, although it is more demanding in terms of information processing. The situation is quite different for understanding written language which, at least in alphabetic systems, requires well-specified phoneme representations.

Arguments in support of a coupling failure in predispositions conducive to an allophonic mode of speech perception in dyslexia for learning to read are provided by computer simulations. It has been shown that deleting "phonological attractions" between phonetic features, which are conceptually similar to "phonological couplings", has strong negative effects on the reading performance of a connectionist network (Harm & Seidenberg, 1999). This suggests that reduced phonological couplings or attractions are at the root of allophonic perception in dyslexics and might be the key problem in dyslexia.

While the problem raised by allophonic perception will be present even in a perfectly transparent orthography, i.e., with a one-to-one correspondence between phonemes and graphemes, it will increase exponentially with the adjunction of many-to-one correspondences between graphemes and phonemes (see the cross-linguistic studies presented in chapters 2 and 3), as suggested by the examples presented in Figures 5.1a, 5.1b, and 5.1c. When, for example, a child perceives two different phonemes for /g/ and for /k/, instead of one (allophonic perception) and when, in addition, he or she mixes up /g/ and /k/ (less well-specified phonemic categories), that will indeed raise a serious problem for reading acquisition.

More precisely, based on the "g" and "k" examples, only two connections are necessary when the phonemic categories of the reader are not impaired and when the orthography offers consistent grapheme–phoneme mappings (Figure 5.1a). The number of connections increases when, in a consistent orthography, the phonemic categories of the reader are impaired (when he or she mixes up /k/ and /g/ and perceives two different allophones for the phonemes /k/ and /g/, Figure 5.1b). Finally, 20 connections are necessary when grapheme to phoneme relationships are impeded both by an impairment of the reader's phonemic categories and inconsistencies in the graphemic representations of the same phoneme in the orthography (Figure 5.1c).

A very small deficit in speech perception may therefore have a very strong negative influence on the acquisition of reading which is heightened by the inconsistencies of the relations between graphemes and phonemes in the orthography. When this is so, compensatory strategies can be used. These strategies can be based either on larger grain size (rhyme, syllable), or on top-down lexical and semantic information.

To conclude, as the allophonic mode of perception provides a straightforward explanation of dyslexia and is fairly robust across studies and prevalent across individuals (see chapter 4, pp. 168–170), the "allophonic theory" is not very far from the core deficit in dyslexia. However, some important questions remain to be solved. The most important one is to understand exactly how allophonic perception interferes with the acquisition of the written-word identification "reflex". Here, the parallel between reading and speech perception might provide some clues. Speech perception calls on highly automatic

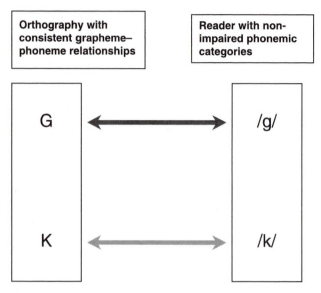

Figure 5.1(a). Orthography with consistent grapheme–phoneme relationships and reader with non-impaired phonemic categories: one-to-one mapping (two connections).

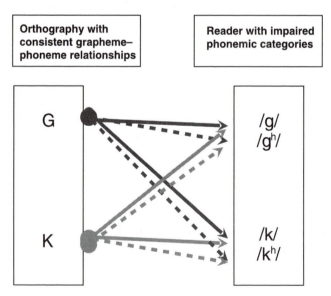

Figure 5.1(b). Orthography with consistent grapheme–phoneme relationships and reader with impaired phonemic categories (confusion between /k/ and /g/ plus allophonic perception of two different allophones for the phonemes /k/ and /g/): eight connections.

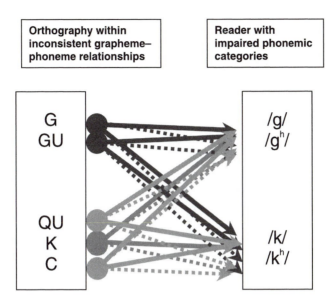

Figure 5.1(c). Orthography with inconsistent grapheme–phoneme relationships and reader with impaired phonemic categories: 20 connections.

processes, anterior to reading in both phylogenetic and ontogenetic terms. Yet, reading affects speech perception. As indicated in chapter 4 (pp. 144–146), several studies show that printed letters affect the perception of speech sounds when presented simultaneously. Further, fRMI investigations suggest that these interactions take place in brain areas that are also involved in the audiovisual integration of speech sounds with lip movements, and within a time window comparable to the one used for natural cross-modal associations between single neurones in animals. This suggests that fairly ancient phylogenetic circuits are recycled for the sake of audiovisual integration of lip movements and speech sounds, and probably also to integrate letters and speech sounds. Further investigations on the connexions between perception of speech and print should provide deeper insights into the acquisition of the written-word identification reflex.

Second, it is important to understand why allophonic discrimination does not show up in some studies. A possible answer to this question arises from the fact that at least some dyslexics achieve categorical perception through different neural pathways (chapter 4, p. 160), thus suggesting reliance on compensatory strategies. These compensatory strategies could be based on lexical processes. As a matter of fact, lexical biases in phonological perception are greater for dyslexics (see p. 136). By way of such lexical compensatory strategies, some dyslexics might attain categorical perception through lexical channels.

Compensatory strategies

As was just emphasized, top-down lexical processes might help dyslexics to achieve categorical perception. Reliance on compensatory strategies might also help us understand why children learning to read in a shallow orthography rely on the sublexical reading procedure, and children learning in a deep orthography rely to a lesser extent on this procedure and to a greater extent on compensatory strategies based on top-down lexical processes that supplement error-prone bottom-up processes based on grapheme–phoneme correspondences (chapter 2, pp. 35–38).

Heavy reliance on top-down lexical processing is a defining trait of beginning readers and of individuals with more or less severe reading disabilities (chapter 1, pp. 3–7; chapter 3, pp. 130–131). More specifically, the performance of fluent readers is predominantly achieved via very rapid, automatic written-word identification, which is largely independent of contextual and semantic effects. In contrast, less fluent readers, especially young children and dyslexics, rely more extensively on top-down compensatory strategies. For instance, as compared to same-reading-level average readers, dyslexics make greater use of the sentence context (chapter 1, pp. 5–7) or the semantic properties of words (e.g., meaningful morphological information; chapter 3, pp. 41–52).

Superior cognitive capacities, like a larger vocabulary, for example, may help in establishing these compensatory strategies (chapter 3, pp. 73, 104). When a word is in the spoken-language vocabulary, beginning readers may recognize it even if they can only partially sound it out. It is probably by way of such compensatory strategies that the smartest dyslexics manage to partially overcome the deficit of their sublexical reading route. These strategies allow them to minimize the consequences of their phonological deficit, in such a way that some adult dyslexics may be indistinguishable from unimpaired readers on measures of reading comprehension (chapter 1, pp. 5–7). However, keep in mind that the diagnosis of unimpaired phonological skills may be erroneous if it is based solely on accuracy scores and not on processing speed. In addition, even when the phonological deficit is not visible at the behavioral level, it may still be possible to observe traces of this disability in its neural correlates (see pp. 185–189).

In the light of these results and the findings of group studies demonstrating the high reliability of the deficit of the dyslexic sublexical reading route (chapter 3, pp. 78–92) and of single and multiple case studies (chapter 3, pp. 123–127) indicating the high prevalence of this deficit, the phonological profile may be seen as the only true type of developmental dyslexia, not as a subtype of it.

Behavioral and neuroimaging data

As argued in chapter 1 (pp. 14–15), it is generally accepted today that the functional neuroanatomy of reading is widely distributed but dominated by a left-sided network, with one anterior component centered in the inferior frontal gyrus implicated in phonological output, especially at the articulatory level. This area is connected to two posterior pathways. The ventral pathway (which includes occipito-temporal areas) is centered in the posterior fusiform gyrus, possibly representing an automatically accessed visual word-form area. The dorsal pathway (which includes temporo-parietal areas, especially the angular and supramarginal gyri) is devoted to phonology-based reading processes.

In normally developing readers, the relatively slow dorsal circuit predominates at first (chapter 1, pp. 15–16). However, reading tasks in which phonological processing is mandatory (for example, judging whether written words sound alike) give rise to greater activation in the angular gyrus for adults than for children (chapter 1, pp. 15–16). This pattern of findings is consistent with behavioral data showing that skilled readers have faster and more automatic access to the phonological code of the written word than children (chapter 1, p. 16). In adults with dyslexia, activation along the two posterior pathways is reduced compared to controls. On the one hand, key components of the dorsal pathway (left angular gyrus) show activity positively correlated with reading scores in normal readers and negatively correlated in dyslexic adults. On the other hand, an activation deficit in the ventral pathway is observed in dyslexics as compared to controls, irrespective of the opacity of their writing system (for Italian, French, and English, see for example, Paulesu et al., 2001).

Neurofunctional indices have been investigated in a similar way to assess phonological processing in auditory tasks (phonemic awareness, phonological short-term memory, and categorical perception of speech sounds). In their review of the literature, Démonet et al. (2004) pointed out that most studies have shown that dyslexic individuals have reduced activity in the left, rather than bilateral, perisylvian regions, especially in the left supramarginal gyrus, an important area for phonological processing. Such a pattern has been observed in dyslexics' implicit perception of phonemic contrasts even when their behavioral performance on the same task is normal, thus suggesting the existence of compensatory mechanisms.

One basic question is whether the neural circuits for visual word perception develop independently of those responsible for auditory word recognition (McCandliss et al., 2003). The fact that the visual word form area (VWFA) does not respond to a passive presentation of the spoken word does not invalidate the hypothesis that visual word perception might be derived from processes prevailing in speech perception. The VWFA is activated when subjects are engaged in a spelling task of auditory words (Booth, Burman, Meyer, Gitelman, Parrish, & Mesulam, 2003a). While this might only reveal optional top-down activation under the demands of an orthographic task (Cohen & Dehaene, 2004), it nevertheless demonstrates the existence of a direct link between VWFA and speech perception.

Words, like any other speech segments, should be affected by allophonic representations and this should have important consequences for reading if speech perception processes transfer to the visual perception of words. The question then is whether there are arguments for a specifically visual deficit. Some studies suggest strong increases in activation of the fusiform gyrus in adults compared to children during reading (chapter 1, p. 16). Other studies suggest that the VWFA fails to increase its activity in response to word forms in adult dyslexics compared to average readers (see for a discussion, McCandliss et al., 2003). However, this might be a further consequence of the "Matthew effect", i.e., the lesser exposure to written words for chidren vs. adults or for adult dyslexics vs. adult average readers.

This is the perspective offered by McCandliss and Noble (2003) who proposed a simple cascading model in which differences in brain areas associated with phonological processing influence the specialization of visual areas involved in the rapid processing of written words. Specifically, disrupted functioning of the perisylvian regions associated with phonological deficits would affect the long-lasting specialization processes that occur in the left fusiform areas during reading acquisition. In normal reading acquisition, the focus on grapheme–phoneme correspondences might act as an incentive for a gradual specialization of the VWFA. To answer these questions, it is necessary to carry out studies which follow children longitudinally with fMRI and include comprehensive behavioral testing to determine what influences on the development of this region.

A causal model of developmental dyslexia

As proposed by Shaywitz and Shaywitz (2005), rather than the smoothly operating, integrated reading systems observed in unimpaired readers, disruption of the posterior reading systems might cause dyslexics to attempt to compensate their deficit by shifting to other ancillary systems, especially anterior sites in the inferior frontal gyrus. These sites are crucial for articulation, and so their activation may help dyslexics develop a motor trace of the phonology of the word they are trying to read by producing more or less overt subvocalization movements. This compensatory strategy may allow them to process written words, although more slowly and less efficiently than if they relied on the fast occipito-temporal word identification system. These findings are consistent with the large body of evidence indicating that the deficit of the dyslexic sublexical reading route can be lessened by the use of compensatory strategies (see p. 184). The greater number of ancillary systems observed in compensated adult dyslexics compared to persistent dyslexics could represent the neural correlates of some of these compensations (Shaywitz & Shaywitz, 2005).

Figure 5.2 presents a framework that schematically depicts the main arguments we have developed to explain developmental dyslexia. This framework takes into account the neurobiological, cognitive, and behavioral levels of description. It also includes the role of environmental factors and compensatory strategies.

At the neurobiological level, the main dysfunctions supposed to be linked to reading are revealed by underactivation of some left perisylvian areas, especially temporo-parietal and occipito-temporal areas. The underactivation of these areas might be neural correlates of the dyslexics' disabilities in two cognitive domains: first, of their "deficit" in processing phonemes (based on allophonic rather than on phonemic representations); second of their word-reading impairment, especially that of their sublexical reading route (which necessitates mapping graphemes with phonemes).

At the behavioral level, the deficit of phonemic processes might explain dyslexics' impaired skills in the three main domains that underlie classical phonological explanation concerning reading acquisition and developmental dyslexia. The fact that dyslexics have difficulty in phonemic segmentation and phonemic discrimination tasks can obviously be conceived as being a mere consequence of their poor phonemic categories. Limitations in phonological short-term memory might also be a side effect of allophonic rather than phonemic representations of speech sounds. The number of elements required for storing words is larger with allophones as they are more numerous than phonemes. While this possibility remains to be investigated, it would imply that problems in verbal memory associated with dyslexia arise from a larger sized memory repertoire rather than from intrinsic difficulties in memory. Likewise, problems in rapid automatic naming (RAN) might derive from the fact that the dyslexics' phonemic categories are not well specified. Indeed, RAN depends on both quick retrieval of words in the mental lexicon and rapid articulatory processing, each of these two factors having phonological components.

The deficit of the sublexical reading route is evidenced at the behavioral level by the strong difficulties that dyslexics have to read new words (i.e., the pseudoword reading deficit), for which it is not possible to rely on lexical knowledge. This impairment can also be due to the fact that the dyslexics have deficits in phonemic discrimination and in phonemic segmentation, as well as in phonological short-term memory and in rapid naming (i.e., the classical phonological explanation). Since establishing a lexical reading route depends on the efficiency of the sublexical reading route, the lexical reading route of dyslexics is also impaired. Moreover, as the efficiency of text reading

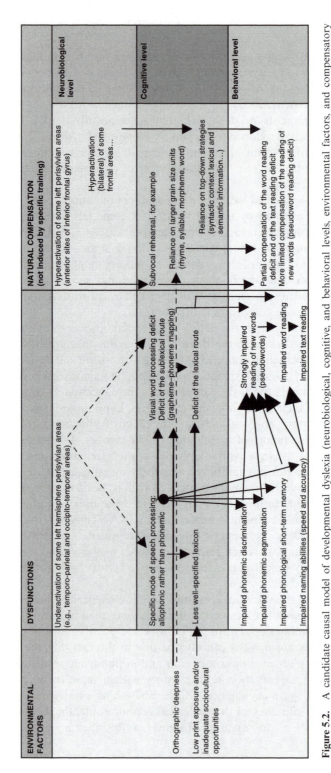

Figure 5.2. A candidate causal model of developmental dyslexia (neurobiological, cognitive, and behavioral levels, environmental factors, and compensatory strategies).

depends on the efficiency of written-word identification processes, text reading is also impaired.

Environmental factors, such as an opaque orthography, in which the connections between graphemes and phonemes are not consistent, may also aggravate the deficit of the sublexical reading route, and lead dyslexics to rely on larger grain size units, such as rhyme, syllable, morpheme or words. In addition, low print exposure and/or inadequate sociocultural opportunities may reduce the size of their spoken lexicon and, consequently, aggravate the deficit of their lexical reading route.

As regards natural compensation (not induced by special training), hyperactivation of some left perisylvian areas (anterior sites of inferior frontal gyrus, areas crucial for articulation), may help dyslexics develop a motor trace of the phonology of the word they are trying to read. Finally, bilateral hyperactivation of some frontal areas may be the neural correlates of the top-down strategies (use of syntactic context, and of semantic information) dyslexics rely on. It is probably by way of such compensatory strategies, including reliance on larger grain size units (such as rhyme, syllable, morpheme and words), that dyslexics do manage partially to compensate their word reading and text reading deficit, these strategies having a more limited incidence on their reading of new words.

CONCLUSION

The framework we are proposing allows us to integrate the many pieces of the puzzling problems of reading acquisition and developmental dyslexia, at least for alphabetic writing systems. It also allows us to highlight some important issues that have not been properly examined so far. Concerning the grain size of processing units in particular, given that most studies have focused on letter-sound *versus* rhyme units, it would be worthwhile to thoroughly examine the role of other units such as the syllable and the morpheme. These units are assumed to be conditioned by both their weight and consistency in the language, and by the child's reading level.

Above all, a number of phenomena demonstrate the crucial importance of phonological factors in reading. A critical issue is thus to understand how these factors enter into the word-reading reflex. To this end, examining the relationship between reading and speech perception, itself a highly automatic process, seems promising. Ascribing dyslexia to an allophonic mode of speech perception illustrates how this approach might contribute to the field.

Notes

Introduction

1 For instance, a Pinyin script that uses the Roman alphabet was introduced in the 1970s in Mainland China as an aid for teaching reading. This script is now compulsory in elementary schools. Children learn to read and write Roman letters and pronounce Chinese syllables before they embark on the long task of learning Chinese characters.

1 What have we learned from studies with skilled adult readers?

1 Other techniques exist, such as the recording of electrical (EEG) or magnetic (MEG) activity in the brain; each has its own limitations.
2 There is a limited amount of published work on children, and most ERP research has been done on infants and young children; but see for example Licht, Bakker, Kok, and Bouma (1992).
3 One can also find the term "orthographic processing" which refers to the visual encoding of written words. The studies typically compared activations between two conditions with the same task but different types of visual stimuli (e.g., words versus false-font strings). Regions more activated during visual encoding of words relative to control stimuli are believed to be specifically involved in orthographic processing.

2 Reading acquisition in deep and shallow orthographies

1 For instance, the concept "speech therapy" is transcribed by two words in English and by one in French: "orthophonie". This word contains sub-units which also

have a meaning, the morphemes *ortho-* (such as in *orthodox, orthography*) and *phon-* (such as in *phonecard, phonetics*).

2 Pre-reading strategies are not examined in this chapter because, apart from a few words that could have been learned by heart, these strategies, called logographics, do not seem to play a significant role in reading acquisition, at least in relatively transparent orthographies (for German: Wimmer & Hummer, 1990; for French: Sprenger-Charolles & Bonnet, 1996). Likewise, studies conducted with English-speaking children suggest that from the very beginning, children make more use of phonological information than visual information in written words (Ehri, 1992; Ehri & Wilce, 1985; Laing & Hulme, 1999; Stuart & Coltheart, 1988). In addition, logographic strategies do not seem to have any generative power (Masonheimer, Drum, & Ehri, 1984).

3 A monophthong is a "pure" vowel whose articulation at both beginning and end is relatively stable, and which does not glide up or down towards a new position of articulation (as "e" in *bed*). A diphthong begins with one vowel and gradually changes to another vowel within the same syllable (as "oi" in *boil*).

4 For French, the analyses were based on the Brulex database (Content et al., 1990). For English, the database contained virtually all monosyllabic words found in Kucera and Francis (1967).

5 All analyses were confined to monosyllabic words occurring in the Celex database for English (Baayen, Piepenbrock, & Gulikers, 1995) and in the Brulex database for French (Content et al., 1990).

6 MANULEX is a web-accessible database that provides word-frequency lists of non-lemmatized and lemmatized words, by school level (Grades 1 to 5).

7 In the study by Defior, Martos, and Cary (2002), Spanish children were also found to make fewer errors and to be faster than Portuguese children on pseudoword reading (Portuguese and Spanish may both be considered as having transparent orthographies; however, GPCs are more consistent in Spanish than in Portuguese).

8 Processing speed was not taken into account, for the same reason as for the Seymour et al. (2003) study.

9 Ages 6.3, 6.9, 7.5, and 6.11 for English-, French-, German-, and Spanish-speaking first graders, respectively; ages 7.4, 7.8, 8.10, and 7.10 for second graders; 7.10, 8.8, 9.10, and 8.11 for third graders; and 8.10, 9.9, 10.7, and 9.10 for fourth graders.

10 Another issue is whether readers process letters or graphemes. This question has been examined especially in French and in Dutch, where there are many long graphemes (more than one letter for one phoneme). For example, differences between regular words containing one- and two-letter graphemes (*ch, ou, on*, etc.) were assessed in French first, second, third, and fourth graders on accuracy, latency, and duration of the vocal response (Sprenger-Charolles et al., 2005). Items including a digraph were never read less well than those with one-letter graphemes only. The duration of the vocal response was consistently shorter on these items. In addition, the presence of a digraph had a positive effect on accuracy for all grade levels taken together, and on latency in the first three grades. The results obtained for the younger children replicate those obtained for French-speaking beginning readers (Sprenger-Charolles et al., 1998b). The latency results for the fourth graders are in line with those of French-speaking adults, at least for frequent words (Rey, Jacobs, Schmidt-Weigand, & Ziegler, 1998). This can be explained by

two facts. If the basic unit of sublexical processing is the grapheme rather than the letter, then first, readers have fewer units to decode and assemble when the items contain a digraph than when they are composed of only one-letter graphemes. Second, they have fewer phonemic units to program in order to produce an oral response. Thus, the presence of a digraph may have an overall facilitatory effect on reading when the reader relies strongly on grapheme–phoneme correspondences, and when this kind of processing has not yet been automatized, as in the youngest children. However, when the letters that correspond to a single phoneme are visually separate, the reading performance of adult English (Pring, 1981) and Dutch (Martensen, Maris, & Dijkstra, 2003) speakers declines, suggesting that graphemes are functional reading units, even for adults.

11 Children also seem to learn other non-phonology-based regularities quite quickly (in English: Cassar & Treiman, 1997; in French: Pacton, & Fayol, 2000; Pacton, Perruchet, Fayol, & Cleeremans, 2001). However, it has not yet been shown that mastery of these regularities plays an important role in reading acquisition.

12 This task is a visual version of the syllable monitoring technique developed by Mehler, Dommergues, Frauenfelder, and Segui (1981).

13 This appears to be the case for skilled French readers when they read low-frequency words, but not high-frequency ones (Colé et al., 1999). However, the results on this topic are not clear-cut (e.g., Brand, Rey, & Peereman, 2003; Ferrand, Segui, & Grainger, 1996). Other phonological features affect syllable processing, such as the sonority of phonemes situated at syllabic boundaries. According to Clements (1990), every phoneme can be defined in terms of its sonority, and a well-formed syllable is made up of a sequence of phonemes that increases in sonority up to the vowel and then decreases. Vowels are the most sonorous phonemes, plosives the least, with liquids (*l* and *r*) occupying an intermediate position on the sonority dimension. Children appear to be sensitive to the sonority principle very early on (see Sprenger-Charolles & Siegel, 1997). Sonority also seems to play a role in syllable segmentation for skilled French readers (Bedoin & Dissart, 2002) but not for skilled English readers processing monosyllabic items (Gross, Treiman, & Inmann, 2000). For the role of sonority in syllabic segmentation of speech by adults, see also Content, Kearns, & Frauenfelder, 2001; Content, Meunier, Kearns, & Frauenfelder, 2001).

14 For each category, the test items were matched on number of letters and number of syllables, and because latencies were examined, on the phoneme corresponding to their first grapheme. The pseudowords, which were matched to the regular words on orthographic difficulty, shared no analogical relationships with the words (i.e., they did not have the same beginnings or endings as real French words).

15 Statistics were computed on the accuracy scores. To make the accuracy and speed differences easier to understand, Figure 2.15a presents the mean error percentages, which increased in the same way as the latencies. Latency was only taken into account starting at the end of Grade 2, because at the end of Grade 1 too many children produced fewer than 50% correct responses.

16 In the study by Sprenger-Charolles et al. (2003), the same children were asked to spell the same items. The most striking finding was that regular words were never spelled better than pseudowords. These results might be due to the strong asymmetry between GPC (used to read) and PGC (used to spell) in French (see

Table 2.1a,b,c). Similar results are reported in other studies on French-speaking children (Alegria & Mousty, 1996; Leybaert & Content, 1995; Sprenger-Charolles & Casalis, 1995) and English-speaking children (Bruck & Waters, 1990; Foorman, Jenkins, & Francis, 1993; Foorman, Novy, Francis, & Liberman, 1991; Juel, 1988; Juel et al., 1986; Lennox & Siegel, 1993; Stage & Wagner, 1992). Most studies in this field have been aimed at determining whether the same procedures are used in reading and spelling (e.g., for English: Bruck & Waters, 1990; Foorman et al., 1991, 1993; Juel, 1988; Juel et al., 1986; Stage & Wagner, 1992; Waters, Bruck, & Seidenberg, 1985; for Spanish: Cuetos, 1989; for German: Wimmer & Hummer, 1990; for French: Eme & Golder, 2005; Leybaert & Content, 1995; Sprenger-Charolles & Casalis, 1995; Sprenger-Charolles et al., 1998b, 2003). The main findings are that the patterns for the regularity effect are similar in reading and spelling (Bruck & Waters, 1990; Foorman et al., 1991, 1993; Sprenger-Charolles et al., 1998b, 2003), and that, based on correlation analyses, there are strong relationships between these two skills (e.g., Juel, 1988; Juel et al., 1986; Stage & Wagner, 1992; Sprenger-Charolles et al., 1998b), thus suggesting quantitative differences between reading and spelling, with substantial reliance on similar processes.

17 Similar results were found in studies in which the effects of regularity, frequency, and/or lexicality were assessed (e.g., for English: Backman, Bruck, Hebert, & Seidenberg, 1984; Waters, Seidenberg, & Bruck, 1984; for French: Leybaert & Content, 1995; Sprenger-Charolles et al., 1998b).

18 Treiman, Broderick, Tincoff, and Rodriguez (1998) also showed that performance on phonemic tasks is dependent on what phonemes are involved. The performance of kindergartners on phoneme identification tasks was found to be better with occlusive consonants (/t/, /d/) than with fricatives (/v/, /z/).

19 Bentin, Hammer, and Cahan (1991) tried to distinguish the effects of age and instruction on the development of phonemic awareness. Using a regression analysis on a sample of 352 kindergartners and 319 children first graders, they found that schooling accounted for 32% of the variance in the children's phonemic performance, while age accounted for only 9%. The effect of schooling was thus four times greater than that of age.

20 Danish, Dutch, Finnish, German, Norwegian, Spanish, Swedish, and Hebrew.

21 Even though phonological awareness precedes morphological awareness, the question of the relationship between the two is still unanswered. Correlation studies have indicated that phonological and morphological awareness are highly correlated (Carlisle, 1995; Fowler & Liberman, 1995), even though these abilities contribute to separate parts of the variance in learning to read and may therefore involve common skills. At the same time, it is not possible to determine whether one of these abilities depends on the other. As we have already mentioned, it is generally agreed that phonological awareness plays an important role in reading in the first grades, while morphological awareness may make a greater contribution in later grades (Carlisle, 2000). But this does not imply that morphological awareness depends on phonological awareness from a developmental point of view. Such a relationship, if it exists, has to be demonstrated.

3 Reliability and prevalence of dyslexic reading deficits

1 Approximately 4% of all children are thought to be dyslexic according to a pre-liminary study on the entire population of 10- to 14-year-old children on the Isle of Wight, and approximately 6% or more according to another study of 14-year-old children in the City of London (Yule, Rutter, Berger, & Thompson, 1974). Data from a longitudinal study of 414 Connecticut children are similar (Shaywitz, Escobar, Shaywitz, Fletcher, & Makuch, 1992; see also Shaywitz et al., 1999).

2 Long items were processed less accurately and less rapidly than short ones by both dyslexics and controls, but the length effect was the same for the two groups, whatever the type of item. However, the younger dyslexics made more errors on both short and long pseudowords. Given that latencies were only calculated for correct responses, this could have biased the overall picture of the results.

3 This footnote was from a personal communication from Castles.

4 The norms were obtained from a control group assessed in a study by Friedrich et al. (1985).

5 Averaged over inconsistent and highly inconsistent words.

6 We did not include four more recent studies, three because there were no reading-level comparisons (Castles et al., 1999; Milne, Nicholson, & Corbalis, 2003; Zabell & Everatt, 2002) and one because the classification was based on regular-word reading instead of pseudoword reading (McDougall, Borowsky, MacKinnon, & Hymel, 2004).

7 Only the controls' individual results for the word and pseudoword reading aloud tasks were reported in the book, so it was not possible to calculate the means and standard deviations of the control group on the visual tasks.

8 $RT = A + B(L)$, where L is the item length, A the zero intercept, and B the slope.

9 The dyslexics and controls came from a cohort of roughly 550 children attending 21 kindergartens located near Paris. Almost 400 children were included in the study on the basis of the classic exclusionary criteria and were followed from age 5 to 8 years. None of the children were readers at the beginning of the study. The dyslexics came from a subgroup of 52 poor readers whose reading scores were found to deviate from the norms according to a standardized reading test (BATELEM; Savigny, 1974) when they were 8 years old. We were able to re-examine 45 of these poor readers 2 years later. The 33 poorest readers (two stand-ard deviations below the mean of the controls according to the ANALEC reading aloud subtest; Inizan, 1995) were classified as dyslexics. The control group came from a subset of the same longitudinal cohort. It included almost 40 children that we were able to follow and to examine thoroughly between the ages of 5 and 10 (e.g., Colé & Sprenger-Charolles, 1999; Sprenger-Charolles & Bonnet, 1996; Sprenger-Charolles & Siegel, 1997; Sprenger-Charolles et al., 1998a, 1998b, 2003). Only the 19 average readers were included in the control groups; the 10 above-average readers, and the 13 below-average readers were excluded.

4 Phonological and sensori-motor explanations of dyslexia

1 As already underlined, the dyslexics and controls came from a cohort of roughly 550 kindergartners. The control group came from a subset of the same longitudinal

cohort. It included almost 40 children that we were able to follow and to examine thoroughly between the ages of 5 and 10. Only the 19 average readers were included in the control groups; the 10 above average readers, and the 13 below average readers were not included.

2　The distinction between transitional and stable segments corresponds more or less to that between consonants and vowels, although stable parts tend to disappear in rapid speech. There are also cross-language differences in the relative contributions of transitions and stable parts to vowel perception, the perceptual weight of transitions being larger in English compared to French (Gottfried, 1984).

3　Effect of training on children in special schools for phonemic awareness might explain the relatively low prevalence of both phonological deficits in children versus adults. The same is true for auditory deficits, for which the PCC is only of 61% in children studies (from Heim et al., 2001; Kronbichler et al., 2002; Marshall et al., 2001; Rosen & Manganari, 2001; Van Ingelghem, Van Wieringen, Wouters, Vandenbussche, Onghena, & Ghesquiere, 2001), against 81% in adults studies (from Amitay et al., 2002; Ramus et al., 2003b; Witton, Stein, Stoodley, Rosner, & Talcott, 2002). However, at least for the moment and at least to our knowledge, no study has shown the prevalence of a categorical perception deficit before reading acquisition in future dyslexics, compared to future average readers, whereas data on the prevalence of a phonemic awareness deficit are available (see pp. 134–139).

5 Explaining normal and impaired reading acquisition

1　Regarding the issue of processing speed, remember also that in studies showing specific visual deficits in developmental dyslexia, children's phonological skills are generally assessed using tasks with no time constraints and without taking processing speed into account. Visual skills, on the other hand, are generally examined with timed measures and/or time-constrained tasks (chapter 3, pp. 90–92, 106–108; see pp. 114–119 for a noteworthy exception). This is also the case when dyslexics' processing speed on rapid naming of frequent words is compared to their accuracy scores on classic phonological tasks (pp. 90–91, 134–139). These methodological problems strongly lessen the significance of the comparisons, because they make it impossible to state that dyslexics' phonological skills are actually unimpaired.

References

Adlard, A., & Hazan, V. (1998). Speech perception in children with specific reading difficulties (dyslexia). *Quarterly Journal of Experimental Psychology, 51A,* 153–177.

Aghababian, V., & Nazir, T. (2000). Developing normal reading skills: Aspects of visual processes underlying word recognition. *Journal of Experimental Child Psychology, 76,* 123–150.

Agnew, J. A., Dorn, C., & Eden, G. F. (2004). Effect of intensive training on auditory processing and reading skills. *Brain and Language, 88,* 21–25.

Alegria, J., & Morais, J. (1979). Le développement de l'habileté d'analyse phonétique consciente de la parole et l'apprentissage de la lecture [The development of phonetic awareness and learning to read]. *Archives de Psychologie, 183,* 251–270.

Alegria, J., & Mousty, P. (1996). The development of spelling procedures in French-speaking, normal and reading-disabled children: Effects of frequency and lexicality. *Journal of Experimental Child Psychology, 63*(2), 312–338.

Alegria, J., Pignot, E., & Morais, J. (1982). Phonetic analysis, speech and memory codes in beginning readers. *Memory and Cognition, 10,* 451–456.

Alvarez, C., Carreiras, M., & Taft, M. (2001). Syllables and morphemes: Contrasting frequency effects in Spanish. *Journal of Experimental Psychology: Learning, Memory, and Cognition, 27*(2), 545–555.

Amitay, S., Ben, Y. G., Banai, K., & Ahissar, M. (2002). Disabled readers suffer from visual and auditory impairments but not from a specific magnocellular deficit. *Brain, 125, Part 10,* 2272–2285.

Anglin, J. M. (1993). Vocabulary development: A morphological analysis. *Monographs of the Society for Research in Child Development, 58,* 1–166.

Anthony, J. L., & Lonigan, C. J. (2004). The nature of phonological awareness:

Converging evidence from four studies of preschool and early grade school children. *Journal of Educational Psychology, 96*, 43–55.

Anthony, J. L., Lonigan, C. J., Burgess, S. R., Driscoll, K., Phillips, B. M., & Cantor, B. G. (2002). Structure of preschool phonological sensitivity: Overlap sensitivity to rhyme, words, syllables, and phonemes. *Journal of Experimental Child Psychology, 82*, 65–92.

Anthony, J. L., Lonigan, C. J., Driscoll, K., Phillips, B. M., & Burgess, S. R. (2003). Phonological sensitivity: A quasi parallel progression of word structure units and cognitive operation. *Reading Research Quarterly, 38*(4), 470–487.

Arnbak, E., & Elbro, C. (2000). The effect of morphological awareness training on the reading and spelling skills of young dyslexics. *Scandinavian Journal of Educational Research, 44*(3), 229–251.

Aro, M., & Wimmer, H. (2003). Learning to read: English in comparison to six more regular orthographies. *Applied Psycholinguistics, 24* (4), 621–635.

Aslin, R. N., Pisoni, D. B., Hennessy, B. L., & Perrey, A. V. (1981). Discrimination of voice onset time by human infants: New findings and implications for the effect of early experience. *Child Development, 52*, 1135–1145.

Baayen, R. H., Piepenbrock, R., & Gulikers, L. (1995). *The CELEX Lexical Database.* Philadelphia, PA: Linguistic Data Consortium, University of Pennsylvania.

Backman, J., Bruck, M., Hebert, M., & Seidenberg, M. S. (1984). Acquisition and use of spelling sound correspondences in reading. *Journal of Experimental Child Psychology, 38*, 114–133.

Baddeley, A. D., Ellis, N. C., Miles, T. R., & Lewis, V. J. (1982). Developmental and acquired dyslexia: A comparison. *Cognition, 11*, 185–196.

Bailey, C. E., Manis, F. R., Pedersen, W. C., & Seidenberg, M. S. (2003). Variations among developmental dyslexics: Evidence from a printed-word-learning task. *Journal of Experimental Child Psychology, 87*, 125–154.

Barber, H., Dominguez, A., & De Vega, M. (2002). Human brain potentials indicate morphological decomposition in visual word recognition. *Neuroscience Letters, 318*, 149–152.

Beauvois, M. F., & Derouesné, J. (1979). Phonologica alexia: Three dissociations. *Journal of Neurology, Neurosurgery and Psychiatry, 42*, 1115–1124.

Bedoin, N., & Dissard, P. (2002). Sonority and syllabic structure in reading: Differences between French and English readers. *Current Psychology Letters: Behavior, Brain and Cognition.* http://cpl.revues.org/document207.html

Beech, J. R., & Harding, L. M. (1984). Phonemic processing and the poor reader from a developmental lag viewpoint. *Reading Research Quarterly, 19*, 357–366.

Bentin, S., Hammer, R., & Cahan, S. (1991). The effects of aging and first grade schooling on the development of phonological awareness. *Psychological Science, 2*(4), 271–274.

Bentin, S., Mouchetant-Rostaing, Y., Giard, M. H., Echallier, J. F., & Pernier, J. (1999). ERP manifestations of processing printed words at different psycholinguistic levels: Time course and scalp distribution. *Journal of Cognitive Neuroscience, 11*(3), 235–260.

Bertram, R., & Hyönä, J. (2003). The length of a complex word modifies the role of morphological structure: Evidence from eye movements when reading short and long Finnish compounds. *Journal of Memory and Language, 48,* 615–634.

Bertram, R., Schreuder, R., & Baayen, R. H. (2000). The balance of storage and computation in morphological processing: The role of word formation type, affixal homonymy, and productivity. *Journal of Experimental Psychology: Learning, Memory, and Cognition, 26*(2), 489–511.

Besner, D., Twilley, L., McCann, R. S., & Seergobin, K. (1990). On the connection between connexionism and data: Are a few words necessary? *Psychological Review, 97,* 432–446.

Blachman, B. A. (1997). *Foundations of reading acquisition and dyslexia: Implications for early intervention.* Mahwah, NJ: Lawrence Erlbaum Associates, Inc.

Blomert, L. (2005). *Dyslexie in Nederland: Theorie, praktijk en beleid* [Dyslexia in The Netherlands: Theory, practice & policy]. Amsterdam: Nieuwezijds.

Blomert, L., & Mitterer, H. (2003). The fragile nature of the speech-perception deficit in dyslexia: Natural vs. synthetic speech. *Brain and Language, 89,* 21–26.

Boder, E. (1971). Developmental dyslexia. A new diagnostic approach based on the identification of three subtypes. *Journal of School Health, 40*(6), 289–290.

Boder, E. (1973). Developmental dyslexia: A diagnostic approach based on three atypical reading-spelling patterns. *Developmental Medicine and Child Neurology, 15*(5), 663–687.

Bogliotti, C. (2003). *Relation between categorical perception of speech and reading acquisition.* Proceedings of the 15th International Congress of Phonetic Sciences (pp. 885–888). Barcelona, Spain.

Bogliotti, C. (2005). *Perception catégorielle et perception allophonique: Incidences de l'âge, du niveau de lecture et des couplages entre prédispositions phonétiques* [Categorical perception and allophonic perception: Incidence of age, reading level and couplings between phonetic predispositions]. Unpublished doctoral dissertation, Université Denis Diderot, Paris, France.

Bogliotti, C., Messaoud-Galusi, S., & Serniclaes, W. (2002). *Relations entre la perception catégorielle de la parole et l'apprentissage de la lecture* [Categorical perception of speech sounds and reading acquistion]. Proceedings of the XXIVèmes Journées d'Etudes sur la Parole (pp. 197–200). Le Chesnay, France: INRIA.

Bogliotti, C., Serniclaes, W., Messaoud-Galusi, S., & Sprenger-Charolles, L. (in prep.) Discrimination of speech sounds by dyslexic children: Comparisons with chronological age and reading level controls.

Boissel-Dombreval, M., & Bouteilly, H. (2003). *Comparaison des performances de perception catégorielle de dyslexiques avec des contrôles de même âge chronologique et de même niveau de lecture.* [Categorical perception of speech sounds by dyslexics: Comparisons with chronological age and reading level controls]. Unpublished master's dissertation. Université Pierre et Marie Curie, Hôpital de la Salpétrière (Dpt. of Speech Therapy).

Bolger, D. J., Perfetti, C. A., & Schneider, W. (2005). Cross-cultural effect on the brain revisited: Universal structures plus writing system variation. *Human Brain Mapping, 25*(1), 92–104.

Booth, J. R., Burman, D. D., Meyer, J. R., Gitelman, D. R., Parrish, T. B., & Mesulam, M. M. (2003a). Relation between brain activation and lexical performance. *Human Brain Mapping, 19,* 155–169.

Booth, J. R., Burman, D. D., Meyer, J. R., Gitelman, D. R., Parrish, T. B., & Mesulam, M. M. (2004). Development of brain mechanisms for processing orthographic and phonologic representations. *Journal of Cognitive Neuroscience, 16*(7), 1234–1249.

Booth, J. R., Burman, D. D., Meyer, J. R., Lei, Z., Choy, J., Gitelman, D. R., Parrish, T. B., et al., (2003b). Modality-specific and -independent developmental differences in the neural substrate for lexical processing. *Journal of Neurolinguistics, 16*, 383–405.

Booth, J. R., Perfetti, C. A., & MacWhinney, B. (1999). Quick, automatic and general activation of orthographic and phonological representations in young readers. *Developmental Psychology, 35*(1), 3–19.

Booth, J. R., Perfetti, C. A., MacWhinney, B., & Hunt, S. B. (2000). The association of rapid temporal perception with orthographic and phonological processing in children and adults with reading impairment. *Scientific Studies of Reading, 4*(2), 101–132.

Borsting, E., Ridder, W. H., Dudeck, K., Kelley, C., Matsui, L., & Motoyama, J. (1996). The presence of a magnocellular defect depends on the type of dyslexia. *Vision Research, 36*(7), 1047–1053.

Bowers, P., & Wolf, M. (1993). Theoretical links among naming speed, precise timing mechanisms and orthographic skill in dyslexia. *Reading and Writing: An Interdisciplinary Journal, 5*, 69–95.

Bradley, L., & Bryant, P. (1983). Categorizing sounds in learning to read: A causal connection. *Nature, 301*, 419–421.

Bradlow, A. R., Kraus, N., Nicol, T. G., McGee, T. J., Cunningham, J., Zecker, S. G., et al. (1999). Effects of lengthened formant transition duration on discrimination and neural representation of synthetic CV syllables by normal and learning disabled children. *Journal of the Acoustical Society of America, 106*, 2086–2096.

Brady, S. A., Shankweiler, D., & Mann, V. A. (1983). Speech perception and memory coding in relation to reading ability. *Journal of Experimental Child Psychology, 35*, 345–367.

Brand, M., Rey, A., & Peereman, R. (2003). Where is the syllable priming effect in visual word recognition? *Journal of Memory and Language, 48*, 435–443.

Brannan, J., & Williams, M. (1987). Allocation of visual attention in good and poor readers. *Perception and Psychophysics, 41*, 23–28.

Breier, J. I., Gray, L., Fletcher, J. M., Diehl, R. L., Klaas, P., Foorman, B. R., et al. (2001). Perception of tone onset time continua in children with dyslexia and with and without attention deficit/hyperactivity disorder. *Journal of Experimental Child Psychology, 80*, 245–270.

Breitmeyer, B. G., & Ganz, L. (1976). Implications of sustained and transient channels for theories of visual pattern masking, saccadic suppression and information processing. *Psychological Review, 83*, 1–36.

Breitmeyer, B. G., & Ritter, A. (1986). The role of visual pattern persistence in bistable stroboscopic motion. *Vision Research, 26*, 1801–1806.

Brown, G. D. A., & Deavers, R. P. (1999). Units of analysis in nonword reading: Evidence from children and adults. *Journal of Experimental Child Psychology, 73*, 208–242.

Bruck, M. (1988). The word recognition and spelling of dyslexic children. *Reading Research Quarterly, 23*, 51–69.

Bruck, M. (1990). Word-recognition skills of adults with childhood diagnoses of dyslexia. *Developmental Psychology, 26*, 439–454.

Bruck, M. (1992). Persistence of dyslexics' phonological awareness deficits. *Developmental Psychology, 28*, 874–886.

Bruck, M., Genesee, F., & Caravolas, M. (1997). A cross linguistic study of early literacy acquisition. In B. Blachman (Ed.), *Foundations of reading acquisition and dyslexia: Implications for early intervention* (pp. 145–162). Mahwah, NJ: Lawrence Erlbaum Associates, Inc.

Bruck, M., & Treiman, R. (1990). Phonological awareness and spelling in normal children and dyslexics: The case of initial consonant clusters. *Journal of Experimental Child Psycholology, 50*, 156–178.

Bruck, M., & Waters, G. (1990). An analysis of component spelling and reading skills of good readers–good spellers, good readers–poor spellers and poor readers–poor spellers. In T.H. Carr, & B.A. Levy (Eds.), *Reading and its development: Component skills approaches* (pp. 161–206). San Diego: Academic Press.

Brunswick, N., McCrory, E., Price, C. J., Frith, C. D., & Frith, U. (1999). Explicit and implicit processing of words and pseudowords by adult developmental dyslexics: A search for Wernicke's Wortschatz? *Brain, 122*, 1901–1917.

Bryant, P. E., & Impey, L. (1986). The similarities between normal readers and developmental and acquired dyslexic children. *Cognition, 24*, 121–137.

Bryant, P. E., MacLean, M., Bradley, L. L., & Crossland, J. (1990). Rhyme and alliteration, phoneme detection, and learning to read. *Developmental Psychology, 26*, 429–438.

Bryant, P., Nunes, T., & Bindman, M. (1998). Awareness of language in children who have reading difficulties: Historical comparisons in a longitudinal study. *Journal of Child Psychology and Psychiatry, 39*(4), 501–510.

Bryson, S. E., & Werker, J. F. (1989). Toward understanding the problem in severely disabled readers. Part I: Vowel errors. *Applied Psycholinguistics, 10*, 1–12.

Burani, C., Marcolini, S., & Stella, G. (2002). How early does morpholexical reading develop in readers of a shallow orthography? *Brain and Language, 81*(1–3), 568–586.

Burnham, D. (2003). Language specific speech perception and the onset of reading. *Reading and Writing: An Interdisciplinary Journal, 16*, 573–609.

Burr, D. C., Morrone, M. C., & Ross, J. (1994). Selective suppression of the magnocellular visual pathway during saccadic eye movements. *Nature, 371*, 511–513.

Bus, A. G., & Van Ijzendoorn, M. H. (1999). Phonological awareness and early reading: A meta-analysis of experimental training studies. *Journal of Educational Psychology, 91*(3), 77–85.

Byrne, B., Freebody, P., & Gates, A. (1992). Longitudinal data on the relations of word-reading strategies to comprehension, reading time and phonemic awareness. *Reading Research Quarterly, 27*, 141–151.

Campbell, R., & Butterworth, B. (1985). Phonological dyslexia and dysgraphia in a highly literate subject: A developmental case with associates deficits of phonemic processing and awareness. *Quarterly Journal of Experimental Psychology, 37A*, 435–475.

Caravolas, M., Hulme, C., & Snowling, M. (2001). The foundation of spelling abilities: Evidence from a 3 year longitudinal study. *Journal of Memory and Language, 45*, 751–774.

Cardoso-Martins, C. (1995). Sensitivity to rhymes, syllables, and phonemes in literacy acquisition in Portuguese. *Reading Research Quarterly, 30*, 808–828.

Carlisle, J. F. (1995). Morphological awareness and early reading achievement. In L. B. Feldman (Ed.), *Morphological aspects of language processing* (pp. 189–209). Hillsdale, NJ: Lauwrence Erlbaum Associates, Inc.

Carlisle, J. F. (2000). Awareness of the structure and meaning of morphologically complex words: Impact on reading. *Reading and Writing: An Interdisciplinary Journal, 12*(3–4), 169–190.

Carlisle, J. F., & Nomanbhoy, D. M. (1993). Phonological and morphological awareness in first graders. *Applied Psycholinguistics, 14*, 177–195.

Carlisle, J. F., & Stone, C. A. (2003). The effects of morphological structure on children's reading of derived words in English. In E. M. H. Assink & D. Sandra (Eds.), *Reading complex words: Cross-language studies* (pp. 27–52). New York: Kluwer.

Carroll, J., Snowling, M., Hulme, C., & Stevenson, J. (2003). The development of phonological awareness in pre-school children. *Developmental Psychology, 39*, 913–923.

Casalis, S. (1995). *Lecture et dyslexies de l'enfant*. Paris: Septentrion.

Casalis, S. (2003). The delay-type in developmental dyslexia: Reading processes. *Current Psychology Letters: Behavior, Brain and Cognition, 10*. http://cpl.revues.org/document95.html

Casalis, S., Colé, P., & Sopo, D. (2004). Morphological awareness in developmental dyslexia. *Annals of Dyslexia, 54*(1), 114–138.

Casalis, S., & Louis Alexandre, M. F. (2000). Morphological analysis, phonological analysis and learning to read French: A longitudinal study. *Reading and Writing: An Interdisciplinary Journal, 12*, 303–335.

Casalis, S., Mattiot, E., Bécavin, A. S., & Colé, P. (2003). Conscience morphologique chez des lecteurs tout venant et en difficultés. [Morphological awareness in average and below average readers]. *Silexicales, 3*, 57–66.

Cassar, M., & Treiman, R. (1997). The beginning of orthographic knowledge: Children's knowledge of double letters in words. *Journal of Educational Psychology, 89*(4), 631–644.

Castles, A., & Coltheart, M. (1993). Varieties of developmental dyslexia. *Cognition, 47*, 149–180.

Castles, A., & Coltheart, M. (1996). Cognitive correlates of developmental surface dyslexia: A single case study. *Cognitive Neuropsychology, 13*, 25–50.

Castles, A., & Coltheart, M. (2004). Is there a causal link from phonological awareness to success in learning to read? *Cognition, 91*, 77–111.

Castles, A., Datta, H., Gayan, J., & Olson, R. K. (1999). Varieties of reading disorder: Genetic and environmental influences. *Journal of Experimental Child Psychology, 72*, 73–94.

Catach, N. (1980). *L'orthographe française: Traité théorique et pratique* [French orthography: Theoretical and practical treatise]. Paris: Nathan.

Catts, H. W. (1986). Speech production/phonological deficits in reading-disordered children. *Journal of Reading Disabilities, 19*, 504–508.

Catts, H. W. (1993). The relationship between speech-language impairments and reading disabilities. *Journal of Speech and Hearing Research, 36,* 948–958.

Cestnick, L., & Coltheart, M. (1999). The relationship between language-processing and visual-processing deficits in developmental dyslexia. *Cognition, 71*(3), 231–255.

Champion, A. (1997). Knowledge of suffixed words: A comparison of reading disabled and non disabled readers. *Annals of Dyslexia, 47,* 29–55.

Chiappe, P., Stringer, N., Siegel, L. S., & Stanovich, K. (2002). Why the timing deficit hypothesis does not explain reading disability in adults. *Reading and Writing: An Interdisciplinary Journal, 15,* 73–107.

Clements, G. N. (1990). The role of the sonority cycle in core syllabation. In J. Kingston & M. E. Beckman (Eds.), *Papers in laboratory phonology 1: Between the grammar and physics of speech* (pp. 283–333). Cambridge: Cambridge University Press.

Cohen, J. (1988). *Statistical power analysis for the behavioural sciences.* Hillsdale, NJ: Lawrence Erlbaum Associates, Inc.

Cohen, L., & Dehaene, S. (2004). Specialization in the ventral stream: The case for the visual word form area. *Neuroimage, 22,* 466–476.

Cohen, L., Dehaene, S., Naccache, L., Lehericy, S., Dehaene-Lambertz, G., Henaff, M. A., et al. (2000). The visual word form area – spatial and temporal characterization of an initial stage of reading in normal subjects and posterior split-brain patients. *Brain, 123, Part 2,* 291–307.

Colé, P., Leuwers, C., & Sprenger-Charolles, L. (2005, September). *Morphologically-based compensatory reading strategy in adult dyslexics.* Paper presented at the ESCOP Conference, Leiden, Netherlands.

Colé, P., Magnan, A., & Grainger, J. (1999). Syllable-sized units in visual word recognition: Evidence from skilled and beginning readers. *Applied Psycholinguistics, 20,* 507–532.

Colé, P., Royer, C., Leuwers, C., & Casalis, S. (2004). Les connaissances morphologiques dérivationnelles et l'apprentissage de la lecture chez l'apprenti-lecteur français du CP au CE2 [Morphological (derivational morphology) awareness and learning to read: Data from French first and second graders]. *L'Année Psychologique, 104,* 701–750.

Colé, P., Segui, J., & Taft, M. (1997). Words and morphemes as units for lexical access. *Journal of Memory and Language, 37,* 312–330.

Colé, P., & Sprenger-Charolles, L. (1999). Traitement syllabique au cours de la reconnaissance de mots écrits chez des enfants dyslexiques, lecteurs en retard et normo-lecteurs de 11 ans [Syllabic-based processing in written-word recognition: Data from 11 year-old dyslexics, backward readers and average readers]. *Revue de Neuropsychologie, 4,* 323–360.

Colé, P., Sprenger-Charolles, L., Siegel, L., & Jimenez-Gonzales, J. E. (2004, June). *Syllables in learning to read in English, French and Spanish.* Paper presented at the SSS-R Congress, Amsterdam, Netherlands.

Coltheart, M., Curtis, B., Atkins, P., & Haller, M. (1993). Models of reading aloud: Dual route and parallel processing approaches. *Psychological Review, 100,* 589–608.

Coltheart, M., Masterson, J., Byng, S., Prior, M., & Riddoch, J. (1983). Surface dyslexia. *Quarterly Journal of Experimental Psychology, 35,* 469–595.

Coltheart, M., Rastle, K., Perry, C., Langdon, R., & Ziegler, J. (2001). DRC: A dual route cascaded model of visual word recognition and reading aloud. *Psychological Review*, *108*, 204–256.

Content, A., Kearns, R. K., & Frauenfelder, U. H. (2001). Boundaries versus onsets in syllabic segmentation. *Journal of Memory and Language*, *45*, 177–199.

Content, A., Meunier, C., Kearns, R. K., & Frauenfelder, U. K. (2001). Sequence detection in pseudo-words in French: Where is the syllable effect? *Language and Cognitive Processes*, *16*(5/6), 609–636.

Content, A., Mousty, Ph., & Radeau, M. (1990). Brulex: Une base de données lexicales informatisée pour le Français écrit et parlé [A computarized lexical database: Spoken and written French]. *Année Psychologique*, *90*, 551–566.

Cornelissen, P. L., Bradley, L., Fowler, S., & Stein, J. F. (1992). Covering one eye affects how some children read. *Developmental Medicine and Child Neurology*, *34*, 296–304.

Cornelissen, P. L., Bradley, L., & Stein, J. F. (1991). What children see affects how they read. *Developmental Medicine and Child Neurology*, *33*, 755–762.

Cornelissen, P. L., Hansen, P. C., Hutton, J. L., Evangelinou, V., & Stein, J. F. (1997). Magnocellular visual function and children's single word reading. *Vision Research*, *38*, 471–482.

Cornelissen, P., Richardson, A., Mason, A., Fowler, S., & Stein, J. (1995). Contrast sensitivity and coherent motion detection measured at photopic luminance levels in dyslexics and controls. *Vision Research*, *35*(10), 1483–1494.

Cossu, G., Shankweiler, D., Liberman, I. Y., & Gugliotta, M. (1995). Visual and phonological determinants of misreadings in a transparent orthography. *Reading and Writing: An Interdisciplinary Journal*, *7*, 235–256.

Coulmas, F. (1996). *The Blackwell Encyclopedia of Writing Systems*. Oxford: Blackwell.

Critchley, M. (1970). *The dyslexic child*. London: Heinemann.

Cuetos, F. (1989). Lectura y escritura de palabras a traves de la ruta phonologica [Involvement of the phonological reading route in word reading and spelling. *Infencia y aprendizaje*, *45*, 71–84.

Davis, C., Castles, A., McAnally, K., & Gray, J. (2001). Lapses of concentration and dyslexic performance on the Ternus task. *Cognition*, *81*, B21–B31.

Deacon, S. H., & Kirby, J. R. (2004). Morphological awareness: Just "more phonological"? The roles of morphological and phonological awareness in reading development. *Applied Psycholinguistics*, *25*, 223–238.

Defior, S., Martos, S., & Cary, L. (2002). Difference in reading acquisition development in two shallow orthographies: Portuguese and Spanish. *Applied Psycholinguistics*, *23*, 135–148.

de Gelder, B., & Vroomen, J. (1998). Impaired speech perception in poor readers: Evidence from hearing and speech reading. *Brain and Language*, *64*, 269–281.

Dehaene, S., Le Clec'h, G., Poline, J.B., Le Bihan, D., & Cohen, L. (2002). The visual word form area: A prelexical representation of visual words in the fusiform gyrus. *Neuroreport*, *13*, 321–325.

Dehaene-Lambertz, G., Pallier, C., Serniclaes, W., Sprenger-Charolles, L., Jobert, A., & Dehaene, S. (2005). Neural correlates of switching from auditory to speech perception. *NeuroImage*, *24*, 21–33.

Dehaene-Lambertz, G., Sprenger-Charolles, L., & Serniclaes, W. (in preparation).

ERP differences between dyslexics and controls when switching from auditory to speech perception.

Delattre, P. (1965). *Comparing the phonetic features of English, French, German and Spanish*. Heidelberg: Jumius Gross Verlag.

Delattre, P. (1966). *Studies in French and comparative phonetics*. The Hague: Mouton.

De Luca, M., Borrelli, M., Judica, A., Spinelli, D., & Zoccolotti, P. (2002). Reading words and pseudowords: An eye movement study of developmental dyslexia. *Brain and Language, 80*, 617–626.

De Luca, M., Di Pace, E., Judica, A., Spinelli, D., & Zoccolotti, P. (1999). Eye movement patterns in linguistic and non linguistic tasks in developmental surface dyslexia. *Neuropsychologia, 37*, 1407–1420.

Demb, J. B., Poldrack, R. A., & Gabrieli, J. D. (1999). Functional neuroimaging of word processing in normal and dyslexic readers. In R. M. Klein & P. A. McMullen (Eds.), *Converging methods for understanding reading and dyslexia* (pp. 243–304). London: MIT Press.

Démonet, J.-F., Taylor, M. J., & Chaix, Y. (2004). Developmental dyslexia. *The Lancet, 363*, 1451–1460.

Dijkstra, T., Schreuder, R., & Frauenfelder, U. H. (1989). Grapheme context effects on phonemic processing. *Language and Speech, 32*, 89–108.

Ducrot, S., Lété, B., Sprenger-Charolles, L., Pynte, P., & Billard, C. (2003). The optimal viewing position effect in beginning and dyslexic readers. *Current Psychology Letters: Behavior, Brain and Cognition, 10*. http://cpl.revues.org/document99.html

Dufor, O., Serniclaes, W., Balduyck, S., Sprenger-Charolles, L., & Démonet, J.-F. (2005, June). *Learning of phonemic categorical perception in dyslexia: A speech perception study using PET*. Poster presented at the 11th Annual Meeting of the Organization for Human Brain Mapping (OHBM, 1128), Toronto, Canada.

Dufor, O., Serniclaes, W., Sprenger-Charolles, L., & Démonet, J.-F. (submitted). The brain substrates of phoneme categorization in dyslexia: Left temporal parietal deficit and crossmodal effects.

Duncan, L. G., & Seymour, P. H. K. (2003). How do children read multisyllabic words? Some preliminary observations. *Journal of Research in Reading, 26*(2), 101–120.

Duncan, L. G., Seymour, P. H., & Hill, S. (1997). How important are rhyme and analogy in beginning reading? *Cognition, 63*, 171–208.

Durgunoglu, A. Y., & Oney, B. (2002). Phonological awareness in literacy development: It's not only for children. *Scientific Studies of Reading, 6*, 245–266.

Ehri, L. C. (1976). Do words really interfere in naming pictures? *Child Development, 47*, 502–505.

Ehri, L. C. (1992). Reconceptualizing the development of sight word reading and its relationship to recoding. In P. B. Gough, L. E. Ehri, & R. Treiman (Eds.), *Reading acquisition* (pp. 105–143). Hillsdale, NJ: Lawrence Erlbaum Associates, Inc.

Ehri, L. C. (1998). Grapheme–phoneme knowledge is essential for learning to read words in English. In J. L. Metsala, & L. Ehri (Eds.), *Word recognition in beginning literacy* (pp. 3–40). Mahwah, NJ: Lawrence Erlbaum Associates, Inc. ·

Ehri, L. C., Nunes, S. R., Stahl, S. A., & Willows, D. M. (2001b). Systematic phonics instruction helps students learn to read: Evidence from the National Reading Panel's meta-analysis. *Review of Educational Research, 71*(3), 393–447.

Ehri, L. C., Nunes, S. R., Willows, D. M., Schuster, B. V., Yaghoub-Zadeh, Z., & Shanahan, T. (2001a). Phonemic awareness instruction helps children learn to read: Evidence from the National Reading Panel's meta-analysis. *Reading Research Quarterly, 36*(3), 250–287.

Ehri, L., & Wilce, L. S. (1985). Movement into reading: Is the first stage of printed word learning visual or phonetic? *Reading Research Quarterly, 20,* 163–179.

Eilers, R. E., Gavin, W., & Wilson, W. (1979). Linguistic experience and phonetic perception in infancy: A cross-linguistic study. *Child Development 50,* 14–18.

Eimas, P. D., Siqueland, E. R., Jusczyk, P., & Vigorito, J. (1971). Speech perception in infants. *Science, 171,* 303–306.

Elbro, C. (1989). Morphological awareness in dyslexia. In C. V. Euler, I. Lundberg, & C. Lennerstrand (Eds.), *Brain and reading: Structural and functional anomalies in developmental dyslexia with special reference to interactions, memory functions, linguistic processes and visual analysis in reading* (pp. 189–209). London: Macmillan.

Elbro, C., & Arnbak, E. (1996). The role of morpheme recognition and morphological awareness in dyslexia. *Annals of Dyslexia, 46,* 209–238.

Elbro, C., Borstrom, I., & Peterson, D. K. (1998). Prediction dyslexia from kindergarten: The importance of distinctness of phonological representations of lexical items. *Reading Research Quarterly, 33,* 36–60.

Elbro, C., Nielsen, I., & Petersen, D. K. (1994). Dyslexia in adults: Evidence for deficits in non-word reading and in the phonological representation of lexical items. *Annals of Dyslexia, 44,* 205–226.

Ellis, N. C., & Hooper, A. M. (2001). Why learning to read is easier in Welsh than in English: Orthographic transparency effects evinced with frequency-matched tests. *Applied Psycholinguistics, 22,* 571–599.

Eme, E., & Golder, C. (2005). Word-reading and word-spelling styles of French beginners: Do all children learn to read and spell in the same way? *Reading and Writing: An Interdisciplinary Journal, 18*(2), 157–188.

Fadiga, L., Fogassi, L., Pavesi, G., & Rizzolatti, G. (1995). Motor facilitation during action observation: A magnetic stimulation study. *Journal of Neurophysiology, 73,* 2608–2611.

Fawcett, A. J., & Nicolson, R. I. (1994). Persistence of phonological awareness deficit in older children with dyslexia. *Reading and Writing: An Interdisciplinary Journal, 7,* 361–376.

Feldman, L. B., Rueckl, J., DiLiberto, K., Pastizzo, M., & Vellutino, F. (2002). Morphological analysis by child readers as revealed by the fragment completion task. *Psychonomic Bulletin, 9*(3), 529–535.

Ferrand, L., & Grainger, J. (1992). Phonology and orthography in visual word recognition: Evidence from masked non-word priming. *Quarterly Journal of Experimental Psycholology, 45*(A), 353–372.

Ferrand, L., & Grainger, J. (1993). The time course of orthographic and phonological code activation in the early phases of visual word recognition. *Bulletin of the Psychonomic Society, 31,* 119–122.

Ferrand, L., Segui, J., & Grainger, J. (1996). Masked priming of words and picture naming: The role of syllabic units. *Journal of Memory and Language, 35,* 708–723.

Fischer, F. W., Liberman, I. Y., & Shankweiler, D. (1977). Reading reversals and developmental dyslexia: A further study. *Cortex, 14*(4), 496–510.

Foorman, B. R., Jenkins, L., & Francis, D. J. (1993). Links between segmenting, spelling and reading words in first and second grades. *Reading and Writing: An Interdisciplinary Journal, 5,* 1–15.

Foorman, B. R., Novy, D. M., Francis, D. J., & Liberman, D. (1991). How letter-sound instruction mediates progress in first grade reading and spelling. *Journal of Educational Psychology, 83,* 456–469.

Foqué, E. (2004). *Lezen, Dyslexie en Spraakperceptie.* [Reading, dyslexia and speech perception]. Unpublished Bachelor dissertation. Eindverhandeling ingediend voor het behalen van de graad van licentiaat taal- en letterkunde: Germaanse talen – optie Gemengd. Universiteit Antwerpen, Faculteit Letteren en Wijsbegeerte.

Forster, K. I. (1981). Priming and the effects of sentence and lexical contexts on naming time: Evidence for autonomous lexical processing. *Quarterly Journal of Experimental Psychology, 33A,* 465–495.

Fowler, A. E., & Liberman, A. M. (1995). The role of phonology and orthography in morphological awareness. In L. B. Feldman (Ed.), *Morphological aspects of language processing* (pp. 157–188). Hillsdale, NJ: Lawrence Erlbaum Associates, Inc.

Fowler, C. A., Liberman, I. Y., & Shankweiler, D. (1977). On interpreting the error pattern of beginning readers. *Language and Speech, 20,* 162–173.

Fowler, C. A., Shankweiler, D., & Liberman, I. (1979). Apprehending spelling pattern for vowels: A developmental study. *Language and Speech, 22*(22), 243–251.

Fox, B., & Routh, D. K. (1984). Phonemic analysis and synthesis as word attack skills: Revisited. *Journal of Psycholinguistic Research, 4,* 331–342.

Friedrich, F. J., Walker, J. A., & Posner, M. I. (1985). Effects of parietal lesions on visual matching. *Cognitive Neuropsychology, 2,* 253–264.

Frith, U. (1985). Beneath the surface of developmental dyslexia. In K. E. Patterson, J. C. Marshall, & M. Coltheart (Eds.), *Surface dyslexia: Neuropsychological and cognitive studies of phonological reading* (pp. 301–330). Hove, UK: Lawrence Erlbaum Associates Ltd.

Frith, U. (1986). A developmental framework for developmental dyslexia. *Annals of Dyslexia, 36,* 69–81.

Frith, U., & Snowling, M. J. (1983). Reading for meaning and reading for sound in autistic and dyslexic children. *British Journal of Developmental Psychology, 1,* 329–342.

Frith, U., Wimmer, H., & Landerl, K. (1998). Differences in phonological recoding in German- and English-speaking children. *Scientific Studies of Reading, 2*(1), 31–54.

Gabor, D. (1947). Acoustical quanta and the theory of hearing, *Nature, 159,* 591–594.

Galaburda, A. M., & Livingstone, M. (1993). Evidence for a magnocellular defect in developmental dyslexia. *Annals New York Academy of Sciences, 682,* 70–82.

Gelb, I. J. (1952). *A study of writing: The foundations of grammatology.* Chicago: University of Chicago Press.

Génard, N., Mousty, P., Content, A., Alegria, J., Leybaert, J., & Morais, J. (1998). Methods to establish subtypes of developmental dyslexia. In P. Reitsma & L. Verhoeven (Eds.), *Problems and interventions in literacy development* (pp. 163–176). Dordrecht: Kluwer.

Geng, C., Mády, K., Bogliotti, C., Messaoud-Galusi, S., Medina, V., & Serniclaes, W. (2005, June). Do palatal consonants correspond to the fourth category in the perceptual F2–F3 space? *Proceedings of the ISCA Workshop on Plasticity in Speech Perception* (pp. 219–222). London.

Gernsbacher, M. A., Varner, K. R., & Faust, M. E. (1990). Investigating differences in general comprehension skills. *Journal of Experimental Psychology: Learning, Memory and Cognition, 16*, 430–445.

Geudens, A., & Sandra, D. (2003). Beyond implicit phonological knowledge: No support for an onset-rime structure in children's explicit phonological awareness. *Journal of Memory and Language, 49*(2), 157–182.

Glushko, R. J. (1979). The organization and activation of orthographic knowledge in reading aloud. *Journal of Experimental Psychology: Human Perception & Performance, 5*(4), 674–691.

Godfrey, J. J., Syrdal-Lasky, A. K., Millay K. K., & Knox, C. M. (1981). Performance of dyslexic children on speech perception tests. *Journal of Experimental Child Psychology, 32*, 401–424.

Goswami, U. (1986). Children's use of analogy in learning to read: A developmental study. *Journal of Experimental Child Psychology, 42*, 73–83.

Goswami, U. (1988). Orthographic analogies and reading development. *Quarterly Journal of Experimental Psychology, 40A*, 239–268.

Goswami, U., & Bryant, P. (1990). *Phonological skills and learning to read.* Hove, UK: Lawrence Erlbaum Associates Ltd.

Goswami, U., & East, M. (2000). Rhyme and analogy in beginning reading: Conceptual and methodological issues. *Applied Psycholinguistics, 21*, 63–93.

Goswami, U., Gombert, J. E., & Barrera, L. F. (1998). Children's orthographic representations and linguistic transparency: Nonsense word reading in English, French and Spanish. *Applied Psycholinguistics, 19*, 19–52.

Goswami, U., Porpodas, C., & Weelwright, S. (1997). Children's orthographic representations in English and Greek. *European Journal of Psychology of Education, 3*, 273–292.

Goswami, U., Thomson, J., Richardson, U., Stainthorp, R., Hughes, D., Rosen, S., et al., (2002). Amplitude envelope onsets and developmental dyslexia: A new hypothesis. *Proceedings of the National Academy of Sciences USA, 99*, 10911–10916.

Goswami, U., Ziegler, J. C., Dalton, L., & Schneider, W. (2001). Pseudohomophone effects and phonological recoding procedures in reading development in English and German. *Journal of Memory and Language, 45*, 648–664.

Goswami, U., Ziegler, J. C., Dalton, L., & Schneider, W. (2003). Nonword reading across orthographies: How flexible is the choice of reading units? *Applied Psycholinguistics, 24*, 235–247.

Gottfried, T. L. (1984). Effects of consonant context on the perception of French vowels. *Journal of Phonetics, 12*, 91–114.

Gough, P. B., & Tunmer, W. E. (1986). Decoding, reading, and reading disability. *Remedial and Special Education, 7*, 6–10.

Goulandris, N., & Snowling, M. J. (1991). Visual memory deficits: A plausible cause of developmental dyslexia? Evidence from a single case study. *Cognitive Neuropsychology, 8*, 127–154.

Grainger, J., Bouttevin, S., Truc, C., Bastien, M., & Ziegler, J. (2003). Word superiority, pseudoword superiority, and learning to read: A comparison of dyslexic and normal readers. *Brain and Language, 87*(3), 432–440.

Grainger, J., & Ferrand, I. (1996). Masked orthographic and phonological priming in visual word recognition and naming: Cross-task comparisons. *Journal of Memory and Language, 35,* 623–647.

Green, L., McCutchen, D., Schwiebert, C., Quinlan, T., Eva-Wood, A., & Juelis, J. (2003). Morphological development in children's writing. *Journal of Educational Psychology, 95*(4), 752–761.

Gross, J., Treiman, R., & Inman, J. (2000). The role of phonology in a letter decision task. *Memory and Cognition, 28*(3), 349–357.

Guenther, F. H., Husain, F. T., Cohen, M. A., & Shinn-Cunningham, B. G. (1999). Effects of categorization and discrimination training on auditory perceptual space. *Journal of the Acoustical Society of America, 106,* 2905–2912.

Guenther, F. H., Nieto-Castanon, A., Ghosh, S. S., & Tourville, J. A. (2004). Representation of sound categories in auditory cortical maps. *Journal of Speech, Language, and Hearing Research, 47,* 46–57.

Guttentag, R. E., & Haith, M. M. (1978). Automatic processing as a function of age and reading ability. *Child Development, 49,* 707–716.

Guttorm, T. K., Leppänen, P. H. T., Poikkeus, A.-M., Eklund, K. M., Lyytinen, P., & Lyytinen, H. (2005). Brain event-related potentials (ERPs) measured at birth predict later language development in children with and without familial risk for dyslexia. *Cortex, 41,* 291–303.

Guttorm, T. K., Leppänen, P. H. T., Richardson, U., & Lyytinen, H. (2001). Event-related potentials and consonant differentiation in newborns with familial risk for dyslexia. *Journal of Learning Disabilities, 34,* 534–544.

Habib, M., Rey, V., Daffaure, V., Camps, R., Espessser, R., Joly-Pottuz, B., et al., (2002). Phonological training in children with dyslexia using temporally modified speech: A three-step pilot investigation. *International Journal of Language and Communication Disorders, 37,* 289–308.

Hanley, J. R., Hastie, K., & Kay, J. (1992). Developmental surface dyslexia and dysgraphia: An orthographic processing impairment. *Quarterly Journal of Experimental Psychology, 44A,* 285–320.

Harm, M. W., & Seidenberg, M. S. (1999). Phonology, reading acquisition, and dyslexia: Insights from connectionist models. *Psychological Review, 106,* 491–528.

Harm, M. W., & Seidenberg, M. S. (2001). Are there orthographic impairments in phonological dyslexia? *Cognitive Neuropsychology, 18,* 71–92.

Harris, M., & Coltheart, M. (1986). *Language processing in children and adults: An introduction.* London: Routledge and Kegan.

Hawelka, S., & Wimmer, H. (2005). Impaired visual processing of multi-element arrays is associated with increased number of eye movements in dyslexic reading. *Vision Research, 45,* 855–863.

Hazan, V., & Barrett, S. (2000). The development of phonemic categorization in children aged 6–12. *Journal of Phonetics, 28,* 377–396.

Heim, S., Freeman, R. B. Jr, Eulitz, C., & Elbert, T. (2001). Auditory temporal processing deficit in dyslexia is associated with enhanced sensitivity in the visual modality. *Neuroreport, 12,* 507–510.

Helenius, P., Uutela, K., & Hari, R. (1999). Auditory stream segregation in dyslexic adults. *Brain, 122,* 907–913.

Hoonhorst, I., Colin, C., Deltenre, P., Radeau, M., & Serniclaes, W. (2006). Emergence of a language specific boundary in perilinguistic infants. *Early Language Development and Disorders. Latsis Colloqium of the University of Geneva, Program and Abstracts, 45.*

Hulme, C., Hatcher, P. J., Nation, K., Brown, A., Adams, J., & Stuart, G. (2002). Phoneme awareness is a better predictor of early reading skill than onset-rime awareness. *Journal of Experimental Child Psychology, 82*(1), 2–28.

Hulme, C., Muter, V. V., & Snowling, M. (1998). Segmentation does predict early progress in learning to read better than rhyme: A reply to Bryant. *Journal of Experimental Child Psychology, 71*(1), 39–44.

Hulme, C., & Snowling, M. (1992). Phonological deficits in dyslexia: A reappraisal of the verbal deficit hypothesis. In N. Singh & I. Beale (Eds.), *Current perspectives in learning disabilities* (pp. 270–331). New York: Springer-Verlag.

Hutzler, F., & Wimmer, H. (2004). Eye movements of dyslexic children when reading in a regular orthography. *Brain and Language, 89,* 235–242.

Hyönä, J., Vainio, S., & Laine, M. (2002). A morphological effect obtains for isolated words but not for words in sentence context. *European Journal of Cognitive Psychology, 14*(4), 417–433.

Inizan, A. (1995). *Analyse de la compétence en lecture (ANALEC)* [A standardized test to assess reading abilities]. Issy-les-Moulineaux: EAP.

Jared, D. (1997). Spelling-sound consistency affects the naming of high-frequency words. *Journal of Memory and Language, 36,* 687–715.

Jimenez, J. E., & Guzman, R. (2003). The influence of code-oriented versus meaning-oriented approaches to reading instruction on word recognition in the Spanish language. *International Journal of Psychology, 38*(2), 65–78.

Jimenez-Gonzalez, J. E., & Ramirez-Santana, G. (2002). Identifying subtypes of reading disability in a transparent orthography. *Spanish Journal of Psychology, 5*(1), 3–19.

Jimenez-Gonzalez, J. E., & Valle, I. H. (2000). Word identification and reading disorders in the Spanish language. *Journal of Learning Disabilities, 33*(1), 44–60.

Joanisse, M. F., Manis, F. R., Keating, P., & Seidenberg, M. S. (2000). Language deficits in dyslexic children: Speech perception, phonology, and morphology. *Journal of Experimental Child Psychology, 77,* 30–60.

Jobard, G., Crivello, F., & Tzourio-Mazoyer, N. (2003). Evaluation of the dual route theory of reading: A metanalysis of 35 neuroimaging studies. *NeuroImage, 20,* 693–712.

Joos, M. (1948). Acoustic Phonetics. *Language, 24,* 1–136.

Jorm, A. F., Share, D. L., MacLean, R., & Matthews, R.G. (1984). Phonological recoding skill and learning to read: A longitudinal study. *Applied Psycholinguistics, 5,* 201–207.

Judica, A., De Luca, M., Spinelli, D., & Zoccolotti, P. (2002). Training of developmental surface dyslexia improves reading performance and shortens eye fixation during reading. *Neuropsychological Rehabilitation, 12*(3), 177–197.

Juel, C. (1988). Learning to read and write: A longitudinal study of 54 children from first through fourth grade. *Journal of Educational Psychology, 80*(4), 437–447.

Juel, C., Griffith, P. L., & Gough, P. B. (1986). Acquisition of literacy: A longitudinal study of children in first and second grade. *Journal of Educational Psychology, 78*(4), 243–255.

Kipffer-Piquard, A. (2003). *Etude longitudinale prédictive de la réussite et de l'échec spécifiques à l'apprentissage de la lecture (suivi de 85 enfants de 4 à 8 ans)*. [Prediction of reading skills: Longitudinal data from 4 to 8 years of age]. Unpublished doctoral dissertation, Université Denis Diderot, Paris.

Kirby, J. R., Parrila, R. K., & Pfeiffer, S. L. (2003). Naming speed and phonological awareness as predictors of reading development. *Journal of Educational Psychology, 95*, 453–464.

Klicpera, C., & Klicpera, B. G. (2001). Does intelligence make a difference? Spelling and phonological abilities in discrepant and non-discrepant reading and spelling disabilities. *Zeitschrift Fur Kinder Und Jugendpsychiatrie Und Psychotherapie, 29*(1), 37–49.

Kronbichler, M., Hutzler, F., & Wimmer, H. (2002). Dyslexia: Verbal impairments in the absence of magnocellular impairments. *Neuroreport, 13*(5), 617–620.

Kucera, H., & Francis, W. (1967). *Computational analysis of present-day American-English*. Providence, RI: Brown University Press.

Kutas, M., & Hilyard, S. A. (1984). Brain potentials during reading reflect word expectancy and semantic association. *Nature, 307*, 161–163.

Laberge, D., & Samuels, S. J. (1974). Toward a theory of automatic information processing in reading. *Cognitive Psychology, 6*, 293–323.

Laing, E., & Hulme, C. (1999). Phonological and semantic processes influence beginning readers' ability to learn to read words. *Journal of Experimental Child Psychology, 73*, 183–207.

Lalain, M., Nguyen, N., & Habib, M. (2002). Particularités articulatoires associées à la dyslexie développementale phonologique: Une évaluation perceptive [Articulatory specificities associated with developmental dyslexia: A perceptual evaluation]. *Proceedings of the 24th Journées d'Etudes sur la Parole* (JEP, pp. 249–252). Le Chesnay, France: INRIA, 193–197.

Landerl, K., & Wimmer, H. (2000). Deficits in phoneme segmentation are not the core problem of dyslexia: Evidence from German and English children. *Applied Psycholinguistics, 21*, 243–262.

Landerl, K., Wimmer, H., & Frith, U. (1997). The impact of orthography consistency on dyslexia: A German–English comparison. *Cognition, 63*, 315–334.

Lasky, R. E., Syrdal-Lasky, A., & Klein, R. E. (1975). VOT discrimination by four to six and a half months old infants from Spanish environments. *Journal of Experimental Child Psychology, 20*, 215–225.

Laxon, V., Rickard, M., & Coltheart, V. (1992). Children read affixed words and non-words. *British Journal of Psychology, 83*, 407–423.

Lecocq, P. (1991). *Apprentissage de la lecture et dyslexie* [Reading acquisition and dyslexia]. Bruxelles: Mardaga.

Lecocq, P. (1996). *E.C.O.S.S.E: Une épreuve de compréhension syntaxico-sémantique* [E.C.O.S.S.E: A standardized test to assess syntactic and semantic abilities]. Lille: Presse du Septentrion.

Lecocq, P., Casalis, S., Leuwers, C., & Watteau, N. (1996). *Apprentissage de la lecture et compréhension d'énoncés* [Reading acquisition and sentence comprehension]. Lille: Presse du Septentrion.

Lefavrais, P. (1967). *Test de l'Alouette: Manuel* [Alouette: A standardized reading test]. Paris: Les Editions du Centre de Psychologie Appliquée.

Lefly, D. L., & Pennington, B. F. (1991). Spelling errors and reading fluency in compensated adult dyslexics. *Annals of Dyslexia, 41*, 143–162.

Legge, G. E., Pelli, D. G., Rubin, G. S., & Schleske, M. M. (1985). Psychophysics of reading: Normal vision. *Vision Research, 25*, 239–252.

Leloup, G. (2001). *Habiletés de perception catégorielle des adultes dyslexiques* [Categorical perception in adult adyslexics]. Unpublished Master's dissertation, Université Denis Diderot, Paris, France.

Lennox, C., & Siegel, L. S. (1993). Visual and phonological spelling errors in subtypes of children with learning disabilities. *Applied Psycholinguistics, 14*, 473–488.

Lété, B., Sprenger-Charolles, L., & Colé, P. (2004). MANULEX: A lexical database from French readers. *Behavioral Research Methods, Instruments and Computers, 36*(1), 156–166.

Leybaert, J., & Content, A. (1995). Reading and spelling acquisition in two different teaching methods: A test of the independence hypothesis. *Reading and Writing: An Interdisciplinary Journal, 7*, 65–88.

Liberman, A. M., Cooper, F. S., Shankweiler, D., & Studdert-Kennedy, M. (1967). Perception of speech code. *Psychological Review, 74*, 431–461.

Liberman, A. M., Harris, K. S., Hoffman, H. S., & Griffith, B. C. (1957). The discrimination of speech sounds within and across phoneme boundaries. *Journal of Experimental Psychology, 54*, 358–368.

Liberman, A. M., & Mattingly, I. G. (1985). The motor theory of speech perception. *Cognition, 21*, 1–36.

Liberman, I. Y., Mann, V. A., & Werfelman, M. (1982). Children's memory for recurring linguistic and non-linguistic material in relation to reading ability, *Cortex, 18*, 367–375.

Liberman, I. Y., Shankweiler, D., Fisher, W. F., & Carter, B. (1974). Explicit syllable and phoneme segmentation in the young child. *Journal of Experimental Child Psychology, 18*, 201–212.

Licht, R., Bakker, D. J., Kok, A., & Bouma, A. (1992). Grade-related changes in event-related-potentials (ERPs) in primary school children: Differences between two reading tasks. *Journal of Clinical and Experimental Neuropsychology, 14*, 193–210.

Lindgren, S. D., De Renzi, E., & Richman, L. C. (1985). Cross-national comparisons of developmental dyslexia in Italy and the United States. *Child Development, 56*, 1404–1417.

Lisker, L., & Abramson, A.S. (1964). A cross-language study of voicing in initial stops: Acoustical measurements. *Word, 20*, 384–422.

Livingstone, M. S., Rosen, G. D., Drislane, F. W., & Galaburda, A. M. (1991). Physiological and anatomical evidence for a magnocellular defect in developmental dyslexia. *Proceedings of the National Academy of Sciences USA, 88*, 7943–7947.

Longtin, C. M., Segui, J., & Hallé, P. (2003). Morphological priming without morphological relationship. *Language and Cognitive Processes, 18*(3), 313–334.

Lorenzi, C., Dumont, A., & Füllgrabe, C. (2000). Use of temporal envelope cues by children with developmental dyslexia. *Journal of Speech Language and Hearing Research, 43*(6), 1367–1379.

Lovegrove, W. J., Bowling, A., Badcock, B., & Blackwood, M. (1980). Specific reading disability: Differences in contrast sensitivity as a function of spatial frequency. *Science, 210*(4468), 439–440.

Lundberg, I., Frost, J., & Peterson, O. (1988). Effects of an extensive program for stimulating phonological awareness in preschool children. *Reading Research Quarterly, 23,* 263–283.

Lundberg, I., & Hoien, T. (1989). Phonemic deficits: A core symptom of developmental dyslexia. *Irish Journal of Psychology, 10*(4), 579–592.

Lyytinen, H., Guttorm, T. K., Huttunen, T., Hämäläinen, J., Leppänen, P. H. T., & Vesterinen, M. (2005). Psychophysiology of developmental dyslexia: A review of findings including studies of children at risk for dyslexia. *Journal of Neurolinguistics, 18,* 167–195.

Lyytinen, H., Leinonen, S., Nikula, M., Aro, M., & Leiwo, M. (1995). In search of the core features of dyslexia: Observations concerning dyslexia in the highly orthographically regular Finnish language. In V. Berninger (Ed.), *The varieties of orthographic knowledge II: Relationships to phonology, reading, and writing* (pp. 177–204). Dordrecht: Kluwer.

Maassen, B., Groenen, P., Crul, T., Assman-Hulsmans, C., & Gabreëls, F. (2001). Identification and discrimination of voicing and place-of-articulation in developmental dyslexia. *Clinical Linguistics and Phonetics, 15,* 319–339.

Mahony, D., Singson, M., & Mann, V. (2000). Reading ability and sensitivity to morphological relations. *Reading and Writing: An Interdisciplinary Journal, 12*(3–4), 191–218.

Manis, F. R., Custodio, R., & Szeszulski, P.A. (1993). Development of phonologic and orthographic skills: A 2-year longitudinal study of dyslexic children. *Journal of Experimental Child Psychology, 56,* 64–86.

Manis, F. R., & Keating, P. (2004). Speech perception in dyslexic children with and without language impairments. In H. W. Catts & A. G. Kamhi (Eds.), *The connections between language and reading disabilities.* (pp. 77–99). Mahwah, NJ: Lawrence Erlbaum Associates, Inc.

Manis, F. R., McBride-Chang, C., Seidenberg, M. S., Keating, P., Doi, L. M., Munson, B., et al. (1997). Are speech perception deficits associated with developmental dyslexia? *Journal of Experimental Child Psychology, 66,* 211–235.

Manis, F. R., Seidenberg, M. S., Doi, L. M., McBride-Chang, C., & Peterson, A. (1996). On the basis of two subtypes of developmental dyslexia. *Cognition, 58,* 157–195.

Manis, F. R., Szeszulsli, P. A., Holt, L. K., & Graves, K. (1990). Variation in component word recognition and spelling skills among dyslexic children and normal readers. In T. H. Carr & B. A. Levy (Eds.), *Reading and its development: Component skills approaches* (pp. 207–259). New York: Academic Press.

Mann, V. A. (1986). Phonological awareness: The role of reading experience. *Cognition, 24,* 65–92.

Mann, V. A., & Liberman, I. Y. (1984). Phonological awareness and verbal short term memory: Can they presage early reading problems? *Journal of Learning Disabilities, 17,* 592–599.

Mann, V. A., & Singson, M. (2003). Linking morphological knowledge to English decoding ability: Large effects of little suffixes. In E. M. H. Assink & D. Sandra (Eds.), *Reading complex words: Cross-language studies* (pp. 1–24). New York: Kluwer.

Mann, V., & Wimmer, H. (2002). Phoneme awareness and pathways into literacy: A comparison of German and American children. *Reading and Writing: An Interdisciplinary Journal, 15*, 653–682.

Marec-Breton, N., Gombert, J.-E., & Colé, P. (2005). Traitements morphologiques lors de la reconnaissance des mots écrits chez des apprenti-lecteurs [Morphological processing in written-word recognition: Data from beginning readers]. *L'Année Psychologique, 105*, 9–45.

Marmurek, H. H. C., & Rinaldo, R. (1992). The development of letter and syllable effects in categorisation, reading aloud and picture naming. *Journal of Experimental Child Psychology, 53*, 277–299.

Marsh, G., Friedman, M., Welch, V., & Desberg, P. (1981). A cognitive developmental theory of reading acquisition. In G. E. MacKinnon & T. G. Waller (Eds.), *Reading research: Advances in theory and practice* (Vol. 3, pp. 199–231). Hillsdale, NJ: Lawrence Erlbaum Associates Inc.

Marshall, C. M., Snowling, M. J., & Bailey, P. J. (2001). Rapid auditory processing and phonological ability in normal readers and readers with dyslexia. *Journal of Speech Language and Hearing Research, 44*, 925–940.

Marshall, J. C., & Cossu, G. (1991). Poor readers and black swan. *Mind and Language, 6*, 135–138.

Martensen, H., Maris, E., & Dijkstra, T. (2003). Phonological ambiguity and context sensitivity: On sublexical clustering in visual word recognition. *Journal of Memory and Language, 89*, 375–395.

Martin, F., & Lovegrove, W. J. (1987). Flicker contrast sensitivity in normal and specifically disabled readers. *Perception, 16*(2), 215–221.

Masonheimer, P. E., Drum, P. A., & Ehri, L. C. (1984). Does environmental print identification lead children into word reading? *Journal of Reading Behavior, 16*, 257–271.

Maurer, U., Bucher, K., Brem, S., & Brandeis, D. (2003). Development of the automatic mismatch response: From frontal positivity in kindergarten children to the mismatch negativity. *Clinical Neurophysiology, 114*, 808–817.

McAnally, K. I., Hansen, P. C., Cornelissen, P. L., & Stein, J. F. (1997). Effect of time and frequency manipulation on syllable perception in developmental dyslexics. *Journal of Speech Language and Hearing Research, 40*, 912–924.

McAnally, K. I., & Stein, J. F. (1996). Auditory temporal coding in dyslexia. *Proceedings of the Royal Society London, B, Biological Sciences, 263*(1373), 961–965.

McCandliss, B. D., Cohen, L., & Dehaene, S. (2003). The visual word form area: Expertise for reading in the fusiform gyrus. *Trends in Cognitive Sciences, 7*, 293–299.

McCandliss, B. D., & Noble, K. G. (2003). The development of reading impairment: A cognitive neuroscience model. *Mental Retardation and Developmental Disabilities Research Reviews, 9*, 196–205.

McCarthy, G., Nobre, A. C., Bentin, S., & Spencer, D. D. (1995). Language-related field potentials in the anterior medial temporal lobe: I. Intracranial distribution and neural generators. *Journal of Neuroscience, 15*, 1080–1089.

McCrory, E., Frith, U., Brunswick, N., & Price, C. (2000). Abnormal functional activation during a simple word repetition task: A PET study of adult dyslexics. *Journal of Cognitive Neurosciences, 12*, 753–762.

McDougall, P., Borowsky, R., MacKinnon, G. E., & Hymel, S. (2004). Process dissociation of sight vocabulary and phonetic decoding in reading: A new perspective on surface and phonological dyslexias. *Brain and Language, 92*, 185–203.

McDougall, S., Hulme, C., Ellis, A., & Monk, A. (1994). Learning to read: The role of short term memory and phonological skills. *Journal of Experimental Child Psychology, 58*, 112–133.

Medina, V., Geron, M.-P., & Serniclaes, W. (2006). Late development of the categorical perception of speech sounds in pre-adolescent children. *Early Language Development and Disorders, Latsis Colloqium of the University of Geneva, Program and Abstracts, 31*.

Mehler, J., Dommergues, J. Y., Frauenfelder, U., & Segui, J. (1981). The syllable's role in speech segmentation. *Journal of Verbal Learning and Verbal Behavior, 20*, 298–305.

Messaoud-Galusi, S., Carré, R., Bogliotti, C., & Serniclaes, W. (2002). Origine du déficit de perception catégorielle des dyslexiques [Origin of the categorical perception deficit in dyslexics]. *Proceeding of the 14th Journées d'Etudes sur la Parole* (JEP, pp. 193–196). Le Chesnay, France: INRIA, 193–197.

Metsala, J. L., Stanovich, K. E., & Brown, G. D. A. (1998). Regularity effects and the phonological deficit model of reading disabilities: A meta-analytic review. *Journal of Educational Psychology, 90*(2), 279–293.

Milne, R. D., Nicholson, T., & Corballis, M. C. (2003). Lexical access and phonological decoding in adult dyslexic subtypes. *Neuropsychology, 17*(3), 362–368.

Milner, A. D., & Goodale, M. A. (1995). *The visual brain in action*. Oxford: Oxford University Press.

Mody, M., Studdert-Kennedy, M., & Brady, S. (1997). Speech perception deficits in poor readers: Auditory processing or phonological coding? *Journal of Experimental Child Psychology, 64*, 199–231.

Molfese, D. L. (2000). Predicting dyslexia at 8 years of age using neonatal brain responses. *Brain and Language, 72*, 238–245.

Morais, J., Bertelson, P., Cary, L., & Alegria, J. (1986). Literacy training and speech segmentation. *Cognition, 24*, 45–64.

Morais, J., Cary, L., Alegria, J., & Bertelson, P. (1979). Does awareness of speech as a sequence of phones arise spontaneously? *Cognition, 7*, 323–333.

Morton, J. (1989). An information-processing account of reading acquisition. In A. M. Galaburda (Ed.), *From reading to neurons* (pp. 43–66). Cambridge, MA: MIT Press.

Muneaux, M., Ziegler, J. C., Truc, C., Thomson, J., & Goswami, U. (2004). Deficits in beat perception and dyslexia: Evidence from French. *Neuroreport, 15*, 1–5.

Murphy, L., & Pollatsek, A. (1994). Developmental dyslexia: Heterogeneity without discrete subgroups. *Annals of Dyslexia, 44*, 120–146.

Muter, V., Hulme, C., Snowling, M. J., & Stevenson, J. (2004). Phonemes, rimes, vocabulary, and grammatical skills as foundations of early reading development: Evidence from a longitudinal study. *Developmental Psychology, 40*(5), 665–681.

Muter, V., Hulme, C., Snowling, M., & Taylor, S. (1998). Segmentation, not rhyming, predicts early progress in learning to read. *Journal of Experimental Child Psychology, 71*(1), 3–27.

Nagy, W., Berninger, V., Abbott, R., Vaughan, K., & Vermeulen, K. (2003). Relationship of morphology and other language skills to literacy skills in at-risk second-grade readers and at-risk fourth-grade writers. *Journal of Educational Psychology*, *95*(4), 730–742.

Nation, K., & Hulme, C. (1997). Phonemic segmentation, not onset-rime segmentation, predicts early reading and spelling skills. *Reading Research Quarterly*, *32*, 154–167.

Newsome, W. T., Britten K. H., & Movshon, J. A. (1989). Neuronal correlates of a perceptual decision. *Nature*, *341*, 52–54.

Nicolson, R. I., & Fawcett, A. J. (1990). Automaticity: A new framework for dyslexia research? *Cognition*, *35*, 159–182.

Nicolson, R. I., Fawcett, A. J., Berry, E. L., Jenkins, I. H., Dean, P., & Brooks, D. J. (1999). Association of abnormal cerebellar activation with motor learning difficulties in dyslexic adults. *Lancet*, *353*(9165), 1662–1667.

Nicolson, R. I., Fawcett, A. J., & Dean, P. (2001). Dyslexia, development and the cerebellum. *Trends in Neuroscience*, *24*, 515–516.

Nittrouer, S. (1999). Do temporal processing deficits cause phonological processing problems? *Journal of Speech, Language, and Hearing Research*, *42*(4), 925–942.

Nunes, T., Bryant, P. E., & Bindman, M. (1997). Spelling and grammar. The necsed move. In C. A. Perfetti, L. Rieben, & M. Fayol (Eds.), *Learning to spell: Research, theory, and practice across languages* (pp. 151–170). Mahwah, NJ: Lawrence Erlbaum Associates, Inc.

Olson, R. K., Forsberg, H., Wise, B., & Rack, J. (1994). Measurement of word recognition, orthographic and phonological skills. In G. R. Lyon (Ed.), *Frames of reference for the assessment of learning disabilities: New views on measurement issues* (pp. 243–275). Baltimore: Paul H. Brookes.

Olson, R. K., Kliegl, R., Davidson, B., & Foltz, G. (1985). Individual and developmental differences in reading disability. In G. E. Mackinnon & T. G. Waller (Eds.), *Reading research: Advances in theory and practice* (Vol. 4, pp. 1–64). San Diego: Academic Press.

Olson, R. K., Wise, B. W., Ring, J., & Johnson, M. (1997). Computer-based remedial training in phoneme awareness and phonological decoding: Effects on the post-training development on word recognition. *Scientific Studies of Reading*, *1*, 235–253.

O'Regan, J. K., & Jacobs, A. M. (1992). Optimal viewing position effect in word recognition: A challenge to current theory. *Journal of Experimental Psychology: Human Perception & Performance*, *18*, 185–197.

Pacton, S., & Fayol, M. (2000). The impact of phonological cues on children's judgements of nonwords: The case of double letters. *Current Psychology Letters: Behaviour, Brain and Cognition*, *1*, 39–54.

Pacton, S., Perruchet, P., Fayol, M., & Cleeremans, A. (2001). Implicit learning out of the lab: The case of orthographic regularities. *Journal of Experimental Psychology General*, *130*(3), 401–426.

Parrila, R., Kirby, J. R., & McQuarrie, L. (2004). Articulation rate, naming speed, verbal short-term memory and phonological awareness: Longitudinal predictors of early reading development? *Scientific Study of Reading*, *8*(1), 3–26.

Pate, T. K., Snowling, M. J., & De Jonc, P. F. (2004). A cross-linguistic comparison of children learning to read in English and Dutch. *Journal of Educational Psychology* *96*(4), 785–779.

Paulesu, E., Démonet, J.-F., Fazio, F., McCrory, E., Chanoine, V., Brunswick, N., et al. (2001). Dyslexia, cultural diversity and biological unity. *Science, 291*, 2165–2167.

Peereman, R., & Content, A. (1998). *Quantitative analysis of orthography to phonology mapping in English and French (on-line)*. http://homepages.vub.ac.be/~acontent/OPMapping.html

Peereman, R., & Content, A. (1999). LEXOP: A lexical database providing orthography-phonology statistics for French monosyllabic words. *Behavioral Methods, Instruments and Computers, 31*, 376–379.

Pelli, D., Burns, C. W., Farell, B., & Moore, D. C. (accepted). Identifying letters. *Vision Research*.

Pelli, D., Farell, B., & Moore, D. C. (2003). The remarkable inefficiency of word recognition. *Nature, 423*, 752–756.

Pennington, B. F., Cardoso-Martins, C., Green, P., & Lefly, D. L. (2001). Comparing the phonological and double deficit hypothesis for developmental dyslexia. *Reading and Writing: An Interdisciplinary Journal, 14*(7–8), 707–755.

Perea, M., & Gotor, A. (1997). Associative and semantic priming effects occur at very short stimulus-onset asynchronies in lexical decision and naming. *Cognition, 62*, 223–240.

Perfetti, C. A. (1985). *Reading ability*. New York: Oxford University Press.

Perfetti, C. A. (1994). Psycholinguistics and reading ability. In M. A. Gernsbacher (Ed.), *Handbook of psycholinguistics* (pp. 849–916). San Diego: Academic Press.

Perfetti, C. A., Beck, I., Bell, L., & Hughes, C. (1987). Phonemic knowledge and learning to read are reciprocal: A longitudinal study of first grade children. *Merrill-Palmer Quarterly, 33*, 283–319.

Perfetti, C. A., Goldman, S. R., & Hogaboam, T. W. (1979). Reading skill and the identification of words in discourse context. *Memory and Cognition, 7*(4), 273–282.

Perfetti, C. A., & Zhang, S. (1995). The universal word identification reflex. In D. L. Medin (Ed.), *The psychology of learning and motivation* (Vol. 33, pp. 159–189). San Diego: Academic Press.

Plaut, D. C., & Booth J. R. (2000). Individual and developmental differences in semantic priming: Empirical and computational support for a single mechanism account of lexical processing. *Psychological Review, 107*, 786–823.

Plaut, D. C., McClelland, J. L., Seidenberg, M. S., & Patterson, K. E. (1996). Understanding normal and impaired word reading: Computational principles in quasi-regular domain. *Psychological Review, 103*, 56–115.

Pollack, I., & Pisoni, D. (1971). On the comparison between identification and discrimination tests in speech perception. *Psychonomic Science, 24*, 299–300.

Posner, M. I., & McCandliss, B. D. (1999). Brain circuitry during reading. In R. M. Klein & P. A. McMullen (Eds.), *Converging methods for understanding reading and dyslexia* (pp. 305–337). Cambridge, MA: MIT Press.

Pring, L. (1981). Phonological codes and functional spelling units: Reality and implications. *Perception and Psychophysics, 30*, 573–578.

Pugh, K. R., Mencl, W. E., Jenner, A. R., Katz, L., Frost, S. J., Lee, J. R., et al. (2000). Functional neuroimaging studies of reading and reading disability (developmental dyslexia). *Mental Retardation and Development Disabilities Research Reviews*, 6(3), 207–213.

Rack, J., Hulme, C., Snowling, M. J., & Wightman, J. (1994). The role of phonology in young children learning to read words: The direct mapping hypothesis, *Journal of Experimental Child Psychology*, 57, 42–71.

Rack, J., Snowling, M. J., & Olson, R. K. (1992). The nonword reading deficit in developmental dyslexia: A review. *Reading Research Quarterly*, 27, 29–53.

Raduege, T. A., & Schwantes, F. M. (1987). Effects of rapid word recognition training on sentence context effects in children. *Journal of Reading Behavior*, 19(4), 395–414.

Ramus, F. (2001). Talk of two theories. *Nature*, 412, 393–395.

Ramus, F. (2003). Developmental dyslexia: Specific phonological deficit or general sensorimotor dysfunction? *Current Opinion in Neurobiology*, 13, 212–218.

Ramus, F., Pidgeon, E., & Frith, U. (2003a). The relationship between motor control and phonology in dyslexic children. *Journal of Child Psychology and Psychiatry*, 44, 712–722.

Ramus, F., Rosen, S., Dakin, S. C., Day, B. L., Castellote, J. M., White, S., & Frith, U. (2003b). Theories of developmental dyslexia: Insights from a multiple case study of dyslexic adults. *Brain*, 126, 841–865.

Rastle, K., Harrington, J., Coltheart, M., & Palethorpe, S. (2000). Reading aloud begins when the computation of phonology is complete. *Journal of Experimental Psychology Human Perception and Performance*, 26(3), 1178–1191.

Rayner, K. (1998). Eye movements in reading and information processing: 20 years of research. *Psychological Bulletin*, 124(3), 372–422.

Reed, M.A. (1989). Speech perception and the discrimination of brief auditory cues in dyslexic children. *Journal of Experimental Child Psychology*, 48, 270–292.

Rey, A., Jacobs, A. M., Schmidt-Weigand, F., & Ziegler, J. C. (1998). A phoneme effect in visual word recognition. *Cognition*, 68, B71-B80.

Rizzolatti, G., Fadiga, L., Gallese, V., & Fogassi, L. (1996). Premotor cortex and the recognition of motor actions. *Cognitive Brain Research*, 3, 131–141.

Roach, N. W., Edwards, V. T., & Hogben, J. H. (2004). The tale is in the tail: An alternative hypothesis for psychophysical performance variability in dyslexia. *Perception*, 33, 817–830.

Rocheron, I., Lorenzi, C., Füllgrabe, C., & Dumont, A. (2002). Temporal envelope perception in dyslexic children. *Auditory and Vestibular Systems*, 13, 1–4.

Rosen, S. (2003). Auditory processing in dyslexia and specific language impairment: Is there a deficit? What is its nature? Does it explain anything? *Journal of Phonetics*, 31, 509–527.

Rosen, S., & Manganari, E. (2001). Is there a relationship between speech and non-speech auditory processing in children with dyslexia? *Journal of Speech Language and Hearing Research*, 44(4), 720–736.

Ruff, S., Cardebat, D., Marie, N., & Démonet, J.-F. (2002). Enhanced response of the left frontal cortex to slowed down speech in dyslexia: An fMRI study. *Neuroreport*, 13(10), 1285–1289.

Savigny, M. (1974). *Bat-Elem* [BATELEM: A standardized reading test]. Issy-les-Moulineaux: Editions de Psychologie Appliquée.

Schatschneider, C., Carlson C. D., Francis, D. J., Foorman, B. R., & Fletcher, J. M.

(2002). Relationship of rapid automatized naming and phonological awareness in early reading development: Implications for the double-deficit hypothesis. *Journal of Learning Disabilities, 35*(3), 245–256.

Schatschneider, C., Fletcher, J. M., Francis, D. J., Carlson C. D., & Foorman, B. R. (2004). Kindergarten prediction of reading skills: A longitudinal comparative analysis. *Journal of Educational Psychology, 96*, 265–282.

Schneider, W., Kuespert, P., Roth, E., & Vise, M. (1997). Short- and long-term effects of training phonological awareness in kindergarten: Evidence from two German studies. *Journal of Experimental Child Psychology, 66*, 311–340.

Schulte-Körne, G., Deimel, W., Bartling, J., & Remschmidt, H. (1998). Auditory processing and dyslexia: Evidence for a specific speech processing deficit. *Neuroreport, 9*(2), 337–340.

Seidenberg, M. S., & McClelland, J. L. (1989). A distributed developmental model of word recognition and naming. *Psychological Review, 96*, 523–568.

Serniclaes, W. (1987). *Etude expérimentale de la perception du trait de voisement des occlusives du français* [Experimental study of the perception of the voicing feature in French stop consonants]. Unpublished doctoral dissertation, Université Libre de Bruxelles. http://www.vjf.cnrs.fr/umr8606/DocHtml/PAGEPERSO/WSerniclaes.htm

Serniclaes, W. (2000). La perception de la parole [Speech perception]. In P. Escudier, G. Feng, P. Perrier, & J.-L. Schwartz (Eds.), *La parole, des modèles cognitifs aux machines communicantes* [Speech, from cognitive models to communicating engines] (pp. 159–190). Paris: Hermès.

Serniclaes, W. (2006). Allophonic perception in developmental dyslexia: Origin, reliability and implications of the categorical perception deficit. *Written Language & Literacy, 9* (1), 135–152.

Serniclaes, W., Bogliotti, C., & Carré, R. (2003). Perception of consonant place of articulation: Phonological categories meet natural boundaries. In M. J. Solé, D. Recaesens, & J. Romero (Eds.), *Proceeding of the 15th International Congress on Phonetic Sciences*, 391–394.

Serniclaes, W., Bogliotti, C., Messaoud-Galusi, S., & Sprenger-Charolles, L. (submitted). Categorical perception and dyslexia: A meta-analysis.

Serniclaes, W., Sprenger-Charolles, L., Carré, R., & Démonet, J.-F. (2001). Perceptual discrimination of speech sounds in dyslexics. *Journal of Speech Language and Hearing Research, 44*, 384–399.

Serniclaes, W., Van Heghe, S., Mousty, Ph., Carré, R., & Sprenger-Charolles, L. (2004). Allophonic mode of speech perception in dyslexia. *Journal of Experimental Child Psychology, 87*, 336–361.

Serniclaes, W., Ventura, P., Morais, J., & Kolinsky, R. (2005). Categorical perception of speech sounds in illiterate adults. *Cognition, 98*, B35–44.

Seymour, P. H. K. (1986). *A cognitive analysis of dyslexia*. London: Routledge and Kegan Paul.

Seymour, P. H. K. (1997). Foundations of orthographic development. In C. A. Perfetti, L. Rieben, & M. Fayol (Eds.), *Learning to Spell: Research, theory, and practice across languages* (pp. 319–337). Mahwah, NJ: Lawrence Erlbaum Associates, Inc.

Seymour, P. H. K., Aro, M., & Erskine, J. M. (2003). Foundation literacy acquisition in European orthographies. *British Journal of Psychology, 94*, 143–174.

Seymour, P. H. K., & Porpodas, C. D. (1980). Lexical and non-lexical processing of spelling in dyslexia. In U. Frith (Ed.), *Cognitive processes in spelling* (pp. 443–473). London: Academic Press.

Shankweiler, D. P., Crain, S., Katz, L., Fowler, A., Liberman, A., Brady, S., et al. (1995). Cognitive profiles of reading disabled children: Comparison of language skills in phonology, morphology and syntax. *Psychological Science, 6*, 149–156.

Share D. L. (1995). Phonological recoding and self-teaching: Sine qua non of reading acquisition. *Cognition, 55*, 151–218.

Share, D. L. (1999). Phonological recoding and orthographic learning: A direct test of the self-teaching hypothesis. *Journal of Experimental Child Psychology, 72*, 95–129.

Share, D. L., Jorm, A. F., MacLean, R., & Matthews, R. (1984). Sources of individual differences in reading acquisition. *Journal of Educational Psychology, 76*, 1309–1324.

Share, D. L., Jorm, A. F., MacLean, R., & Matthews, R. (2002). Temporal processing and reading disability. *Reading and Writing: An Interdisciplinary Journal, 15*, 151–178.

Shaywitz, S. E., Escobar, M. D., Shaywitz, B. A., Fletcher, J. M., & Makuch, R. (1992). Evidence that dyslexia may represent the lower tail of a normal distribution of reading ability. *New England Journal of Medicine, 326*(3), 145–150.

Shaywitz, S. E., Fletcher, J. M., Holahan, J. M., Shneider, A. E., Marchione, K. E., Stuebing, K. K., et al. (1999). Persistence of dyslexia: The Connecticut Longitudinal Study at Adolescence. *Pediatrics, 104*(6), 1351–1359.

Shaywitz, S. E., Fletcher, J. M., & Shaywitz, B. A. (1994). Issues in the definition and classification of attention deficit disorder. *Topic in Language Disorders, 14*, 1–25.

Shaywitz, S. E., & Shaywitz, B. A. (2005). Dyslexia (specific reading disability). *Biological Psychiatry, 57*, 1301–1309.

Siegel, L. S. (1992). An evaluation of the discrepancy definition of dyslexia. *Journal of Learning Disabilities, 25*(10), 618–629.

Siegel, L. S., & Faux, D. (1989). Acquisition of certain grapheme–phoneme correspondences in normally achieving and disabled readers. *Reading and Writing: An Interdisciplinary Journal, 1*, 37–52.

Siegel, L. S., & Ryan, E. B. (1988). Development of grammatical sensitivity, phonological, and short-term memory skills in normally achieving and learning disabled children. *Developmental Psychology, 24*, 28–37.

Simon, C., & Fourcin, A. J. (1978). Cross-language study of speech-pattern learning. *Journal of the Acoustical Society of America, 63*, 925–935.

Singson, M., Mahony, D., & Mann, V. (2000). The relation between reading ability and morphological skills: Evidence from derivational suffixes. *Reading and Writing: An Interdisciplinary Journal, 12*(3–4), 219–252.

Skottun, B. C. (2000). The magnocellular deficit theory of dyslexia: The evidence from contrast sensitivity. *Vision Research, 40*, 111–127.

Slaghuis, W., & Davidson, J. (1993). Visual and language processing deficits are concurrent in dyslexia. *Cortex, 29*, 601–615.

Slaghuis, W., & Lovegrove, W. J. (1985). Spatial-frequency mediated visible persistence and specific reading disability. *Brain and Cognition, 4*, 219–246.

Slaghuis, W. L., & Ryan, J. F. (1999). Spatio-temporal contrast sensitivity, coherent motion, and visible persistence in developmental dyslexia. *Vision Research*, *39*(3), 651–668.

Slaghuis, W. L., Twell, A., & Kingston, K. (1996). Visual and language processing deficits are concurrent in dyslexia and continue into adulthood. *Cortex*, *32*, 413–438.

Snowling, M. J. (1981). Phonemics deficits in developmental dyslexia. *Psychological Research*, *43*, 219–234.

Snowling, M. J. (2000). *Dyslexia*. Oxford: Blackwell.

Snowling, M. J., Bryant, P., & Hulme, C. (1996a). Theoretical and methodological pitfalls in making comparisons between developmental and acquired dyslexia: Some comments on A. Castles and M. Coltheart (1993). *Reading and Writing: An Interdisciplinary Journal*, *8*, 443–451.

Snowling, M., Goulandris, N., Bowlby, M., & Howel, P. (1986b). Segmentation and speech processing in relation to reading skills: A developmental analysis. *Journal of Experimental Child Psychology*, *41*(3), 489–507.

Snowling, M. J., Goulandris, N., & Defty, N. (1996b). A longitudinal study of reading development in dyslexic children. *Journal of Educational Psychology*, *88*, 653–669.

Snowling, M. J., Hulme, C., Smith A., & Thomas, J. (1994). Effect of phonetic similarity and word length on children's sound categorization performance. *Journal of Experimental Child Psychology*, *57*, 42–71.

Snowling, M. J., Nation, K., Moxham, P., Gallagher, A., & Frith, U. (1997). Phonological processing skills of dyslexic students in higher education: A preliminary report. *Journal of Research in Reading*, *20*(1), 31–41.

Snowling, M. J., Stackhouse, J., & Rack, J. (1986a). Phonological dyslexia and dysgraphia: A developmental analysis. *Cognitive Neuropsychology*, *3*(3), 309–339.

Solomon, J. A., & Pelli, D. (1994). The visual filter mediating letter identification. *Nature*, *369*, 395–397.

Spencer, L. H., & Hanley, J. R. (2003). Effects of orthographic transparency on reading and phoneme awareness in children learning to read in Wales. *British Journal of Psychology*, *94 Part 1*, 1–28.

Sprenger-Charolles, L. (2003). Reading acquisition: Cross linguistic data. In T. Nunes & P. Bryant (Eds.), *Handbook of children's literacy* (pp. 43–66). Dordrecht: Kluwer.

Sprenger-Charolles, L., & Bonnet, P. (1996). New doubts on the importance of the logographic stage. *Current Psychology of Cognition*, *15*, 173–208.

Sprenger-Charolles, L., & Casalis, S. (1995). Reading and spelling acquisition in French first graders: Longitudinal evidence. *Reading and Writing: An Interdisciplinary Journal*, *7*, 1–25.

Sprenger-Charolles, L., Colé, P., Béchennec, D., & Kipffer-Piquard, A. (2005). French normative data on reading and related skills: From EVALEC, a new computerized battery of tests. *European Review of Applied Psychology*, *55*, 157–186.

Sprenger-Charolles, L., Colé P., Lacert, P., & Serniclaes, W. (2000). On subtypes of developmental dyslexia: Evidence from processing time and accuracy scores. *Canadian Journal of Experimental Psychology*, *54*, 88–104.

Sprenger-Charolles, L., & Siegel, L. S. (1997). A longitudinal study of the effects of syllabic structure on the development of reading and spelling skills in French. *Applied Psycholinguistics*, *18*, 485–505.

Sprenger-Charolles, L., Siegel, L. S., & Béchennec, D. (1998a). Phonological mediation and semantic and orthographic factors in silent reading in French. *Scientific Studies of Reading, 2*(1), 3–29.

Sprenger-Charolles, L., Siegel, L. S., Béchennec, D., & Serniclaes, W. (2003). Development of phonological and orthographic processing in reading aloud, in silent reading and in spelling: A four year longitudinal study. *Journal of Experimental Child Psychology, 84*, 194–217.

Sprenger-Charolles, L., Siegel, L. S., & Bonnet, P. (1998b). Phonological mediation and orthographic factors in reading and spelling. *Journal of Experimental Child Psychology, 68*, 134–155.

Stage S. A., & Wagner R. K. (1992). Development of young children's phonological and orthographic knowledge as revealed by their spellings. *Developmental Psychology, 28*, 287–296.

Stanovich, K. E. (1986). Matthew effects in reading: Some consequences of individual differences in the acquisition of literacy. *Reading Research Quarterly, 21*, 360–407.

Stanovich, K. E. (2000). *Progress in understanding reading: Scientific foundations and new frontiers*. New York: Guilford Press.

Stanovich, K. E., Nathan, R. G., & Zolman, J. E. (1988). The developmental lag hypothesis in reading: Longitudinal and matched reading-level comparisons. *Child Development, 59*, 71–86.

Stanovich, K. E., & Siegel, L. S. (1994). Phenotypic performance profile of children with reading disabilities: A regression-based test of the phonological-core variable-difference model. *Journal of Educational Psychology, 86*, 24–53.

Stanovich, K. E., Siegel, L. S., & Gottardo, A. (1997). Converging evidence for phonological and surface subtypes of reading disability. *Journal of Educational Psychology, 89*, 114–127.

Stein, J. (2001). The magnocellular theory of developmental dyslexia. *Dyslexia, 7*, 12–36.

Stein, J. (2003). Visual motion sensitivity and reading. *Neuropsychologia, 41*, 1785–1793.

Stein, J. F., & Fowler, M. S. (1982). Diagnosis of dyslexia by means of a new indicator of eye dominance. *British Journal of Ophthalmology, 66*, 332–336.

Stein, J. F., Richardson, A. J., & Fowler, M. S. (2000). Monocular occlusion can improve binocular control and reading in dyslexics. *Brain, 123*, 164–170.

Stein, J. F., Riddell, P., & Fowler, M. S. (1988). Disordered vergence eye movement control in dyslexic children. *British Journal of Ophthalmology, 72*, 162–166.

Stein, J., & Walsh, W. (1997). To see but not to read: The magnocellular theory of dyslexia. *Trends in Neuroscience, 20*, 147–152.

Strange, W., & Dittmann, S. (1984). Effects of discrimination on the perception of /r-l/ by Japanese adults learning English. *Perception & Psychophysics, 36*, 131–145.

Stroop, J. R. (1935). Studies of interference in serial verbal reactions. *Journal of Experimental Psychology, 18*, 643–662.

Stuart, M. (1995). Prediction and qualitative assessment of five- and six-year-old children's reading: A longitudinal study. *British Journal of Educational Psychology, 65*(3), 287–296.

Stuart, M., & Coltheart, M. (1988). Does reading develop in a sequence of stages? *Cognition, 30*, 139–151.

Studdert-Kennedy, M. (2002). Deficits in phoneme awareness do not arise from failures in rapid auditory processing. *Reading and Writing: An Interdisciplinary Journal, 15*, 5–14.

Studdert-Kennedy, M. (2005). How did language go discrete? In M. Tallerman (Ed.), *Evolutionary prerequisites of language*. Oxford: Oxford University Press.

Stuebing, K. K., Fletcher, J. M., LeDoux, J. M., Lyon, G. R., Shaywitz, S. E., & Shaywitz, B. A. (2002). Validity of IQ-discrepancy classifications of reading disabilities: A meta-analysis. *American Educational Research Journal, 39*(2), 469–518.

Swan, D., & Goswami, U. (1997a). Picture naming deficits in developmental dyslexia: The phonological representations hypothesis. *Brain and Language, 56*, 334–353.

Swan, D., & Goswami, U. (1997b). Phonological awareness deficits in developmental dyslexia and the phonological representations hypothesis. *Journal of Experimental Child Psychology, 66*(1), 18–41.

Szeszulski, P. A., & Manis F. R. (1987). A comparison of word recognition processes in dyslexic and normal readers at two reading-age levels. *Journal of Experimental Child Psychology, 44*(3), 364–376.

Tallal, P. (1980). Auditory temporal perception, phonics and reading disabilities in children. *Brain and Language, 9*, 182–198.

Tekieli, M. E., & Cullinan, W. L. (1979). The perception of temporally segmented vowels and consonant-vowel syllables. *Journal of Speech and Hearing Research, 22*, 103–121.

Temple, C. M., & Marshall, J. C. (1983). A case study of developmental phonological dyslexia. *British Journal of Psychology, 74*, 517–533.

Ternus, J. (1938). The problem of phenomenal identity. In D. W. Ellis (Ed.), *A sourcebook of gestalt psychology*. London: Routledge and Kegan Paul.

Thorndike, R. L. (1973). *Reading comprehension education in fifteen countries: An empirical study*. New York: Halsted.

Treiman, R., & Baron J. (1983). Phonemic analysis training helps children benefit from spelling-sound rules. *Memory and Cognition, 11*, 382–389.

Treiman, R., Broderick, V., Tincoff, R., & Rodriguez, K. (1998). Children's phonological awareness: Confusions between phonemes that differ only in voicing. *Journal of Experimental Child Psychology, 68*, 3–21.

Treiman, R., & Cassar, M. (1997). Can children and adults focus on sound as opposed to spelling in a phoneme counting task? *Developmental Psychology, 33*, 771–781.

Treiman, R., & Hirsh-Pasek, K. (1985). Are there qualitative differences in reading behavior between dyslexics and normal readers? *Memory and Cognition, 13*, 357–364.

Treiman, R., Mullennix, J., Bijeljac-Babic, R., & Richmond-Welty, E. D. (1995). The special role of rimes in the description, use, and acquisition of English orthography. *Journal of Experimental Psychology: General, 124*, 107–136.

Valdois, S. (1996). A case study of developmental surface dyslexia and dysgraphia. *Brain and Cognition, 32*, 229–231.

Valdois, S., Bosse, M. L., Ans, B. Carbonnel, S., Zorman, M., David, D., et al. (2003). Phonological and visual processing deficits can dissociate in developmental dyslexia: Evidence from two case studies. *Reading and Writing: An Interdisciplinary Journal, 16*, 541–572.

Valtin, R. (1989). Dyslexia in the German language. In P. G. Aaron & R. M. Joshi

(Eds.), *Reading and writing disorders in different orthographic systems* (pp. 119–136). Dordrecht: Kluwer.

van Atteveldt, N., Formisano, E., Blomert, L., & Goebel, R. (submitted). The effect of temporal asynchrony on the multisensory integration of letters and speech sounds.

van Atteveldt, N., Formisano, E., Goebel, R., & Blomert, L. (2004). Integration of letters and speech sounds in the human brain. *Neuron, 43*, 1–12.

Van der Leij, A., Van Daal, V., & De Jong, P. (2002). Task related factors in reading efficiency of dyslexic children. In L. Verhoeven, C. Elbro, & P. Reitsma (Eds.), *Precursors of functional literacy* (pp. 229–245). Amsterdam: John Benjamins.

Van Ijzendoorn, M. H., & Bus, A. G. (1994). Meta-analytic confirmation of the non-word reading deficit in developmental dyslexia. *Reading Research Quarterly, 29*, 266–275.

Van Ingelghem, M., Van Wieringen, A., Wouters, J., Vandenbussche, E., Onghena, P., & Ghesquiere, P. (2001). Psychophysical evidence for a general temporal processing deficit in children with dyslexia. *Neuroreport, 12*, 3603–3607.

Van Orden, G. C., Pennington, B. F., & Stone, G. O. (2001). What do double dissociations prove? *Cognitive Science, 25*(1), 111–172.

Vellutino, F. R., Fletcher, J. M., Snowling, M. J., & Scanlon, D. M. (2004). Specific reading disability (dyslexia): What we have learned in the past four decades? *Journal of Child Psychology and Psychiatry, 45*(1), 2–40.

Vellutino, F. R., Scanlon, D. M., & Lyon, G. R. (2000). Differentiating between difficult-to-remediate and readily remediated poor readers: More evidence against the IQ-achievement discrepancy definition of reading disability. *Journal of Learning Disabilities, 33*, 223–238.

Verhoeven, L., Schreuder, R., & Baayen, R. H. (2003). Units of analysis in reading dutch bisyllabic pseudowords. *Scientific Studies of Reading, 7*(3), 255–271.

Véronis, J. (1986). Etude quantitative sur le système graphique et phono-graphique du français [Quantitative study of the French graphemic and phono-graphemic writing system]. *European Bulletin of Cognitive Psychology, 6*, 501–553.

Vitu, F., O'Regan, J. K., & Mittau, M. (1990). Optimal landing position in reading isolated words and continuous text. *Perception & Psychophysics, 47*, 583–600.

Wagner, R. K., & Torgesen, J. K. (1987). The nature of phonological processing and its causal role in the acquisition of reading-skills. *Psychological Bulletin, 101*(2), 192–212.

Wagner, R. K., Torgesen, J. K., & Rashotte, C. A. (1994). Development of reading related phonological processing abilities: New evidence of bi-directional causality from a latent variable longitudinal study. *Developmental Psychology, 30*, 73–87.

Wagner, R. K., Torgesen, J. K., Rashotte, C. A., Hecht, S. A., Barker, T. A., Burgess, S. R., et al. (1997). Changing relations between phonological processing abilities and word-level reading as children develop from beginning to skilled readers: A five year longitudinal study. *Developmental Psychology, 33*: 468–479.

Waters, G. S., Bruck, M., & Seidenberg, M. S. (1985). Do children use similar cognitive processes to read and spell words? *Journal of Experimental Child Psychology, 39*, 511–530.

Waters, G. S., Seidenberg, M. S., & Bruck, M. (1984). Children's and adults' use of spelling sound information in three reading tasks. *Memory and Cognition, 12,* 293–305.

Watson, B. U. (1992). Auditory temporal acuity in normally achieving and learning-disabled college students. *Journal of Speech & Hearing Research, 35*(1), 148–156.

Werker, J. F. (2003). The acquisition of language specific phonetic categories in infancy. *Proceeding of the 15th International Congress of Phonetic Sciences* (pp. 21–24). Barcelona, Spain.

Werker, J. F., & Logan, J. S. (1985). Cross-language evidence for three factors in speech perception. *Perception & Psychophysics, 37,* 35–44.

Werker, J. F., & Tees, R. C. (1984a). Cross-language speech perception: Evidence for perceptual reorganization during the first year of life. *Infant Behavior and Development, 7,* 49–63.

Werker, J. F., & Tees, R. C. (1984b). Phonemic and phonetic factors in adult cross-language speech perception. *Journal of the Acoustical Society of America, 75,* 1866–1878.

Werker, J. F., & Tees, R. C. (1987). Speech perception in severely disabled and average reading children. *Canadian Journal of Psychology, 41,* 48–61.

Werker, J. F., & Tees, R. C. (1999). Influences on infant speech processing: Towards a new synthesis. *Annual Review of Psychology, 50,* 509–535.

West, R. F., & Stanovich, K. E. (1978). Automatic contextual facilitation in readers of three ages. *Child Development, 49,* 717–727.

White, S., Milne, E., Rosen, S., Hansen, P., Swettenham, J., Frith, U., et al. (2006). The role of sensorimotor impairments in dyslexia: A multiple case study of dyslexic children. *Developmental Science, 9,* 237–269.

Wilson, A. M., & Lesaux, N. K. (2001). Persistence of phonological processing deficits in college students with dyslexia who have age-appropriate reading skills. *Journal of Learning Disabilities, 34*(5), 394–400.

Wimmer, H. (1993). Characteristics of developmental dyslexia in a regular writing system. *Applied Psycholinguistics, 14,* 1–33.

Wimmer, H. (1995). The nonword deficit in developmental dyslexia: Evidence from German children. *Journal of Experimental Child Psychology, 61,* 80–90.

Wimmer, H. (1996). The early manifestation of developmental dyslexia: Evidence from German children. *Reading and Writing: An Interdisciplinary Journal, 8,* 171–188.

Wimmer, H., & Goswami, U. (1994). The influence of orthographic consistency on reading development: Word recognition in English and German children. *Cognition, 51,* 91–103.

Wimmer, H., & Hummer, P. (1990). How German speaking first graders read and spell: Doubts on the importance of the logographic stage. *Applied Psycholinguistics, 11,* 349–368.

Wimmer, H., & Mayringer, H. (2002). Dysfluent reading in the absence of spelling difficulties: A specific disability in regular orthographies. *Journal of Educational Psychology, 94*(2), 272–277.

Witton, C., Stein, J. F., Stoodley, C. J., Rosner, B. S., & Talcott, J. B. (2002). Separate influences of acoustic AM and FM sensitivity on the phonological decoding skills of impaired and normal readers. *Journal of Cognitive Neuroscience, 14,* 866–874.

Witton, C., Talcott, J. B., Hansen, P. C., Richardson, A. J., Griffiths, T. D., Rees, A., et al. (1998). Sensitivity to dynamic auditory and visual stimuli predicts nonword reading ability in both dyslexic and normal readers. *Current Biology, 8*(14), 791–797.

Wolf, M., & Bowers, P. (1999). The question of naming speed deficits in developmental reading disabilities: An introduction to the double-deficit hypothesis. *Journal of Educational Psychology, 19*, 1–24.

Wolf, M., Bowers, P. G., & Biddle, K. (2000). Naming-speed processes, timing, and reading: A conceptual review. *Journal of Learning Disabilities, 33*(4), 387–407.

Wolf, M., Goldberg O'Rourke, A., Gidney, C., Lovett, M., Cirino, P., & Morris, R. (2002). The second deficit: An investigation of the independence of phonological and naming-speed deficits in developmental dyslexia. *Reading and Writing: An Interdisciplinary Journal, 15*, 43–72.

Wolff, P. H., Cohen, C., & Drake, C. (1984). Impaired motor timing control in specific reading retardation. *Neuropsychologia, 22*(5), 587–600.

Wolff, P. H., Michel, G. F., & Ovrut, M. (1990). The timing of syllable repetition in developmental dyslexia. *Journal of Speech and Hearing Research, 33*, 281–289.

Wood, C. C. (1976). Discriminability, response bias, and phoneme categories in discrimination of voice onset time. *Journal of the Acoustical Society of America, 60*, 1381–1389.

World Health Organization (1993). *The international classification of diseases. Classification of mental and behavioural disorders* (Vol. 10). Geneva: World Health Organization Publications.

Wright, B. A., Lombardino, L. J., King, W. M., Puranik, C. S., Leonard, C. M., & Merzenich, M. M. (1997). Deficits in auditory temporal and spectral resolution in language-impaired children. *Nature, 387*, 176–178.

Yule, W., Rutter, M., Berger, M., & Thompson, J. (1974). Over- and under-achievement in reading: Distribution in the general population. *British Journal of Educational Psychology, 44*, 1–12.

Zabell, C., & Everatt, J. (2002). Surface and phonological subtypes of adult developmental dyslexia. *Dyslexia, 8*, 160–177.

Ziegler, J. C. (1998). La perception des mots, une voie à double sens? *Annales de la fondation Fyssen, 13*, 81–88.

Ziegler, J., & Goswami, U. (2005). Reading acquisition, developmental dyslexia and skilled reading accross languages: A psycholinguistic grain size theory. *Psychological Bulletin, 13*(1), 3–29.

Ziegler, J. C., Jacobs, A. M., & Stone, G. O. (1996). Statistical analyses of the bidirectional inconsistency of spelling and sound in French. *Behavior Research Methods Instruments and Computers, 28*(4), 504–515.

Ziegler, J. C., Perry, C., Ma-Wyatt, A., Ladner, D., & Schule-Körne, D. (2003). Developmental dyslexia in different languages: Language-specific or universal? *Journal of Experimental Child Psychology, 86*, 169–193.

Ziegler, J. C., Stone, G. O., & Jacobs, A. M. (1997). What is the pronunciation for -ough and the spelling for /u/? A data base for computing feedforward and feedback consistency in English. *Behavior Research Methods Instruments and Computers, 29*(4), 600–618.

Zoccolotti, P., De Luca, M., Di Pace, E., Judica, A., Orlandi, M., & Spinelli, D. (1999). Marker of developmental surface dyslexia in a language (Italian) with high grapheme-phoneme correspondence. *Applied Psycholinguistics*, *20*, 191–216.

Author index

Zabell, C. 127, 128, 137, 195
  (Note 6)
Zecker, S.G. 150
Zhang, S. 7, 130, 173
Ziegler, J. 10, 20, 21, 22, 23, 28, 29, 36,
  37, 38, 39, 40, 41, 55, 59, 68, 74, 78,

83, 84, 86, 87, 89, 101, 102, 128, 150,
  176, 192 (Note 10)
Zoccolotti, P. 90, 91, 92, 101, 129
Zolman, J.E. 81
Zorman, M. 103, 106, 107, 108, 127,
  128, 129, 130

Subject index